WARPATH

THE STUNNING PERSONAL STORY

WARPATH

ONE VIETNAM VETERAN'S JOURNEY THROUGH WAR, DISILLUSIONMENT, GUILT AND RECOVERY

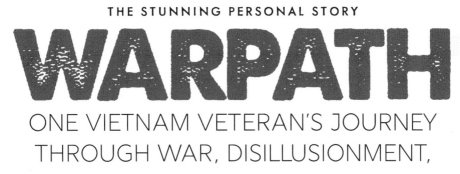

A.J. MOORE

APACHE PRESS BOOKS

For inquiries, please visit: www.ApachePressBooks.com

Published by Apache Press Books.

ISBN: 979-8-9855434-0-7

Editor: David Larkin
Cover concept: Kevin Moore
Cover design & interior formatting: Mark Thomas / Coverness.com

To my wife, Norma, and our two wonderful children, Tina Price and Kevin Moore. I hope this book helps them better understand some of my wacky behavior over the years.
I could not have made it without their love and support.

I owe a huge debt to my VA counselors Mel Pol and Nancy Edenfeld, and my VA psychiatrist, Dr. Belina R. Alfonso. Their guidance and patience over the years made my recovery possible.

Several names have been changed to protect the incompetent.

TABLE OF CONTENTS

FOREWORD 1

THE CALL 3

BEGINNING 10

ADVANCED INDIVIDUAL TRAINING (AIT) 24

ASSIGNMENT 32

ARRIVAL 48

ACCLIMATION 56

GROUND CREW 71

TRANSFER 98

HUNTING CHUCK 129

THE U MINH 200

SHORT 212

DEPARTURE 218

HOME 223

SEPARATION 235

CIVILIAN 239

REVELATION 259

HELP 263

RECOVERY & REWARD 271

EPILOGUE 277

APPENDIX "A" GLOSSARY 281

APPENDIX "B" QUOTED AUTHORS 291

ABOUT THE AUTHOR 295

FOREWORD

"Once you've flown Scouts, what else is there?"

Anonymous helmet art

How do you describe the impact of life-changing disillusionment and the loss of faith in the things you hold sacred?

This collection of stories is my attempt to explain the most tumultuous year in my life and the ongoing impact those months would have on me. It is difficult to describe such emotional intensity, especially when endured over a long duration.

Some will question the validity of the "duration" comment, especially those who recall the four-year-plus service of many WWII veterans. However, the Vietnam combat experience was a twenty-four-hour, 365-day grind for most of us. There were no rear lines where you could go for peace and quiet. The only break was one short week of R&R. Otherwise, you were "ON" for the entire twenty-four hours of each and every day.

Even the noncombat time was intense. We spent those same twenty-four hours working with the same individuals day after day, month after month. You got to know each other intimately. I cannot think of any other experience that would form the type of bonds we created among us.

When one considers the cycle of events, it may have been a twelve-month tour, but it was more like three years on a nine-to-five job.

My first ten years following Vietnam were ones of great confusion. I could not understand how my country had executed such an immoral war. I knew from direct experience with the South Vietnamese people and their army that something was seriously wrong, but I did not know what it was. I researched the history of our involvement relentlessly, reading well over forty books. When I learned the truth about our participation, I spent the next forty years coping with overwhelming feelings of guilt.

I do not consider myself a victim. I had sought out the experiences that later caused me so much discomfort. I never expected to be made whole or returned to the person I was before 1969.

I now have it partially sorted out. Thanks to the support of the Best Wife in the World, the continuing love of our children and grandchildren, and two wonderfully effective VA counselors, I am no longer incapacitated by feelings of guilt or confusion. While some PTSD symptoms persist, they are more manageable.

I am still proud of my service and even prouder of the actions of the individuals with whom I served in the Scout platoon and the 370th Transportation Company Detachment. While proud of our actions, I have never sought to glorify combat or in any way make it sound attractive.

THE CALL

"War is delightful to those who have had no experience of it."

Desiderius Erasmus

I was eager to go, and I was not waiting for the draft.

My calling started as early as the second grade. One of our two TV networks began airing the series *West Point* in 1956. I loved it and decided then that I wanted to be a career army officer, which appeared to me at the time, and remained for the next twelve years, to be the highest possible service to the country.

Reinforcing this feeling was that my dad had served as a rifleman during WWII. He was assigned to the Seventh Armored Division, arriving in Belgium in late December 1944. After a few months in the field, he and a part of his platoon were captured by a German panzer division and marched deep into Germany. It was a traumatic event, but he always downplayed the incident, never wanting to draw attention to himself or his experiences. Fortunately, he was liberated after fourteen days and rotated back to the US. He wanted to return to his unit, but army policy required that all former POWs be returned to the States for R&R.

While he was always guarded about his combat experience, he did enjoy talking with my uncles and his cousins about his less-intense army days. My eavesdropping on these exchanges, never directed at me, helped form my sense of duty and patriotism.

Dad was the only combat veteran in a large, close family. His youngest brother had been too young to go. His older brother was protected from the draft because of his oldest-surviving-son status. However, he did enlist in the navy in '45, reportedly to earn the veteran's preference points awarded by the civil service system. My dad's brother-in-law had spent his two-year army career stateside, benefitting from playing for the New York Yankees when he was drafted. Other than basic training, he probably never slept outside. None of Dad's many cousins served.

These gab sessions were frequent, and I loved being in the room so I could overhear them. Most stories were funny and many conveyed miserable experiences, such as sleeping outside in the snow with no cover. All of the tough stories belonged to my dad.

During these exchanges, one subtle message came through to me: Dad's utter contempt for people who had shirked their duty, especially those who worked the system to gain a safe job far from the front lines. While he never bragged or even hinted at boasting about his combat experiences, his feelings about the rear echelon were clear.

In addition to his war experiences, his life up to that point was one of local fame. He was a star athlete in high school, quarterback when his small county school upset the much bigger Norfolk city school for the first time in their existence, and the star pitcher when Norview defeated that same city school in baseball, again for the first time. Mom had a scrapbook full of his athletic accomplishments. As high school drew to a close, he was granted a full scholarship to play either football or baseball for Wake Forest University. The draft eliminated that opportunity.

After the war, he continued his baseball career, playing in the minors, then in the adult city leagues. These stints were an unmistakable testament to his baseball skills. Late each winter, team sponsors would visit our little, 700-square-foot house, hoping to recruit him to their teams. These always resulted in full-time employment with the sponsor, working in their car dealerships or small manufacturing shops.

My sense of having something to live up to was very strong.

This feeling was reinforced to the hilt by my frequent viewing of WWII documentaries and dramas in which the American participants were always infallible, heroic, and perfectly capable of saving the day, regardless of the circumstances. Self-sacrifice for a common cause was the standard of the day.

The Western genre was popular then. The heroic resolution of problems, usually through the use of justifiable violence, was the norm. When the Westerns faded, spy thrillers replaced them as the media authority, defining what it took to be a man. In the '60s, the culture seemed to revolve around the heroic ideal. There was no lack of heroism in the living room of our house.

One incident that I remember vividly, and it had an impact on my thinking, was a movie covering the Korean War. One of the Americans was in minor trouble with his comrades over his hesitancy to shoot an enemy soldier. When I asked my dad what was wrong with this guy, Dad explained that his conscience was bothering him, making it hard for him to kill another human being. I expressed my disbelief, and Dad commented that killing was a far more difficult thing to do than was ever portrayed in the movies.

While I did not argue, I remained skeptical. A few scenes later, the same soldier was stabbed to death by an enemy infiltrator while on guard duty. The message was clear: hesitating to do your duty results in a silent, lonely, and unheroic death. There was an implied dishonor in that.

Other movies, many produced shortly after WWII, contributed to my overdeveloped sense of patriotism. The more memorable ones included:

- *Bataan!* – 1943, starring Robert Taylor
- *The Sands of Iwo Jima* – 1948, starring John Wayne
- *Attack!* – 1956, starring Jack Palance
- *The Longest Day* – 1962, John Wayne
- *The Sand Pebbles* – 1966, Steve McQueen
- *The Professionals* – 1966, Burt Lancaster & Lee Marvin

Each one delivered a strong message on honor and what men were expected to do in times of war. They were indelible messages.

I should have paid more attention to my dad and less to the movies.

I became enamored with anything to do with the military and the army in particular. By the time I was eight, I knew all the moves associated with close order drill. Because Dad had been a drill sergeant when he returned from Europe, I pestered him constantly. He would teach me the moves and then grade me when I thought I had mastered them. He promoted none of this, and it was clear he did not enjoy doing it. But I wasn't to be denied.

I also developed a deep appreciation for firearms. Again, Dad was a master instructor, stressing safety and proper gun handling. When he and his brothers would take their pistols to a local farm and practice shooting, Dad would allow me to take a couple of shots. This was always under intense, close-up supervision, and joking around with a weapon was strictly forbidden. Many of those lessons stuck with me throughout my life, and I can still remember the first time he allowed me to fire his pistol. It made a deep impression.

My parents relocated from Norfolk to Chesapeake during the summer between my junior and senior years, and I got to spend my senior year in a new and strange environment. This turned out to be a positive change for me. I had always excelled in English, history, and literature. My new school offered several courses in the humanities that appealed to me, and I excelled in those as well. Achieving a high degree of literacy and familiarity with the classics fit perfectly with my idea of the warrior-poet.

During my senior year of high school, I met the lady who would become my wife: Norma Potter. Norma and I met on the school bus, no less. Bus number 210. In 1966, the majority of students, including seniors, rode the bus.

Norma and I found ourselves to be extremely close in our attitudes and life goals. We dated throughout the school year and beyond.

By the time I graduated from high school, my intended path was clear: I would join the army and learn to fly helicopters through their Aviation Warrant Officer Program. Too poor for my parents to pay for college, this program opened a path for me to fly and eventually get a college degree. In my eyes, this would be the most glamorous way to serve. I visited the recruiter and scheduled the myriad of tests required for acceptance. Because of my long-time interest in aviation, I was not intimidated.

First came the physical exam, which posed no problem. I had been surfing all spring and was in excellent shape. Next came a basic intelligence test, which I passed with no problem. Remember, this was an army intelligence test.

Then came the FAST – the Flight Aptitude Selection Test. Everyone in the recruiting office warned me of its difficulty and the high failure rate.

Like the physical exam and the intelligence test, the FAST required an overnight trip to Richmond, where the nearest induction center was located. I was slightly apprehensive, having had no real flying experience. However, I felt that my interest in aviation would give me a slight advantage over those candidates to whom the idea of flying helicopters simply looked like a good way to stay out of the mud.

The FAST was challenging, and I could see why the failure rate was high. It included many questions on the theory of flight, basic navigation, and mechanical theory.

The most trying part of the test was the instrumentation section. This presented about twenty or thirty illustrations of an aircraft attitude indicator, or false horizon, and several other instruments representing certain flight conditions. The candidate had to view the indicators, then select what combined action (stick and rudder) was required to bring the aircraft back to level flight. The answers were presented as multiple-choice selections, with each of the four selections describing the action, such as stick back and left, partial left rudder. It was not easy, and I could see how difficult it would be for candidates who had never seen an attitude indicator. Luckily, I was familiar with the instrument because of my reading.

After passing the FAST, the next and final hurdle was the officer candidate selection board: a group interview with a panel of four commissioned officers ranging in rank from captain through lieutenant colonel. *This* was intimidating.

After a series of routine questions, the lieutenant colonel asked if I was aware of my FAST results. My heart began racing and I started sweating. I could not imagine that I had done so poorly that it got a colonel's attention. I weakly stuttered, "No . . . no, sir, I'm not." I assumed I had passed, or I would not have been invited to this interview.

He then said he had the pleasure of informing me that I had recorded the highest score ever achieved in the state of Virginia by a non-flight-licensed individual. I was stunned. At that point, all four officers stood up, offered me their hands, and welcomed me to Army Aviation. I felt my dream was coming true.

This interview took place in late June. The recruiter and I selected early September as an enlistment date, and he initiated the flight school paperwork. I was elated.

1967 - A Summer of Love

Before September rolled around, there was a whole lot of fun to be had.

After graduation, my cousin hooked me up with a truck-driving job at a local print shop. This allowed me to cruise all over Norfolk and Virginia Beach delivering printed materials. The company had a small, 1966 Ford Econoline van – perfect for bobbing around the beach.

On Fridays, I spent the entire afternoon and evening, often beyond midnight, delivering the *Virginia Beach Guide* to about 130 businesses on and around the oceanfront. The publication was a small-format, sixty-page magazine full of ads and info about the beach attractions. Seemingly of limited value, I soon learned that the various hoteliers, restaurateurs, and trinket shop owners would go ballistic if they did not receive their *Guide* on time. The bumper-to-bumper traffic on Atlantic Avenue, combined with the thousands of tourists filling the sidewalks, made getting into and out of the various establishments a daredevil task. It was quite an adrenaline rush. I did not know how much this experience would prepare me for some of my later activities.

An entertaining fringe benefit accrued to the person delivering the *Guide*. I had the chance to meet dozens of college women working at the oceanfront. No matter how pressed I was for time, I always took the opportunity to engage in some small talk before jumping back into the truck. While none of these encounters led to any long-lasting relationships, it was a great deal of fun.

On the weekends, and in the evenings when the tides were right, Norma and I spent all of our time on the beach, either Sandbridge or at the North End. I surfed constantly. I loved the water and the thrill of sliding down the face of a wave and making a big turn at the bottom. I later said that it was the only sensation that compared favorably to flying.

We stayed on the go continually. Movies, concerts, and parties at night, coupled with lots of restaurant visits, prompted my dad to caution us about our spendthrift ways. He would tell Norma, "You're going to wish you'd held onto that money someday." Naturally, we never did. We had so much fun and built so many wonderful memories, neither of us would change a thing about those days. Of course, foremost in my mind was that I was heading into the military and what promised to be a dangerous future.

Maybe I would change one thing.

Our cruising was *not* done in style. At the beginning of my senior year, I needed part-time employment. That meant I needed reliable transportation. Using my father's car was out of the question. He could not buy one for me and could not lend me the necessary money. I had limited, (read *nonexistent*) monetary resources – I was broke. My maternal grandmother was kind enough to step forward and lend me $600 to buy a car.

I ended up with a stripped-down, 1963 Ford Falcon. By stripped-down, I mean in the extreme. Its only chrome was on the two bumpers. It had no radio, air conditioning, or power anything. Until I saw it, I did not know that Ford made such a featureless automobile.

I purchased a $10, battery-powered transistor radio that we used to capture the sounds. We placed it on the dashboard, where it could receive the strongest signal. When we entered a turn, the radio would slide across the dashboard. Norma had to be extra careful to prevent the radio from flying off the dash and out through the open window. It kept her on her toes!

It got me to work and got us to the beach, so I did not complain.

Ten weeks after graduating from high school, I was boarding a Trailways bus and heading to Richmond for my swearing-in ceremony. I was on my way.

BEGINNING

"It is forbidden to kill. Therefore, all murderers are punished, unless they kill in large numbers and to the sound of trumpets."

Voltaire

Life in the army started strangely. After taking the oath at the Richmond Induction Center, a group of thirty of us boarded a train for Columbia, South Carolina, the location of Fort Jackson. We departed late in the afternoon, indicating that it would be an overnight trip. Because this was my first train trip, I had no idea what to expect. I was excited to finally be on the way. I should have known better.

Before leaving Richmond, a lieutenant informed me that I would be in charge of this detachment, making me responsible for getting these thirty individuals to Fort Jackson on time and in one piece. My first reaction was "Why me?" The lieutenant said that I was the only officer candidate in the group, and as such, outranked everyone else. Oh boy.

One fact about military service, you get to meet many interesting individuals, representing every economic and psychological profile on the planet.

I succeeded in getting everyone on the train and in the right car without a problem. As soon as we boarded and got underway, someone discovered the club car and the fun began.

Imagine thirty men, ranging in age from eighteen (me!) to near thirty, departing home for at least two years in the army. On top of that, visualize an open bar with patrons willing to buy drinks for all these doomed servicemen. Checking IDs was out of the question.

Things got out of hand quickly. Guys were running from car to car, shouting and yelling as they played a game similar to tag, but using punches to the biceps instead. Spilling drinks, stumbling around, and talking way too loudly were the mildest behaviors. I spent my evening trying to prevent fistfights and attempting to keep everyone in one car where I could try to watch them.

This went on until about two or three in the morning, when we arrived at Columbia. Almost everyone was still drunk or beginning to feel sick. The sergeants who met us at the train station were quite pissed off and started yelling for, "Private Moore. Private Moore. Get over here right fucking now!"

I had to recount what happened on the train, including a woeful explanation that I could not do anything about the civilians who insisted on buying all the drinks. That all thirty men arrived, that no one was injured, either my guys or the civilian innocents, and that no one was under arrest saved me. The senior sergeant said, "OK. OK. Get your ass on the goddamned bus!"

Basic training at Ft. Jackson was not a problem, largely due to my good physical condition. The rest of the military instruction was not challenging. I made a practice out of remaining anonymous, avoiding the attention of the drill sergeants.

Repetitive training sessions on all things military filled the days. First aid training was nearly a daily topic, so frequent and repetitive that it was hard to endure. Spending so much time on one topic could successfully train a first grader.

Inoculations were nearly a daily occurrence during the first couple of weeks. There were so many shots I lost track of what I was being inoculated against. On one occasion, in the middle of a very hot September day, the entire company of three hundred miserable souls ran about two miles from a training site to a building where the shots were administered. We lined up in our platoon formations, took off our gear and fatigue shirts, and stood at parade rest, awaiting our turn to enter the building.

We stood in a dirt parking lot that was extremely dusty and on the sunny side of the building. The building, like all army buildings, was painted white and reflected the heat back at us. We stood there with our helmets on, sweating.

As one squad was ordered into the line, running at double time as they entered the building, another squad would return from the slaughter. All had blood streaming down their arms. It began at their shoulders, soaked through their white T-shirt sleeves, ran down their biceps, and eventually dripped from their fingertips. When it hit the ground, it formed little red mud pies on both sides of each soldier's feet.

The silence was broken every minute or two by the sound of a helmet liner and skull hitting the ground as soldiers passed out, probably from a combination of heat, dehydration, and an overwhelming fear of needles.

It was enough to make one wonder what in the hell was happening inside that building. I soon found out.

As we entered the building and slowed to a walk, it was like entering a movie theatre after being on a sunny beach. I was blind and disoriented. We all shuffled forward to a gauntlet where four medics were standing on each side of us, waving their pneumatic syringes and yelling at us to "Keep it moving."

As we stepped into position between two of the medics, they would attempt to insult us or make us laugh – it was hard to tell which – by making some comments or asking questions. The first medic asked me where I was from. When I told him I was from Virginia, he said, "Never heard of it. Keep moving." Others would make comments about our mothers or sisters in a constant attempt to humiliate us.

The stars of the show were the pneumatic syringes. These were just coming into use, and rumors were floating around about the damage they could do if something went wrong. One story warned that the syringe could inject air bubbles into your veins, which would kill you when they reached your heart! Or, if you moved while the injection was underway, the air pressure would slice your bicep, leaving you disabled.

These stories achieved instant credibility when we entered the building. In addition to the medics forming the gauntlet, others stood in the background, casually slicing paper with the syringes. They made sure we saw what they were doing. They created anxiety by holding a sheet of notebook paper at shoulder height and using the syringe's pressure to slice the paper into vertical strips. They would finish it off with a horizontal swipe, severing the strips from the sheet and allowing them to fall gently to the floor.

When we ran back to the parking lot, we were greeted by quite a scene. We were in the third platoon, so two platoons had already returned. Scattered on the ground, but within the ranks of the standing soldiers, were a dozen or more people who had passed out. It resembled a Civil War battleground: men standing at attention in orderly, perfectly spaced rows, with streaks of blood running down each arm, and many "dead" guys lying among them. It was certainly motivating. I do not fear needles now.

Basic was not without its entertaining moments. My platoon of forty individuals, whose last names started with either M, N, or O, contained its fair allotment of exceptional individuals.

One was Norris, a twenty-eight-year-old attorney who had been drafted way too late in life. His college and law school deferments had finally run out. He mistakenly thought the Boston Draft Board would overlook him. They didn't.

Norris was a nice guy but a sad soul. He appeared to have abstained from any physical activity for the past fifteen years. He was about five feet seven inches tall and sported a forty-inch-plus waist. His flexibility and range of motion were about the same as a baseball bat. Because his girth was so out of proportion for his height, his fatigue uniform was far too big. Both the sleeves and pant legs were probably six inches too long. He would not be appearing on any recruiting posters.

Everything that one would fear for a person of Norris's stature came true. Any and all parts of physical training, or PT in the army's vernacular, were disastrous for Norris. True to army tradition, the drill instructors identified him as the weak puppy in the litter. This drew their attention, and it was not supportive. Their constant harassment was intended to weed out the weak so they would not fail on the battlefield. At least that is what they'll tell you. It was difficult to know if that was true, or, as most of us believed, Norris gave them an opportunity to indulge their masochistic joy by physically abusing a defenseless individual. All you needed to know about their motivation was contained in one drill instructor (DI) from Georgia who had an eighth-grade education and was working on his GED at night. He struggled mightily with his reading, sometimes asking the recruits for help. The opportunity to make life miserable for a Boston lawyer was too good for him to pass up.

PT occurred at least three times a day, before or after each meal, rain or shine. There were also hour-long sessions devoted to PT, giving poor Norris multiple opportunities to fail. When in the company area, three activities were constants: overhead bars, low crawl, and run-dodge-and-jump. Initially, all three presented new challenges to all the recruits. However, after a week, they were easily mastered. Mastered by everyone except Norris.

The low crawl seemed impossible at first. We had to crawl forty yards while letting only our elbows and toes touch the ground and keep our torso as close to the ground as possible. Naturally, there was a time limit, requiring a considerable amount of speed. Because the Ft. Jackson soil was so sandy, a canvas runner forty yards long and one yard wide was staked to the ground and used as the lane down which all the recruits would crawl. While the canvas may have improved our speed, the coarse material was like crawling on rough sandpaper. Knees and elbows bled frequently, and the black, shiny coating on our combat boots would be destroyed, showing tan, untreated leather where a nice gloss used to be. It was exhausting at first, but after the technique was mastered, it was not difficult. Except for Norris.

It took Norris nearly a month to progress to where he could make it forty yards before collapsing. And it took him forever. As I remember it, he never made the crawl within the maximum time allowed.

Overhead bars are probably familiar to most people. They were comprised of a series of overhead rungs about twenty-four inches wide and about seven or eight feet above the ground. Imagine a ladder hanging horizontally between two uprights. The idea was to hang from the rungs and navigate their twenty-foot length in a specified time without swinging from bar to bar. Good rhythm had a lot to do with success.

Getting an acceptable time was not difficult for the majority of the eighteen-to twenty-five-year-old recruits. You could simply jump up, grab on, and start taking the rungs one or even two at a time, if you had rhythm.

Poor Norris. Getting a passing time was the least of his worries. At first he couldn't jump up to the first rung. He would try and try and try again until he would collapse in the sand. After the first failure, two or three DIs would be standing over him cursing him at the top of their lungs.

It took weeks before Norris could make the leap. When he finally did, he was unable to make it past three or four bars. He simply did not have the arm strength to carry that much weight. He never passed the overhead bars.

His next, and to me his most disturbing challenge, was the run-dodge-and-jump. This probably has no civilian equivalent and, in the way Norris had to attack it, was far outside the norm.

The obstacle had five components, and each had to be taken in the right sequence and right direction. It was a timed event, of course. At each end of the obstacle stood two horizontal railroad ties about three feet apart and five feet in length. They were supported on each end by posts about four feet high. Imagine a western hitching post: two vertical posts topped by a wide horizontal post. They sat side by side, creating a pathway between them. From the opposite end of the obstacle, the horizontal ties were oriented left to right, as though you were looking at a set of hurdles.

In the middle of the obstacle was a pit with railroad ties for walls. It was about eighteen inches deep, eight feet long, and five feet wide. It was oriented across the obstacle, requiring the runner to jump over the five-foot width.

From end to end, the obstacle was about fifty or sixty feet long. Like every other part of Ft. Jackson, the obstacle was covered in loose sand.

The goal was to begin running at one end, leap over the pit, then do a figure eight around the posts at the opposite end. Two laps were required, and your time determined how many points you earned toward your overall PT proficiency score. If you failed to clear the pit, five seconds were added to your time, lowering your score. Clearing the pit was not easy, but most people in reasonably good condition could do it.

Run, Dodge, & Jump Course.

In this case, Norris was able to complete the course every time. However, his times were abysmal and never improved. At first, the DIs tried to motivate him by running beside him and screaming insults for the entire platoon to hear. It was not pretty. Norris would complete the run, then collapse at the DI's feet, nearly in tears. We all felt sorry for him, but there was nothing we could do to help.

That is, until one of the DIs came up with a brilliant motivational technique that gave many of us a chance to participate.

The DI decided that we could help improve Norris's scores by simply running beside him and beating him with our pistol belts. Two platoon members were "volunteered" to help Norris on every one of his attempts. Being beaten with an army pistol belt is serious. The belts are heavy, multi-ply canvas and have almost zero flexibility. They are about three-sixteenths of an inch thick and the ends are folded, making them twice as thick. The buckle mechanism is made of heavy steel rods that are an eighth of an inch in diameter and bent into the proper shape. The body of the belt is reinforced with two rows of heavy brass grommets about four inches apart and covering the entire belt. These grommets are used to attach holsters, canteens, ammo pouches, shovels, and other gear. The belt itself is pretty heavy and easily capable of causing deep bruising when used as a motivational tool. It can do far more damage than a leather belt of the same dimensions.

Three times a day, every day for the remaining six weeks of basic training, Norris received this beating. Those of us "volunteered" for this task were unable to soften the blows. The DIs watched closely and beat the beaters whenever they discovered someone pulling their punches.

This treatment succeeded in bringing tears to Norris's eyes and to the eyes of many of his fellow platoon members. It was brutal and did not result in Norris getting the times required to pass.

Norris lived in fear of getting recycled, that is, being reassigned to another basic training company and going through the entire eight-week training period again. It was a topic of constant conversation for him; he repeatedly asked those closest to him if we thought he would graduate or be recycled. We all encouraged him but secretly agreed that he was headed for the recycle bus. He was a smart guy, but oblivious to the fact that he failed more PT tests than he passed. Any event that required physical exertion defeated him. When we ran to the various training venues that were sometimes five miles away, Norris was always the first to drop out. Near the end of basic training, he was the only one dropping out. His optimism was anchored in the belief that they would not have let him get this far and then recycle him. He had never asked to quit. He was just unable to do what was required. He believed they would surely recognize this and pass him through. He was completely sincere in his attempts to succeed. Others in his predicament may have just taken the easy way out and asked for some form of discharge. Norris was determined to see it through to graduation.

An African American from New Jersey named Nelson was a draftee and former Golden Gloves boxing champion. After a few weeks, Nelson apparently decided the army was not for him. He became "afflicted" with some sort of mental disorder that caused him to walk around in a zombie-like state, saying nothing and rarely responding. He was driven to the medical station every morning after first formation. On one occasion, while the entire company of three hundred men was standing listening to the first sergeant's announcements, Nelson tumbled down the entire flight of stairs descending from the second floor to the first. He hit the exit door at the bottom of the stairs, spilling out and onto the concrete stoop that served as a small porch. Fortunately or unfortunately, depending on your definition of entertainment, our barracks were located directly behind the first sergeant's podium, an elevated and covered structure from which he could look down on his miserable flock of hairless, homesick boys. Our platoon had the best seat in the house for what was to come.

Nelson descended loudly, enhanced by some well-timed and intentional kicks at the walls and banister as he made his way down. When he hit the door, he knocked it off its hinges with an incredible bang. He lay there motionless, in a terrible position, facedown on the concrete stoop with one leg suspended on one of the guardrails.

A couple of platoon members in the front row broke for the stoop, intending to come to Nelson's aid. Before they were two steps away, the first sergeant bellowed, "Stand still! Maintain ranks! I hope the bastard broke his goddamned NECK!"

Nelson stayed there for another ten or fifteen minutes while "Top," the army's nickname for every first sergeant of every company in the world, droned on about our daily schedule. He covered every hour of the day while Nelson lay there, bleeding from a big gash on his forehead, visible to us some forty feet away. Two other drill sergeants eventually came over and carried him away. We never heard from or anything about Nelson again.

Another memorable scene occurred every day we ran to and from the rifle range. Depending on the route chosen by the DIs, it could be three to five miles, one way.

The trails to the ranges were hard-packed dirt that became terribly dusty when three hundred men ran on them. Naturally, they included some pretty severe slopes, making the runs more difficult.

When in route, several trainees would fall out of formation from fatigue. On one particularly hot afternoon, Norris created a memorable experience.

As we ran the trail, the dust rose and became so thick we could not see the head of the formation, nearly two hundred feet in front of us. We were running to the west. The sunlight streamed through the pine trees and dust, creating an almost biblical atmosphere. As we approached another uphill section, several guys began to tire. One was Norris.

People started peeling away from the formation, looking for a place to sit down. As each one fell by the wayside, it reminded me of the old WWII documentaries, the ones in which a B-17 was shown falling out of formation, then spinning toward the ground. One of the more merciful DIs was running with Norris, holding his backpack straps to prevent him from falling.

They were both right beside me, no longer in the actual formation but to the left of it. As we crested the hill and started to run downhill, the DI could carry Norris no longer. He let go of Norris's strap, said something like, "Good luck, buddy," and jogged away.

As soon as Norris was free of the DI's support, he lost his balance and started running sideways and fell off to his left. His knees buckled and he looked over his left shoulder to see where he was going to land. As he did so, his helmet came off and started rolling beside him.

His steps began to quicken as gravity took over. Because he was running sideways, he had to cross one foot in front of the other to keep up. When he realized that he was heading for a large ditch, he let out a high-pitched, long moan. He lost control of his feet and fell to the ground about a foot short of the ditch. Unfortunately, his momentum caused him to bounce once and tumble into the ditch in a cloud of red dust and green battle dress. As he did so, it sounded like all the air was expelled from his lungs. He let out a long, low death moan and disappeared into the ditch.

While the episode only lasted a few seconds after the DI cut him loose, the visual and sound effects were very impressive. We jogged away, and I never found out how he made his way back to the company area.

The eight weeks of basic training dragged on toward graduation. At the beginning of week seven, Norris received the news he feared. Our senior DI came into the barracks one evening, stood at one end of the open bay, and shouted, "Norris! Pack your gear. Secure your weapon and bayonet. Report to the orderly room in ten minutes. You're going to the recycle center!"

Norris broke down, sat on his bunk with his head in his hands, and sobbed quietly. A few of us packed his gear. The DI unlocked the weapons rack, grabbed the M-14 assigned to Norris, and threw it on the bed without another word. He spun on his heels and walked out. Everyone wished Norris well and told him he would probably do much better during his next attempt at completing basic. I think we all knew it was a lie. Norris was never mentioned again.

One of our few breaks from the drudgery of training was an infrequent visit to the on-post beer garden. There was nothing about it that resembled a garden. It was a hundred-foot-long picnic shelter containing dozens of beat-up picnic tables, laid end to end from one end of the garden to the other. At one end was a bar with a couple of ice chests and someone selling cans of beer for about a dollar. Trainees were crammed into the tables, sitting shoulder to shoulder, with very few open seats. You had to wait for someone to stand up and leave before you could sit down. When you did, you were likely to be sitting among a group of strangers. Little conversation took place. First, you didn't know what to talk about. Second, you might be sitting next to a psychopath who was just waiting to explode. Despite being surrounded by two or three hundred men, the feeling of loneliness was overwhelming.

Extreme loneliness was the prevailing emotion throughout basic from the very first day. You did not know whom you could trust, so you stayed to yourself. Remaining anonymous was the best way to avoid the attention of the DIs. Too much attention could bring unpleasant assignments or abuse. Doing exactly what you were told to do, nothing more and nothing less, was a way to maintain anonymity. Do not dare ask the DIs a question! If you missed something, ask another trainee. Do not try to stand out in anything. Just go with the flow.

The challenging environment and loneliness led many guys into depression. While it never got this serious in our company, reports of suicides and emotional breakdowns were numerous.

Probably the worst experience in BT was NBC Training. That's nuclear-biological-chemical warfare. The nuclear part was nearly the same as the duck & cover drills we did in elementary school. At our age, you had to be an idiot to believe lying prone on the ground would save you from a hydrogen bomb.

Biological training wasn't much better. Your first line of defense was to lie on the ground and cover yourself with a poncho. Then there was chemical. This one involved a great deal of anxiety because we had to deal with deadly chlorine gas. We had also heard that we would be gassed with "CS" at some point in the training.

We practiced donning our gas masks repeatedly. It was easy to master, even on those occasions when the DI would scream "GAS!" at the most surprising times. He would run among us, screaming insults directly into our ears as we juggled our weapon, helmet, field gear, gas mask bag, and the mask itself. Once you've done it three times, it's automatic. However, the army was teaching to the lowest common denominator, so we probably did it thirty times before we began the NBC course.

The first exercise was to enter a small building containing chlorine gas, don your gas mask, and show that you had a good, tight seal before being directed to exit the building. After exiting the building, we went to an open space to wait in formation for the others to complete the exercise. Our formation area was a grassy field with a slight depression, making it about two feet lower than the surrounding area. We had removed our shirts so that we could experience the tingling sensation that the poisonous chlorine gas causes on bare skin.

We were standing at ease and chatting when someone yelled, "GAS!" I turned left to see what was happening. One of the instructors was standing to my immediate left, holding a CS gas grenade tied to the end of a three-foot stick. He stuck it right under my nose. Unfortunately, I inhaled a snootful of gas before I could react and stop breathing.

My eyes, ears, nose, throat, and lungs were instantly on fire. I could not breathe because my lungs would no longer inflate. My armpits and crotch were burning, and I could not open my eyes. I started vomiting and thought I might drown. I panicked and ran blindly for the woods about fifty feet away.

I glanced off a tree and fell to all fours, puking and wondering where I was. Every moist surface on my body was burning, including those on the inside. I was on the verge of passing out when I was finally able to catch a shallow breath. Snot was pouring from my nose. Ignoring the pain, I opened my eyes for a micro-second but could only see a blurry scene because of the tears. Two hundred guys were lying all around me, puking, gasping for air, moaning and cussing. Not one soul was still in formation.

The only thought was: CS gas isn't supposed to be lethal. Why am I dying?

After about fifteen minutes, the DIs came by and hustled us back into formation. They hosed down our faces just enough to get the gas out of our eyes, nose, and hair, then we marched back to the company area. It was a tough walk. We still had the gas on our bodies and in our clothes, and our skin was still burning. It was right at the limit of being unbearable. There was nothing we could do but endure it.

My only basic training disappointment was my failure to qualify as an expert in marksmanship. I missed the sixty-point threshold by missing *one shot* and scoring fifty-five on a rainy, windy, and overcast day. The targets were three hundred meters away and nearly invisible in the rain and mist, and I missed one. Qualifying as an expert would have meant a weekend pass and the chance to return home. Because that was the only opportunity for a pass, not making the cut restricted me to the fort for all but one short Saturday afternoon. This meant fifty-five and a half days of seeing no one but other soldiers, most of whom were miserable.

Graduation day finally came. All three hundred of us marched around a dusty field in front of a bunch of officers none of us knew. A few families were on hand to witness a relatively insignificant event. It was over in twenty minutes, including the speeches that kept us standing at attention the entire time.

We marched back to the company area to turn in our weapons and gear, await the delivery of the orders that would send us to our Advanced Individual Training (AIT) assignments, and then wait for the buses that would take us to the train station.

As we sat around waiting, we noticed another training company on the street above our area. They were probably in their first or second week. This was obvious because nearly all of them were playing with their newly issued M-14s, opening the bolt and slamming it shut, mimicking bayonet strokes, and aiming at imaginary enemies as we looked on and laughed. Many insulting jokes and warnings were shouted across the street at the new FNGs (Fucking New Guys). We all enjoyed our old war dog status, having been in the army a total of eight weeks.

For the RAs (Regular Army – those who had voluntarily enlisted), our upcoming training was not a mystery. By enlisting and accepting the obligation of a third year of active duty, you were allowed to select your Military Occupational Specialty, or MOS. The only question was at which fort you would receive your training. For the draftees, whose serial numbers carried the US prefix, it was a total crapshoot. They were at the mercy of the needs of the army and the strength of their general test results. In 1967, the odds of ending up as an infantry rifleman were strong.

A couple of days before graduation, I learned that the army had screwed up my flight school start date. I agreed to begin helicopter maintenance training until a class date opened up.

The DI stood before his forty-man platoon with a stack of papers. He went through the papers in alphabetical order, calling out each man's last name, the name of the fort, and the MOS. "Moore. Fort Eustis, Virginia. Sixty-Seven November. Utility Helicopter Maintenance." Or, in several cases, "Oliver. Fort Polk, Louisiana. Eleven Bravo. Rifleman." This was the one all the draftees feared – basic rifleman – the expressway to a Vietnam combat assignment. While we did not know this at the time, of the 58,200 Americans killed in Vietnam, 20,460 of them would be US Army infantrymen. Hearing that you were going to Fort Polk for infantry training was frightening news.

Fortunately for our platoon, a low percentage of draftees got that assignment. Our platoon was about equally divided between US and RA, meaning about twenty in each category. Of the twenty draftees, only four or five were assigned to the infantry.

After a couple of hours waiting around with absolutely nothing to do but get more and more thirsty, the buses showed up and we were off. For me, it was a trip home. Fort Eustis was only an hour from our home in Chesapeake. I could foresee many weekends with friends and family in my future.

ADVANCED INDIVIDUAL TRAINING (AIT)

The train ride to Ft. Eustis was long, resulting in a late arrival in Richmond and a later bus trip to the fort, about an hour south of the city. The train was a local, stopping about every fifteen minutes. It was a mild form of mental torture. As soon as the train would reach thirty-five to forty miles per hour, it would begin slowing for the next stop. As the trip progressed, the soldiers in the car would let out a groan or rough expletive. Despite leaving Columbia, South Carolina, in the late morning, we did not reach Ft. Eustis until near midnight.

For me, the bus trip was a ride down memory lane. I had spent tons of time driving I-64 between Chesapeake and Richmond. We had relatives in Richmond and made many trips to visit them, so many that I had memorized all the exits and knew what was at the end of each of the exit ramps.

Planning my heroic welcome home, I did not call my parents until I was actually at the fort. I was planning on a big surprise. As soon as I told my dad where I was, he said, "There's a guy there named Vernon Summerell. We know his parents. Get a hold of him and get a ride home." Vernon was arriving from a different Ft. Jackson training company but was also starting the same training. I found him and he agreed to give me a ride home when his wife picked him up. She was on the way. He lived in Virginia Beach, only twenty minutes from my home.

So, I would not be getting the photogenic, run-across-the-flowered-meadow greeting from my fiancé. I would be riding in the back seat of a car with two strangers who desperately wanted to be doing something else. I was in the way. Big time.

Because of the volume of helicopter mechanics needed to support the war effort, class schedules were doubled up, and we were assigned to night classes. This was not ideal, but it did provide some benefits. Because classes did not begin until late in the afternoon and ran past midnight, we were allowed to sleep in as long as we wanted. No activities were scheduled for the daytime hours, so we had plenty of free time to do whatever we pleased.

Because so few of us had cars, most of us had no way to get off the post. We spent hours reading and playing pool. Incredibly, the army had purchased some cheap pool tables and located them in one of the empty barracks buildings. We played pool for hours. The tables weren't great, but they did a good job of defeating boredom. Once we had breakfast, about a dozen of us would head to the pool hall and shoot until lunch. We would then return and shoot until 3 p.m., when classes would begin.

The worst part of being in the night class was the cold. I was amazed at how much colder it was in Newport News than in Chesapeake. While only thirty-two miles north of Chesapeake, it was probably forty miles west. That distance was enough to remove the ocean effect on winter temperatures. If it rained in Chesapeake, it snowed or sleeted in Newport News. Walking back from class in the dark became an adventure as everyone tried to avoid slipping on the ice-covered sidewalks.

The training facilities at Ft. Eustis were unbelievable in their complexity and completeness. Our training started with the use of hand tools, the basic principles of mechanics, and the theory of flight. While many guys had some experience working on cars, some had never turned a wrench. Despite their lack of experience, the army was successful in bringing them along slowly until they became proficient. We were immersed in such topics as sheet metal repair, the concept of torque, hydraulics, electricity, and jet engine mechanics. We spent weeks on these fundamentals before we were allowed to see an actual helicopter. Naturally, proficiency examinations were administered weekly to identify those who needed remedial help. Only a very few guys flunked out.

When we were finally introduced to the UH-1 Iroquois helicopter, it was a spectacular experience. We sat in a normal classroom as one of the instructors ran through some of the general characteristics and evolution of the Huey. This was my first realization that the turbine engine was used only to drive a transmission that in turn drove the rotor blades. I had mistakenly believed that the turbine engine exhaust also provided significant thrust, capable of driving the helicopter at higher speeds. Because the UH-1 had often been referred to as the first jet-powered helicopter, I thought they meant jet in the traditional sense. Wrong.

When we left the classroom, we entered a large hangar through wide double doors, allowing all thirty-five of us to enter almost simultaneously. Before us sat two rows of UH-1As, each row with about ten helicopters. They were parked at an angle, so our primary view was of the nose of each ship. The rotor blades and tail booms had been shortened so the aircraft would fit into the hangar and could be moved around if necessary.

Once introduced to the actual aircraft, the training pace grew more intense. Our eventual job would be that of an aircraft crew chief or a maintenance mechanic (i.e., ground crew). As a crew chief, we would be assigned to an individual aircraft and be responsible for its care and feeding. While the crew chief performed what the army called first echelon maintenance, such as filter changes and minor repairs, the unit's maintenance platoon would perform the heavier repairs, such as engine and transmission replacements, sheet metal repair, and hydraulic or electrical system repair. Regardless of which job we would eventually get, the training at Eustis would prepare us for it. We would become a jack of all trades for everything on the Huey. We would know quite a bit about every system and component on the aircraft, certainly enough to detect and often diagnose problems. If a more specialized mechanic was needed, the maintenance platoon would handle it.

As a person that liked cars and airplanes, the Huey was a wonderland of new technology. Most impressive was the computer-controlled turbine engine. Unlike piston engines of the past, the turbine engine was controlled by a computer that measured engine strain and automatically adjusted the fuel flow. The pilot did not have to adjust the throttle when he took off, hovered, or landed. The computer would make all the adjustments, once the pilot set the turbine at the proper RPM. In 1968, this was pretty remarkable. It was the basic equivalent of fuel injection, but much smarter. I was amazed.

Virtually everything about the Huey fascinated me. One of my earliest questions was, "Who were the geniuses that invented all of this?"

Because I had often worked alongside my father when he was repairing the family car, I was comfortable with mechanical tasks. We undertook repairs that most folks would not. We rebuilt carburetors, generators, and starters, adjusted valves, replaced brakes, shocks, mufflers, and distributors. We never removed or rebuilt an engine, but we did almost everything else. As an eighteen-year-old, I possessed a solid background in mechanics.

Our classes ran from early November through mid-March. I did well on the final exam and ranked number one when the class ended. Finishing at the top had not been a personal goal, but I was proud of the achievement. Because two UH-1 classes were being taught simultaneously, I learned that I had finished at the top of both classes, finishing ahead of some seventy other students.

As a reward for academic performance, the army allowed the top twelve students in each UH-1 class to pursue further training. Better still, we would have our choice of attending Cobra school or OH-6A school. The OH-6A carried the nickname "Loach" as a bastardization of the Light Observation Helicopter (LOH) army acronym. Because Loach crew chiefs flew and Cobra crew chiefs did not, I selected Loach school. It turned out the absolute best choice for me.

Loach school students were always trained as UH-1 mechanics first. The school was only four weeks long. This allowed me to spend another month close to home, so I was very enthused about it. I was also promoted to the rank of Spec-4, the equivalent of a corporal in the infantry.

The Loach was a much simpler aircraft than the Huey. It had no hydraulics or all the requisite lines, tanks, accumulators, and pumps needed for hydraulic flight control. The transmission was the size and shape of an oversized hatbox. The seats weren't even adjustable, but the foot pedals were! The tail rotor driveshaft was a single nine-foot aluminum tube, running from the transmission to the tail rotor gearbox, not the four-section drive shaft of the Huey, with hanger bearings and universal joints between each section. Because the rotor head configuration was completely different than the Huey, the mechanical flight controls were very simple and easy to maintain. Like the Huey, it was also turbine-powered.

I was able to master Loach repair with few problems. The final exam was memorable.

I was sitting next to one of my friends from Huey school, a great guy from New York State named Jim Manley. Our paths would cross again over a year later. Jim was tall, skinny, and always joking around. Somehow, he knew exactly how far he could push an instructor without getting into trouble. He was quick-witted and kept us amused. He was the class clown.

The final exam consisted of a hundred questions. Most were multiple-choice, with a few math problems thrown in. Because the class ended the same day as the final exam, we were required to exchange our test sheets and score each other's tests. There was no time to wait for instructor grading and the posting of grades.

When the scoring was complete, we were instructed to write the number of incorrect answers on the top of the first page, along with the percentage of correct answers. When that was completed, and with the scorers still in possession of their neighbors' tests, the instructor began polling the class to see how we scored. He started, "Who got one wrong? Who got two wrong?" On he went down the scale. When he finished writing down the responses, he threw his pencil on the desk and said, "Dammit! Someone screwed up. I only have twenty-three scores." Manley raised his hand. Prepared for a Manley wise crack, the instructor asked Jim, "What do you want, *Specialist* Manley?" Jim responded, "Well, Mr. Instructor, sir, Sergeant. You did not ask how many people got *zero* wrong, sir."

The instructor smirked and said, "Zero wrong? *Nobody* gets *zero* wrong!"

"Mr. Sergeant, sir. Specialist Moore got all one hundred questions correct. If my math is still correct, sir, that means he got zero wrong, sir."

The instructor walked over to our table and demanded to see my test papers. He held them up to the light, as if he was looking for invisible ink or some kind of coded cheat sheet. He handed them back to Manley.

"Goddamn it, Moore. No one has ever aced the final exam. Congratulations, Specialist!"

As they say, the crowd went wild. All of my classmates started whopping and hollering, shouting their congratulations and clapping. I believe they were more amused by Jim's taunting of the instructor than my test score, but it was fun to watch. They also made sure I understood that the drinks were on me that night.

With Loach class over, I headed home for a long weekend. I would be on leave until the orders to my next duty station arrived. It would turn out to be a very long weekend.

I left the fort on a Friday afternoon. When I woke up Saturday morning, I could not sit up in bed. I was burning up and my throat was on fire. I could barely swallow, and my throat was almost swollen shut. The inside of my mouth was burning too, and my swollen gums felt as though they were about to burst open.

My dad stuck a thermometer into my mouth. Three minutes later, he said, "Oh my God! We've got to get you back to Fort Eustis." He did not say how high my fever was. I really did not care.

He drove me back to the base. It was an hour-long trip, during which I was sleeping in the fetal position. I was semiconscious when we rolled up to the gate.

The guard looked in the backseat and asked, "Who's that, and what's wrong with him?" My dad explained that I was a student there and woke up with a bad temperature. The gate guard said, "Yeah. I'll bet," implying that I was only hung over.

He gave us directions to McDonald Army Hospital, where I checked into the emergency room. An army doctor who looked to be about fifteen years old examined me. He announced that I had tonsillitis and would prescribe some antibiotics. I grunted, "That's nice. I had my tonsils removed about eight years ago."

He said, "Oh. Oh. Let me take another look." I was finally diagnosed with strep throat. They admitted me to an eight-bed ward. I instructed them to inform my company commander, then promptly passed out.

They pumped me with megadoses of penicillin and hooked up an IV. My gums continued to swell, and I was no better three days later. I still did not have the strength to sit up or get out of bed. When two doctors made their rounds the following morning, I could hear their puzzled conversation. They had no idea what was wrong. They started poking around my abdomen and making remarks about something being wrong with my spleen. I was not encouraged.

Things got significantly worse on day four. A nurse came to the ward and let me know that I had to get up and change my own linens! I could barely move but gave it a try. I immediately fell back onto the bed. She walked away saying, "Get it done."

I gradually improved over the next week or so. I lost track of the days because I was barely conscious for most of the time. When I finally got to the point where I could walk, my company CO and the executive officer paid me a visit. When they walked into the ward, my first instinct told me I must be in serious trouble. Maybe the hospital did not inform them of my whereabouts, making them think I was AWOL for something over a week. Maybe they had reported me to the MPs, creating a mess that would take forever to clear up.

I was wrong. They presented me with a certificate, documenting that I had finished as the number one graduate of Loach school. They also presented me with a small, gold tie tack in the shape of a Loach. The certificate was nice, but the tie tack impressed me. They had gone to a local jeweler and had it made at their own expense. They were very excited that the first student to ace the final exam was in their company. It really was touching.

They also informed me that I was being promoted to Spec-5 in recognition of my achievements. This was news. I had only been in the army for seven months and had already made a rank equivalent to buck sergeant. I knew my dad would be very proud in his own silent way.

ASSIGNMENT

"The key is to keep company only with people who uplift you, whose presence calls forth your best."

Epictetus

After discharge from the hospital, I arrived home to find that my orders had arrived the day before. It appeared that I had wasted my leave lying in the hospital.

The orders themselves were incredibly hard to decipher. They looked like they were written in a foreign language, with weird combinations of letters, numbers. and symbols. I found the words, "Ft. Hood, Texas," and knew where I was headed, and it was not Vietnam. I was crushed.

I also found the phrase "370 TC DET." I had no idea what it meant, but it looked like a unit designation. While disappointed at not being assigned to a combat unit, I tried to put a positive spin on the situation. I imagined that I would serve as a crew chief for some general commanding an armored division. I would have a great assignment with little danger, cruising around Texas and impressing everyone with my shiny helicopter and my flight suit.

Such a future did not work for me. I was pissed that I was not going to Vietnam.

Now I had to arrange my transportation to Ft. Hood. Using the family encyclopedia and a map of Texas, I located the town of Waco and saw that it had a regional airport. I selected Waco as my final destination, figuring to arrange ground transportation when I arrived there. I made my one-way reservations with venerable Piedmont Airlines and hoped for the best.

My departure was not all that emotional. After all, I was going to Texas, not the war.

We flew from Norfolk to Dallas, with a stopover in Atlanta. Upon arrival at Dallas's Love Field, I made the connection to Waco. When I walked onto the tarmac to board the plane – these were the days of using steps to board a plane; jetways were rare – I saw that the gate agent was pointing me toward a tiny single-engine airplane. A man who turned out to be the pilot was leaning casually against the fuselage, waving me over. The fun was about to begin.

We boarded the plane and I threw my duffle bag into the small rear seat and prepared to crawl in with it, but the pilot directed me to sit in the front seat beside him.

I sat before a full array of controls, instruments, and switches within easy reach. I wondered if I was going to get any stick time. As we taxied away from the terminal, I noticed that our plane was the only small plane on the facility. We were surrounded by large commercial jets of the day, as well as the large, turboprop-driven airliners that were rapidly becoming obsolete. As we taxied around, we were so low we could actually look *under* the surrounding aircraft to see if the way was clear. It was scary. I wondered if the pilots in the commercial jets could even see us when we crossed in front of them. Worse yet, I feared that one of the larger aircraft could easily blow us over with their exhaust blast, turning us and the plane into a flaming piece of debris, tumbling along the taxiway.

We made it safely from Dallas for the short flight to Waco. Other than having a near miss with an aircraft departing Waco, it was an uneventful flight. Waco was an uncontrolled airport, meaning there was no control tower. Pilots were on their own to navigate as they saw fit. It was the honor system, where a code violation could end up killing someone. Unfortunately for us, the departing plane was taking off in the wrong direction while we were on final approach – the perfect setup for a head-on collision. He was taking off downwind – a flagrant violation of the rules of the road. If my pilot had not been paying attention, we would have died in Waco.

After aborting the first landing attempt, we circled the airport and made our approach. When I looked down, I thought that we had gone to the wrong place. The airport was incredibly small. There were no other aircraft on the ground. I only saw one small building sitting at the side of the active runway. "Is that Waco?" I yelled to the pilot. "Yep. That's it," he replied.

Once on the ground and taxiing toward the building, I asked the pilot again if we really were at Waco. He chuckled and confirmed that we were. He pulled the plane up to the small, concrete-block building, and I jumped out. While I was retrieving my bag, he told me that there were vending machines inside and a bus stop on the other side of the terminal. He said the Ft. Hood bus came by every hour or two, and I just had to wait under the bus stop sign. I walked through the building, observing two half-empty vending machines and nothing else. Health concerns prevented me from buying any of the food or drinks, so I wandered outside and sat on my duffle bag. There was no phone and no other humans in sight. I began to worry about the probability of being stranded with no options. I began to sweat.

About ninety minutes later, miracle of miracles, a bus approached out of the haze. He was coming from the west and blowing up a sizable cloud of dust. The setting sun created quite a visual as my rescuer arrived. Now I only had to hope that this was the Ft. Hood bus.

It was, and I was treated to a sight that I will always remember.

This was mid-April 1968, the week Martin Luther King was assassinated in Memphis. Riots were breaking out in many major cities, and the regular army was called upon to stop the violence.

As we pulled onto the fort property, I saw the entire First Armored Division assembled on a large, empty space beside the road. Anyone familiar with army posts knows that they are characterized by rolling expanses of empty space, usually large enough to build small villages. The division included about 10,000 soldiers and all of their equipment and vehicles, including their tanks. It was an amazing sight. The men were milling around in small groups. All of them carried M-14s, and their field gear was arranged in neat rows on the ground.

The bus was only fifty to seventy-five yards from the formations. The distance and size of the group gave me a strong impression of how interchangeable the individual soldiers appeared. With the exception of the little bit of hair color I could see under their hats and their slight variations in height, they all looked exactly the same. Even their eyeglasses were the same: black frames with square lenses on man after man. Not only did they look interchangeable, but disposable too.

It must have taken about eight to ten minutes to drive past the entire division. The bus driver told me they were being sent to Detroit. Since I was the only passenger on the bus, he could devote his attention to me.

Now we started to hunt for the 370 TC DET, whatever that was. Because it was well after 5 p.m., all of the offices were closed, all except the military police (MP) office, so I had the bus driver drop me there.

I walked up to the desk, showed them my orders, and asked if they had any idea what or where this unit was. They did not. They searched a typed list of units. Not there. They searched a phone directory. Not there. After about twenty minutes of fruitless research, one of the MPs made a phone call. He and his unidentified buddy exchanged "What about . . . ?" questions until one of them suggested a small airstrip outside of the fort. They talked a while longer and convinced each other that that was my destination.

They showed it to me on a large wall map. It was about ten miles away. My heart sank. How in the hell was I going to get there? It was dark and I was on foot. I had no idea where the nearest cab stand was or if one even existed.

One of the MPs offered to give me a ride, so he could get out of the office for a while.

It took about fifteen minutes to get there. Because it was now dark, all I could see were lights and what looked like an airport control tower. The MP dropped me off at one of the main buildings adjacent to the control tower. There wasn't a human in sight, and no vehicles were moving. The setting seemed very, very strange.

I entered the building and met another soldier coming out to greet me. He confirmed that this was where I was supposed to be: the 370th Transportation Detachment. He gave me some linens and pointed me toward a barracks building about 150 yards away. He told me to go over there, pick out a room, and come back at seven thirty in the morning. Pick out *a room*? He said he would get me fed and issue my gear in the morning. He also said I was one of the first men to arrive.

The 370th Transportation Detachment – not a very glorious-sounding name. Was I now a truck driver? I figured I would learn more in the morning and started walking toward the barracks to select *a room*.

As promised, the two-story building was laid out as I imagined a college dorm would: small, four-bunk rooms with built-in wall lockers and a double window. Also, a door that could be closed for privacy. A single latrine and shower area served the entire floor and was capable of handling about fifteen men at a time.

I chose one on the first floor, unpacked my duffle bag, and crashed onto the bed for a night's sleep.

My biological alarm clock woke me up at six in the morning, starving. I had not eaten since lunch in Dallas, so my first priority was finding the mess hall. I jogged over to the main building and found my greeter from the night before. He showed me the mess hall and said to come straight back to get my gear.

The breakfast was not remarkable, but my gear was. The first thing I received was my underwear, and it was olive green. I looked up at the supply clerk, and before I could get a word out, he said, "That's right, buddy. You're heading for the Nam with a build-up unit!"

All right then. I wasn't excited about a build-up unit because that meant the vast majority of us would be Nam rookies. However, it was better than missing the whole war – at least in my naïve opinion.

After receiving the full complement of jungle apparel, I next went to another office to check in. The clerk told me that the 370th was one of six helicopter maintenance units being readied for deployment. He could not name the destination but said the jungle clothing should tell me something: I was not going to Germany or Korea!

He also told me that five or six others had checked in. Because I was the ranking E-5, I would be in charge of the unit until an officer or a senior NCO showed up. Oh God! I had visions of the train ride. But this gig might be weeks long, not the short overnighter that I felt lucky to survive.

He explained my duties and responsibilities and told me to go to my building, introduce myself to the others, and get them into formation at 1300. He planned to come over and make a few announcements.

When I got there, I found two others from my AIT class: Craig Schmidt and Jim Reed. I invited them to my room. We would at least know our roommates.

Craig was a quiet Midwesterner from the St. Louis area. Like me, he enjoyed reading and fast cars. We both tended to be on the quiet side, usually sizing up a group before joining in. Craig and I would become close friends, with him eventually serving as best man in my wedding.

Jim was more on the gregarious side. A proud Texan, Jim was easygoing and outspoken. He treated everyone like a long-lost friend. The three of us got along fine.

We ate lunch and then reported to the designated spot for our 1300 formation. There were about eight of us in the 370th TC Detachment, including my friend Vernon Summerell from Virginia Beach. He and his wife had arrived a few days earlier and had rented a house in Killeen, the small town that bordered the fort on the northeast.

The Spec-4 who checked me in came over to address the formation. He announced that senior NCOs and an officer would be arriving soon and that, for now, I was in charge and why (my AIT grades). Because I had finished first in the class, my date-of-rank positioned me ahead of any other student who had been promoted upon graduation. For the next few days, we were to concentrate on cleaning the barracks building and getting it ready to house about fifty guys – enough to fill the building.

As the week wore on, we held formation twice per day: once at 0700 and once at 1300. More guys trickled in daily, and our headcount began to grow. One of my duties included accounting for all the men and reporting any absences to the Spec-4 in the tower building.

As the group grew with the addition of people with varying occupational specialties, work assignments began to come over from the tower. Most of them were related to housekeeping, moving bunk frames among the buildings, and getting ready to house more men.

The relocation of bunks was particularly exhausting because we were required to move the frames from the second story in one building to the second story in another building. The bunk frames were metal, which had become burred and dinged over the years. Handling them without gloves cut your hands and often left them with painful metal splinters that could quickly become infected.

During one of my visits to the tower, the guy in charge asked if I was going on the work details. I said I was. He admonished me, saying, "You shouldn't be doing this! You should stay in the area in case I need to get in touch with you. All you have to do is assign the other guys to do the work and wait for it to be done." From that point on, I decided to let rank have its privilege.

The work was also getting a little more diverse, requiring me to assign people to teams and appoint a leader for each team. Leveraging the axiom that success is more dependent on who you know than what you know, I naturally appointed my closer friends to the team leader roles and left the grunt work to the strangers. I was also allowed to appoint a deputy to help me keep the paperwork straight. It had to be someone living in the barracks. No problem. I appointed Craig Schmidt.

Leisure Time

During these early weeks in Texas, the workload was not as demanding as it would become in May and June, and there was a great deal of idle time. We were idle, but not free. We were required to remain in the barracks area "in case something comes up." It never did, and the boredom became intense. I spent a lot of time reading and listening to music, as did Craig.

After a while, Craig had a suggestion: he wanted to teach a few of us to play pinochle. He proved to be quite the teacher. In less than a week, almost all of us were playing and playing intensely. We all played single-deck, in which only fifty-two cards were used. This version, as compared to double-deck, seemed more demanding because each card held greater significance in the scoring.

The number of games underway at any one time must have been around eight or ten. Guys paired off into regular two-man teams. A pecking order soon developed, and Craig and I were at the top. Because the barracks had two floors, the residents of each floor usually played each other, with very little cross-floor competition. The relative strengths and weaknesses of the teams were usually spoken of in terms of which floor a certain team represented.

Craig and I remained undefeated for a long, long time. We played together so often we recognized each other's bidding patterns and playing tactics during the hands. We could virtually tell what cards we each held, allowing us to play to our strengths and maximize our opponents' weaknesses. After several weeks, a team from upstairs challenged us to a match. They had made several comments about our streak, asserting that we had to be cheating. Of course, they had not played us. They just could not believe we were *that* good.

In the day or so between the challenge and the game, it started taking on the feel of a grudge match. Significant trash-talking and betting got underway. Each team seemed to be playing for the honor of their respective floor. Things got a little nasty when one of the second-floor guys started talking about what they were going to do to us if they caught us cheating: a certainty in their minds.

On the night of the game, we agreed to play a best three-out-of-five-game match. Because there was no recreation facility, we only had our rooms in which to play. Men from both floors jammed into our room, two or three on each of the four bunks and three or four more standing on the few square feet of floor space available. The card table was a footlocker with a green towel on it, with the players sitting on the floor, cross-legged. Other spectators milled around in the hall, just outside our door.

It was over quickly. We swept them in three games, and they never led a single game. By the time we got to the middle of the second game, they were arguing with each other and cussing profusely. Every hand resulted in more groans from the upstairs contingent. We maintained our cool and put them away silently and efficiently. One of the things that Craig taught me early was the absolute prohibition on criticizing the play of your partner – no groans, eye-rolling, or outward signs of displeasure. I learned that Craig and his family were avid card players and valued maintaining a poker face at all times. This may have been as important to our win as our actual play.

The upstairs boys had to agree that Craig and I were *that* good. There were no more accusations of cheating.

Nearly four years later, when my wife and I were in St. Louis for Craig's wedding, we guessed at the number of pinochle games we might have played between early May and July 25th, when we left for Nam. We figured six games per day for six and a half days per week over twelve weeks came out to 468 games, and that's a pretty conservative estimate. With a level of play that intense over a fairly short period, it is easy to see how we could understand each other's play without cheating.

The work continued, with Craig and I doing very little of it. One of our larger guys, a six four redneck named Edwards, started giving me a hard time about my position of privilege. He made several threats about beating me senseless. Because he was always yelling these threats at the top of his lungs, every guy in the detachment could hear them. He started to attract some allies, so I thought I had better put an end to it before a mutiny occurred.

As we were breaking up our morning formation the next day, Edwards started in on me, bellowing his threats and getting laughs from a few of his friends. I could tell my timing was right because many other guys were giving me a look that said, "Well, Al, what are you going to do about it?"

As Edwards started to walk away, I yelled for him to hold on and come over to where I was standing. Naturally, all forty or so guys stopped and watched what they thought would be a beatdown. Edwards pranced over to where I was standing, a distance of about twenty-five feet. He was nodding his head and making derogatory remarks as he walked over, chest thrust out like a barnyard rooster. He stopped a couple of feet in front of me, with his fists clinched by his side. He looked down at me in contempt.

I said softly, "Edwards, you've been making some noise about the way I'm running things. You think you can beat my ass and intimidate me into giving you your way. Well, neither of those things are going to happen. You can go ahead and throw the first punch if you really want to. Go ahead. I'm ready." I paused for effect while he stood frozen.

"But I just want you to think about one small thing. You are an E-4. I'm an E-5. That makes me your superior in every way the army cares about. No matter what, I outrank you," I continued. "You're not working any harder than anyone else in this outfit. So you can go ahead and throw that punch, but think about the consequences if you do. A court-martial? An Article 15? Busted back to E-2? A little time in the stockade? Go right ahead."

None of this could be heard by his friends, so they had no idea what was going on. All they saw was me talking, and Edwards's shoulders sag as he exhaled a long, relaxing breath. He turned and walked away.

To make sure everyone heard what I wanted them to hear, I yelled after him, "Edwards, if you really wanted to be in charge, all you had to do was study *just a little harder!*" This brought a chuckle from just about everybody. Problem solved. He never mouthed off again.

As the weeks passed, a senior NCO arrived. He was a staff sergeant (E-6) named Davis. He had been in the army about ten years. He was not at all comfortable with the idea of having five or six brand-new E-5s who had been in the army for less than a year. He wanted to let everyone know that he was in charge, so he had us do meaningless tasks that consumed all of our leisure time.

Soon after Davis's arrival, Lieutenant (Lt.). Camp and Sergeant First Class (SFC) Smith arrived. Camp became our CO and Smith became our platoon sergeant. He was an E-7, outranking Davis by one grade. This effectively ended my reign as top dog. I was now one of the worker bees.

I never really had a conversation with Lt. Camp. The only time I saw him was during the formations. I had no idea what he did during the day. Being new and over-respectful of rank, I never asked.

Davis was an odd one. At times he wanted to show that he was hard-core by abusing us. At other times, and especially after a few snorts, he was a completely different person – appealing for friendship in one-on-one encounters, whining about his responsibilities, and blaming Smith and Camp for everything he required of us. I found this strange and incredibly weak.

SFC Smith *was* hard-core. He didn't give a lick about anyone's feelings, sensitivity, or mental well-being. He was almost unapproachable and held us E-5s in total and obvious contempt. At one point, we were moving some bunk frames from one building to another in a very inefficient way. We discovered that he wanted us to move this stuff from building one to building three, then move the stuff in building three to building four. All the frames were the same. Upon hearing his directions, anyone with half a brain could see that all we really needed to do was move the stuff from building one to building four and skip all the movements in between.

To avoid embarrassing him, I stepped up and quietly pointed this out. He exploded. "When I want any shit out of you, *Specialist*, I'll squeeze your fucking head!"

Well. OK, I thought. I certainly know whom I'll be dealing with in the future. This was my first indication of how little respect the lifers had for their subordinates. Initially, I thought it was limited to SFC Smith's particular personality. I later found it to be a rigid caste system that pervaded the army in the late '60s.

Craig Schmidt, LOH Mechanic, St. Louis.

Smith maintained this attitude for the rest of our time at Hood and during my time in the maintenance unit when we arrived in Vietnam. Asking questions about his directions was a no-no. Suggesting a different approach was insubordination, no matter how illogical his orders might be. Needless to say, very few people respected SFC Smith. Both Davis and Smith served as prime examples of the treatment we new soldiers could expect from the senior NCOs. It wasn't encouraging.

Austin

Austin, Texas, was only about sixty miles south of where we were living at Ft. Hood. When we realized that Austin was the home of the University of Texas, it went to the top of our must-see destinations.

Although Austin was beyond our fifty-mile limit, we began to visit regularly. There was a two-lane back road that kept us off of Interstate 35, allowing us to miss the rush hour traffic. Better still, the road had no speed limit, so we could make good time getting there. It was a little tricky at night, but we were immortal, so the dark did not slow us down much.

Typically, we would stuff four guys into Craig's Mustang and hit the trail. Once we arrived in Austin, we would try to get served in the local bars. Despite the presence of all those cute Texas coeds, we were not very popular. Our short hair signaled that we were military, and most folks would not even speak to us. They all assumed we were stationed at Lackland, the local air force base.

San Antonio

The world's fair, or at least a close cousin called Hemisfair, was going on in San Antonio. Because we were accustomed to breaking our fifty-mile travel limit, the 160 miles to San Antonio did not seem like a big deal.

Several of us made the four-hour trip, booked a hotel room, and got ready to party.

We arrived at the fairgrounds and were immediately ensnared by a barker who tried to hustle the passersby into an all-nude review in the style of a French floorshow. He was accompanied by three or four beautiful women, all dressed in revealing costumes. What were a bunch of nineteen-year-olds to do?

We bought tickets and went in. The theatre was full, and as we all moved up to the edge of our expensive seats, the music came on and the curtain rose. Down from the ceiling dropped about twenty semi-nude female dancers dangling from nearly invisible cords – puppets!

The remainder of the weekend was about the same. We did not go up in the

Tower of the Americas, a sort of space needle with a revolving restaurant. It was way beyond our budget, so we passed it by.

Car Crazy

While in Texas, most of my friends developed an obsession for cars. I did not have my '63 Ford Falcon in Texas, and I never considered it much of a permanent vehicle anyway. It was adequate for a high school student but did not cut it for an E-5 of my stature. I began car shopping. During the following months, I probably decided on three or four different manufacturers and models. I was surrounded by experts who never missed an opportunity to share their ever-changing opinions. We spent days cruising the auto dealerships in and around Killeen, Texas, gathering specs and prices.

A factor that added to the pressure was my plan to purchase the car *before* I went to Nam, not after I returned.

After all of the research and fretting over which car to buy, I decided on a new '68 Plymouth Road Runner. They were hot, inexpensive, and purpose-built street racers. I asked my dad to visit our local Plymouth dealer, where I had bought the Falcon, and see what kind of deal they would offer.

He got a sweet one. The car was a hardtop with several options. It lacked air conditioning and power brakes and was generally set up for speed. The option package focused on appearance, so the car had metallic green paint and was quite attractive.

Because I wasn't sure how my girlfriend Norma would react, I told my folks not to show it to her until I came home on leave.

When I did, she wasn't happy. Of course, she saw it as a huge waste of money. I saw it as one last splurge before heading for the combat zone.

Lampasas Riot

Then an event occurred that brought us a little excitement. One of the men in the 370th had been cruising one of the local drive-ins when some civilians jumped him and roughed him up. During the scrape, one of the locals mentioned that they were from Lampasas and if he wanted a real beating, our guy could come over to Lampasas, which was a small town about twenty-five miles west of Ft. Hood. One of the men in the 370th came up with the bright idea of getting about fifty people together, cruising Lampasas until we found the assailant, and starting a riot.

While it appears as a stupid idea now, it seemed to be a *great* idea to a bunch of nineteen- and twenty-year-olds on their way to Vietnam. What did we have to lose?

On the next Saturday afternoon, about twenty cars full of soldiers departed Ft. Hood for Lampasas. We were determined to show the locals a thing or two about fighting.

We hit the two or three drive-ins and hangouts in Lampasas, but our man could not find the perpetrator. After two or three hours of this, we drove back to Ft. Hood unfulfilled.

After that event, I often wondered just how sincere the search really was. Our victim was in the lead car. He was a sensible person. He possibly considered the outcome if we started a real riot. How many times might we have driven past the culprit but left him unmolested? We will never know.

Leave

Several weeks after Smith's arrival, we had all of our equipment prepared and packed and ready to ship to Nam. An advance party was selected to accompany the gear on its trip to Nam – a thirty-day ocean voyage. Volunteers were invited. I avoided it because my father's described his trip to Europe in 1944 on the *Queen Mary* as pure misery, where they had to stay below, even in calm weather. I wanted no part of it. Even when they said our twelve-month clock would begin when we departed the US, sparing us thirty days in-country, I declined.

With the equipment gone, there was absolutely nothing to do. Pinochle continued, along with frequent trips to the NCO club. After a week of this, we were allowed to go home for a two-week leave.

Rather than fly back through Waco, Craig Schmidt offered me a ride to St. Louis, where I could catch a flight home. It was a long drive, and having two drivers would enable him not to stop overnight.

It was a relatively smooth trip and gave me the opportunity to meet Craig's family in St. Louis. His entire family treated me great. They were wonderful people. After I got some sleep, they drove me to the St. Louis airport for my trip home.

The trip was relatively short. After a stop in DC and another in Newport News, we touched down in Norfolk.

We spent most of the days on the beach or visiting friends who were home from college. The evenings were spent cruising the local Shoney's and the Atlantic Avenue strip. This was the peak of the muscle car era, so the Road Runner was incredibly popular. Requests to sound the horn were nonstop; everyone wanted to hear that famous beep-beep. It sounded reasonably close to the cartoon character, so everyone was always pleased.

The car drew people like a magnet. Every gas station stop turned into a car show as people wanted to see the engine, hear the engine, and hear that horn. It was a major ego trip for a nineteen-year-old.

It was during this two-week leave that I decided to solidify my commitment to Norma. I asked her to marry me. I later talked to her dad, and he gave us the OK.

Because I believed I would eventually make my way to a combat assignment, I was opposed to getting married before deployment. I did not want to make Norma a young widow if the worst happened. We agreed to marry when I returned.

We drove to a downtown jeweler to pick out a ring. Being of limited means, affordability was a major factor. I think it was less than one-quarter carat in size. As we were signing up for an installment payment plan, I commented about its weight. The jeweler casually tossed the diamond on a balance scale, then dropped a small rubber band on the opposite scale. They weighed about the same! To say I was deflated is a massive understatement.

The two weeks flew by. After what felt like three days, I was back on a plane and heading for Waco. The departure was tough for me because a yearlong tour sounded like an eternity. Of course, my parents and Norma were worried about my survival. My dad's parting advice was, "Keep your damned head down!"

In those days, the Norfolk airport had no jetways, so passengers walked across the tarmac to go up the stairway and into the plane. After kissing Norma goodbye, I walked straight to the plane and climbed aboard without looking back. It seemed like the macho thing to do. In actuality, I was afraid that I might cry if I looked back and saw Norma standing there. Years later, she told me how much she wanted me to look back, but I did not. It caused her unnecessary pain.

ARRIVAL

"War makes strange giant creatures out of us little routine men who inhabit the earth."

Ernie Pyle

We all came back to Ft. Hood within a day of each other. You could not describe the mood as jovial. Most people were depressed about the twelve-plus months we would be gone. Our twelve-month tour clock did not start ticking until the minute we left the United States, and we had no idea when that would be. For all we knew, we could be sitting around in Texas for another month or two.

It turned out to be about a week – a week of the most intense boredom one could imagine. No transportation was available because private cars were no longer allowed. Taxis would not come in because we were restricted to our little airbase facility. The only form of entertainment was an enlisted man's club about three miles away. That was not a very attractive prospect, considering we were in central Texas in July! We did make the trek a couple of times, but the place resembled a nightclub in a prison. The only women around were the waitresses, all of whom were old enough to be our mothers.

On one of those treks back from the club, a car passed us going in the opposite direction. For some reason the people in the car decided to give us some grief and yelled a string of insults as they went by. Not wanting to appear as pussies, the four of us spun around and yelled back. As we did so, we began running toward the car.

When the car's occupants saw this, they slammed on the brakes and the car slid to a halt about two hundred feet down the road. Two people stepped out. We continued running toward the car until two gunshots rang out! The bullets went right over our heads, emitting high-pitched swooshing noises as they passed by.

It was now our turn to slide to a stop and reverse course. We did so, sprinting back toward the barracks and the safety of the darkness. We heard the shooters laughing as they drove away.

We literally had nothing to do. Our radios and phonographs had been taken home. Pinochle began to get old. As most GIs do, we mainly sat around in the heat, sweated, and bitched.

Finally, on July 25th, we got the word to pack our bags, go outside, and wait for the buses. Even this simple process resulted in more frustration. We got the word shortly before noon, so we didn't eat lunch. We went outside with our duffle bags and tried to find some shade.

The buses finally arrived about seven hours later, and a loud cheer went up from the hundred and thirty men now lying in the grass and fighting off the bugs. One of the Nam vets in our group warned us that we wouldn't be cheering when we got to Nam. Someone told him to go to hell, and we were off.

We were then treated to a three-hour bus ride to Lackland Air Force Base in San Antonio. It was close to 11 p.m. when the buses went through the gate, onto the tarmac, and pulled alongside a Flying Tiger Airlines Boeing 707 airliner. I expected a military transport of some type, so the sight of a civilian plane had promise. Portable floodlights mounted on trucks illuminated the scene. Armed guards surrounded the plane, forming a circle with the men about ten to twenty feet apart. They appeared to be military policemen, but it was hard to tell in the glare of the lights.

I could not imagine why they were present. Perhaps they thought some of us would run away. Or maybe they were expecting some sort of peace protest. In any case, it seemed like a mammoth waste of their evening to me.

In true army tradition, we remained on the bus for about another hour while nothing seemed to be going on. The entire day had been an illustration of the old "hurry up and wait" cliché. This topped it off.

When we boarded the plane, the purpose of this aircraft became obvious. It was a single, uninterrupted aluminum tube from tail to flight deck. No dividers, curtains, or panels broke the line of sight. The seats were typical airliner equipment arranged in rows of three on either side of the aisle. Because we entered through a door in the rear of the plane, the view was pretty dramatic. It made me feel like a piece of ground meat stuffed into a hotdog casing. There appeared to be about forty rows of seats, meaning a capacity of 240 souls, all dressed the same, sporting the exact same baseball caps, with many wearing the same black-rimmed glasses. The army had a variety of ways to strip away a person's sense of individuality. This seemed to be another one.

The flight turned out to be another test of our perseverance over monotony. The flight was over twenty-four hours long, with refueling stops in Hawaii and the Philippines. Stretching your legs was difficult because you had to disturb your neighbors to reach the aisle. Once in the aisle, the presence of other people made it nearly impossible to walk. Cramps were prevalent.

One of the worst things about the trip was the in-flight meals. I use the term "meal" guardedly. The meals consisted of a ham and cheese sandwich on a sub roll accompanied by a six-ounce cup of orange juice. The sandwich was free of any dressing like mayonnaise or mustard. The bread was at least a day old, and the orange juice was room temperature, or plane temperature, which felt like eighty degrees.

What made the meals even worse was the flight attendants' insistence that you eat every three hours, whether you wanted to or not. They would constantly wake you up and have you choke down a sandwich. This was particularly annoying in the middle of the night. You would wake up a little nauseated and have to gag your way through one of these sandwiches and warm juice. The attendants explained that they had strict instructions to see that each of us ate the specified amount of food on the flight to make sure we did not arrive hungry. No one knew when we would eat again, so they made sure our stomachs remained full the entire time we were in their control.

We arrived in Hawaii at 2 a.m. local time. The airport was open, so we went inside to buy cigarettes and look for food while the plane was refueled.

The place was empty and all the shops were closed for the night. The only cigarettes we could find were in a vending machine. The machine price was seventy-five cents per pack, and we were absolutely stunned. We could not imagine paying that much for a pack of smokes, but we coughed up the money anyway.

The flight turned out to be a little worse for me than the other guys because of an experience I had with one of the flight attendants. She had a warped sense of humor, and I was destined to suffer for it.

During the overnight hours of the flight, I suddenly woke up in a choking fit and had a difficult time breathing. The people beside me looked horrified, and the flight attendant was standing in the aisle laughing her head off. When I finally caught my breath, she explained that I had been snoring with my mouth open and she thought it would be funny to pour a bag of sugar down my throat!

I did not think it was at all funny and began cussing her out. Not only had it choked me, but she had also dumped most of the bag of sugar inside my shirt. It began itching right away. My buddies helped me get the shirt off, but by then some of the sugar had worked its way into my pants. It was a mess that would last another thirty-six hours. We were not able to shower when we eventually landed in Long Binh, so I had to suffer from the sugar for over a day and a half. I acted like I had fleas because I could not stop the itching. I would have probably strangled her if I would have seen her again.

Our next fuel stop was at Clark AFB in the Philippines. We arrived around midmorning and it was already very hot. We taxied to the refueling point, where we were ushered off the plane and instructed to sit on the tarmac, but not to smoke.

That morning was my first experience with a true tropical climate. The sky was a brilliant blue, spotted with beautiful, low-hanging cumulous clouds. It was the first of many such sights I would enjoy in Nam.

We suddenly heard a roar and looked toward the runway. A flight of B-52s were departing for a bombing mission somewhere in Southeast Asia. They looked like doomsday machines. Mainly black or dark green, with droopy wings, they seemed to strain to take off. As they gained speed and passed by, they left thick plumes of dense, black smoke. It was so dense that it obscured our view of the planes as they left the runway. Four of them took off. Someone somewhere was going to have a very bad day.

After a little more than an hour of sitting in the Pacific heat, we reboarded the 707 for the final leg of the trip.

The actual arrival provided an exciting start to our tour. When we approached the Vietnamese land mass, we could see nothing but deep green jungle – no roads, no structures, no towns. The trees seemed impenetrable and stretched from the ocean as far as one could see to the west. If an aerial landscape could look foreboding, this was it.

The landing approach was nothing like our landings in Hawaii and Clark. Rather than the slow descent at a modest angle, we were diving toward the ground at a steep angle with the engines roaring. This was an evasive technique used to avoid ground fire. We broke out of the clouds and within seconds were touching down on the runway. I was surprised the landing gear stood up to the strain. We only bounced once, but it was a good one.

As we taxied toward the terminal building, we could see Vietnamese civilians scurrying around the airport. It was a civilian airport after all, so the presence of civilians was not unexpected. However, they were all wearing what looked like black pajamas – the supposed uniform of the Viet Cong. While watching them, I experienced the full force of a new feeling: there are people here who want to kill me for no reason other than my being an American. It was not a fleeting thought. I pondered it and its ramifications for quite a while. I had done nothing to these people, yet given the chance, they would kill me without hesitation. They didn't even know me. It was quite sobering.

I was blown out of this daydream when the aircraft doors opened and we were drowned in an ocean of intense heat and a smell so nauseating we all came close to vomiting. The combination took our breath away. The heat and high humidity had us soaked through before we even disembarked. The stench was worse. It was as though we had parked on top of a sewage treatment plant. Little did we know that this was pretty much the normal atmosphere for Vietnam, especially during monsoon season.

As we grabbed our duffels and walked away from the plane, we could hear artillery explosions in the distance. Some folks speculated that it was either thunder or a construction crew, but we knew what it was.

If the country wanted to make a bad first impression, it did an excellent job.

We took a bus from the airport to the Long Binh Army Base. The windows of the bus were open but covered with chicken wire to stop the locals from throwing grenades into the bus. Why the locals might want to grenade Americans in a bus was beyond me.

I also noticed that poverty showed its presence everywhere I looked. I felt a great deal of sympathy for the Vietnamese and wanted to do everything I could to help them remain free.

We spent two nights in Long Binh being processed by the Ninetieth Replacement Battalion. Again, pure boredom. Because many of us had developed a fascination with fancy knives at Hood, we proudly wore them on our belts and under our fatigue blouses. That is, until one of the NCOs from the Ninetieth informed us that they were unauthorized weapons, and carrying a concealed weapon was a felony. Despite feeling defenseless, most of us stuck the knives into our duffels and forgot about them for a while.

When it came time to head for our assigned units, we were trucked toward the airport where we sat around in the sun for a couple of hours with nothing to drink. Sgt. Smith then informed us that we were taking lunch at an air force facility within walking distance. When we got there, we were shocked to see that they served all the ice cream one could eat! I had no idea that this was the last time I would see ice cream for the next twelve months!

After lunch we boarded an army C-123 "Provider" cargo plane. A C-123 is the downsized version of the C-130 Hercules, of great fame. The 123 has a similar but smaller profile than the 130 with a tail loading ramp and two turboprop engines instead of four. Like a 130, a 123 also has small jet engines mounted on the outer expanses of the wings to assist with short runway takeoffs.

The inside of the 123 is like every other military airplane I ever saw: aluminum and nylon seats, no soundproofing or insulation, miles of exposed tubing and electrical cables, and enough cabin noise to wake the dead. Everything rattled and creaked. Hydraulic fluid dripped from the fittings. To carry on a conversation, you had to yell directly into your friend's ear at the top of your lungs. Chats did not last long. Soon after takeoff, we were all staring silently at the floor.

Then we felt the beginnings of a descent toward an unknown destination. As soon as we felt the drop, Vernon Summerell, who was sitting directly across from me, stood up and placed his face against a small porthole window to look around. After about five seconds, he turned around and leaned back against the airframe. His face was void of all color. His expression was one of shock. His eyes looked like small saucers. He looked like he had seen his own ghost.

Seeing that, I unbuckled and stepped over to the porthole as Vernon sat down. By the time I looked outside, we were on final approach.

All I saw were mangled trees and fresh bomb craters. It gave me the impression that, wherever we were landing, it certainly was not secure. The scene probably shocked Vernon into the reality that I had experienced while seeing people who probably wanted me dead. This place is *serious* business.

We learned that we were now at Vinh Long airbase in the heart of the Mekong Delta. We were joining the Seventh Squadron of the First Air Cavalry; part of the Sixty-Fourth Aviation Group and First Aviation Brigade. The Seventh of the First was referred to as "The Blackhawks," a nickname it had earned during the Blackhawk War of 1833. We would be supporting the aircraft of "A" Troop, commonly called Apache Troop. We soon learned that despite public pronouncements of the opposite, the Delta was not secure and we could expect to be attacked at any time. The VC overran Vinh Long during the Tet Offensive in February, and the VC were active in the area. Nighttime mortar and rocket attacks occurred every three or four days. Sniper shots were frequent.

I was getting closer to where I felt I belonged.

Vernon Summerell, OH-6A mechanic and Crew Chief. Virginia Beach, VA.

ACCLIMATION

"Courage is knowing what not to fear."

Plato

The first thing we noticed when walking away from the C-123 was a group of about ten GIs walking toward it. We could not help noticing them because they began shouting insults upon spotting us. They were going home, and they made sure we knew it. Every possible taunt that could be directed toward a bunch of green rookies came our way. There was nothing we could say in return. They were as good as gone. We had 362 days to go. Amazingly, this scene was one of the first scenes in the movie *Platoon*, released in 1986. It was a near-perfect reenactment of what I had experienced. I never forgot the contrast between our boots and theirs.

What struck me was their physical appearance. They looked worn out. Their fatigues were faded to a pale green and were threadbare in places. The leather on their jungle boots was tan in color because all the black had been worn off. The nylon, a rich forest green on our boots, was pink on theirs, completely overwhelmed by the red clay of the surrounding area. And they were either extremely tanned or extremely dirty – probably a combination of both. I had the mental impression of a group of worn-out tires, used up and thrown away. Next!

And of course, it was hot. We were in the middle of the Delta, which was situated only ten degrees above the equator. Even though we were in the monsoon season, the sun beat down like a blowtorch.

We made our way to Fort Apache, as the A-Troop area was called. The area was comprised of a tropical barracks building (a hooch), an orderly room, which served as the CO's, first sergeant's, and troop clerk's offices, a gazebo-like structure that kept the bulletin boards out of the rain, and the Tactical Operation Center, or TOC. This was where the squadron missions were planned. The area had a concrete sidewalk between the orderly room and TOC. It was large enough to provide a slightly elevated platform for the gazebo.

The other troops, HQ, C, and D, each had their own barracks building. The squadron was constructing a new mess hall, scheduled to open any day. B-Troop was still deployed in Dian (Zee-an), working with the First Infantry Division – the Big Red One. In-country troops referred to it as the Big Dead One because of their high casualty rates.

The barracks and support buildings were brand-new, having been completed just days before our arrival. Each hooch had its own attached shower. This was a great convenience, if and when we had water. They were fed from a common water tank tower that served the entire squadron. Water shortages occurred frequently, especially in the dry season.

Leeches often found their way into the showers. If you were showering at night, which I often did while in the maintenance platoon, these critters could make for some exciting times.

Our first day was spent setting up large tents to create an aircraft maintenance area for A-Troop. It was hard and dirty work because the maintenance area was being created on top of sand. Much of Vinh Long, an old French fort, was built upon sand dredged from the Mekong River. This created acres of sandy terrain that resembled the Sahara. Working in the sand, sweating through my clothes, and having no way to wash put me and everyone else in a foul mood.

That was just an introduction. When we returned to the hooch, we received air mattresses to place over the steel springs of the standard GI double-deck bunks. The air mattresses were nothing like I was used to seeing on Virginia Beach. These were made of thick black rubber similar to that used on automobile inner tubes. They came packed in a talcum-like powder, as if that was supposed to provide some level of dry lubrication, but it was soon gone.

We also learned that we would not be receiving any sheets for a couple of days. This meant sleeping on an uncovered rubber mattress. The prospect of rug burns from the friction loomed large.

Then, the coup de grâce. We learned that the showers had not been hooked up and there was no water in the tank anyway! Instead, we would be allowed to fill our steel pots (helmets) with water from one of the Lister bags. That would be enough to brush our teeth, wash our faces, shave, and do what we could to clean up. We just needed to make sure we got the sequence right.

Now I was worried. I was a longtime acne sufferer. For me, cleanliness was a must. Otherwise, I feared my head would turn into one large pimple. After years of special cleansers, restricted diets, and even X-ray treatments, how was I supposed to keep my face clean? For some reason, this issue had never occurred to me during my boyhood dreams of becoming a successful warrior. Maybe that was an unconscious reason for wanting to fly. Fliers slept in clean places.

When it came time to turn in, I discovered that sleeping in my fatigue pants and T-shirt was mandatory. This provided some protection against the sensation of rubbing my sweaty, sand-encrusted legs and torso against the unforgiving surface of the air mattress. Of course, the added clothing ensured that I sweated profusely throughout the night.

An essential survival technique was the manipulation of your mosquito net. The net always stayed tied to the bunk frame at the top and tucked under your mattress on the bottom. When climbing into bed, we had to make sure we opened this seal for the shortest time possible. Otherwise, mosquitos would follow you into your cocoon and make you miserable for days.

Once inside, we had to reestablish the seal by tucking the net under the mattress. The trick here was to establish a seal that would not unravel during the night but leave the tucked portion easy to break loose in the event of an attack. Many a GI has experienced pure panic when awoken by mortar rounds falling nearby but unable to find his way out of his mosquito net. It happened more often than one would think, and it was never pretty: a grown man yelling and flailing wildly with both arms and legs, unable to get free.

First Meal

When I woke up before sunrise the next morning, I wasn't surprised to find that my clothing was soaking wet – I could wring the sweat out of my trousers and T-shirt. I decided I should shed these clothes and get into some dry duds to face the day. I opened my locker and retrieved a fresh fatigue blouse and set of trousers. Something was wrong. They were wet! Not wet enough to wring out, but close. They had absorbed a huge amount of moisture from the atmosphere because the humidity was somewhere around 99 percent. I saw that everything I had was in the same state: towels, underwear, socks, everything that could soak up moisture had done so. Even a book and several photographs were damp. I realized why the army had moved away from using leather and into nylon: leather would simply rot away in this place.

We shuffled into a few waiting trucks, and they took us to the old mess hall, a collection of three ten-man tents standing in the middle of one of the sandy areas at the end of the flight line. It was still dark, but we could see the outline of several A-Troop aircraft as we whizzed along the perimeter, just feet from the barbed wire. They all had some

Apache Head Logo on an OH-6A
Note the repaired bullet hole in the engine door! (at right)

type of Apache head stenciled on their sides. I also noticed that this ran right beside the perimeter fence. On the other side of that barbed wire was Charlie territory. I felt terribly exposed, expecting to be fired on at any moment.

A cold wind blew. It was probably 75 degrees, but wearing damp clothes and riding in the wind was chilly. I was surprised again.

We filed into the cooking tent and saw a chow line illuminated by three small light bulbs. You could barely see that the cooks were serving scrambled eggs, bacon, and a biscuit. From the serving line, we filed out to one of the two dining tents about fifteen feet away. The wind was howling, and I felt sand blowing into my face. I could also hear grains of sand striking my aluminum mess tray. *This will be great*, I thought.

As I entered the dining tent and began to take a seat at one of the picnic tables, I glanced down at my tray and almost puked.

The powdered eggs had dropped to ambient temperature and solidified into a solid yellow blob. The two bacon strips and biscuit were locked in a small pool of congealed grease about an eighth of an inch thick. But I was starving, so I carved off a portion of the yellow blob and moved it slowly toward my mouth. When I bit in, I experienced a cold, slimy mass completely shot through with sand pebbles. It was so bad I could barely get through it, but I did.

I then went for plan B – the biscuit and bacon. I put down my fork and grabbed the biscuit. When I lifted it, the biscuit, two bacon strips, and a triangular hunk of congealed grease rose to greet me. Thinking one doesn't get to dine on such fare every day, I held it up into the light for a better look. The two bacon strips were dangling from the grease like two legs of a dead animal. The grease, still in the shape of a triangle taken from the aluminum tray compartment in which it had rested, looked like the torso, and the biscuit looked like the poor creature's head. My much-anticipated breakfast had morphed into a grotesque piece of roadkill.

I placed it back on the tray and, not knowing when or what I would eat next, I carefully dissected the creature and ate it. It was pretty bad, but it was filling. However, I could not stop thinking that my dermatologist back in Norfolk would be pissed if he knew I was eating this stuff.

I believe every one of us was having similar thoughts. If not, I am at least sure we were all equally disgusted. No one said a word. I pondered my fate. I was now convinced I would die in Vietnam, becoming a casualty of acne or starvation, depending on whether I chose to eat and become a gigantic pimple or simply starve to death. My prospects looked dim.

We broke into smaller groups in the afternoon and went for different classes. My group went to map-reading class, and I was back in the middle of the Sahara again. The class was being taught by a group of six or eight members of D-Troop. This outfit had armed jeeps instead of helicopters and saw combat regularly. They spent more time outside of the perimeter than inside, often spending a month or more patrolling the Cambodian border. To us, they were the real McCoy. They looked, talked, and acted the part of tough combat troops.

Map reading was always a bore for me, so this simply meant standing in the sun for a few hours. The map course was laid out on a vast expanse of sand, probably 500 yards square. Once we completed the training, we waited until the dumbest of us finally found his way around the course. Several of us were standing beside the course when we saw the D-Troopers start running in tight circles and yelling like they were on fire. We then saw that they were chasing a rat, an actual live rat.

They yelled for us to join the chase and trap the rat by throwing a steel pot over him. The plan was to then draw straws and select a winner. That would entitle the winner to grab the rat and be bitten, which would result in rabies treatments, keeping the trooper in the rear for weeks,

This was freaking crazy! These guys were actually trying to be bitten by a rat so they could take rabies shots! They would rather face those shots than go to the boonies for several weeks and risk getting killed.

The rat escaped, pissing off the D-Troopers immensely. No rabies shots today. This sight, coupled with breakfast, convinced me that I was in a very serious situation indeed. I needed to get my act together.

Guard Duty

When we returned to Ft. Apache, I learned that I had been assigned to guard duty. I had to report to Guard Mount in ten minutes. Because I would not have time to eat in the mess hall, I was given a couple of boxes of C rations. I was totally relieved.

Prior to leaving the barracks for Guard Mount, a Scout wearing a Screaming Eagles patch on his right arm and our First Aviation Brigade patch on his left approached me. I was expecting some form of harassment. He asked if I was headed for guard duty and offered a few tips. He showed me how to arrange my gear and ammo pouches so I could get to them more quickly and how to hang my gas mask where it would not interfere with the more important ammo. Once he had me squared away, he wished me good luck and headed back toward the Scout section of the barracks.

He had gone out of his way to help me, and I thought it a pretty nice gesture for someone not in his platoon. I asked about him a week or so later and found out he had been sent home early. Evidently, he became a little too enthusiastic about the body counts and started exhibiting some bizarre behavior in the Area of Operations ("AO") – like wanting to land the Loach so he could get out and chase VC. He was considered "kill crazy" and unreliable. He had to leave.

Guard Mount consisted of about fifteen guys standing in formation while the officer of the guard inspected us and our gear and then assigned us to our posts. Because I was the rookie of the group, I was assigned to walk the flight line and guard the aircraft. The officer of the guard ("OG") was a D-Troop lieutenant called Pappy, and the sergeant of the guard was an A-Troop Scout who I would later learn was Jimmie Banlow.

Just after sundown, they trucked us out to our posts, and I was the last to be dropped off. Banlow, who was driving the truck, jumped out and showed me where I was to walk. He pointed out a damaged pagoda about two hundred yards away and told me to keep an eye on it. They had occasionally received sniper fire from there, but no one had been hit.

Less than five seconds after he said that, I heard a loud pop over my head and saw Banlow drop into a crouch. He yelled, "Get down!" and I did. We duckwalked over to one of the revetments and got behind it. He started laughing, saying, "Can you believe that shit? No sooner did I say it than he took a shot at us. It went high and he missed, as usual."

I did not even realize that the "pop" was a shot directed at me, so I did not know enough to be scared. If Banlow had not been there, I do not know if I would have recognized it as a gunshot. In any event, I had officially become the first member of the 370th TC Detachment to experience enemy fire. I made sure I would remember that sound.

The next day was more work and a trip outside the perimeter for a weapons demonstration. We were shown an M-79, an M-2 .50 caliber machine gun, a claymore mine, and a 106-mm recoilless rifle. The 106 stole the show with a high-explosive (HE) round and a flechette round, which explodes at a preset distance and fires thousands of tiny steel arrows out the front of the round, shotgun-style. The "arrows" were about 1.25 inches in length and about one-sixteenth of an inch in diameter. The nose is pointed and the rear has tiny fletching formed from the steel of the shaft and served the same function as the feathers of an arrow. When we saw it happen, I could not imagine how anyone could survive being fired upon with that device.

After dinner, we had our first mail call. Several letters from Norma and my folks finally caught up with me. We had sent our postal address home while we were at Long Binh so our loved ones could reach us.

One of my fellow AIT students approached me while I was standing in the mail line and told me something that would change my life. He implored me to join the Scout platoon as soon as I could. He was in the Scouts and told me that was where all the action happened; it was *the* job for a crew chief. I thanked him and he walked away. He remembered me because I had aced the Loach school final and thought I would enjoy the Scouts more than the maintenance platoon. Unfortunately, I later learned that he was wounded and sent home before I became a Scout, so I never saw him again.

The next day, I approached Sgt. Smith and requested a transfer to the Scout platoon. He said OK, and that I would get the next opening. That was it.

The "Attack"

Work continued on the maintenance area the next day. Things became interesting in the late afternoon when the troop CO, Major Ron White, gathered us for an announcement. He explained that we would be on high alert tonight because intelligence indicated a VC attack was being planned for 2 a.m. He further explained that VC agents had purchased all of the antibiotics and bandages in the town. This was typically seen just prior to an attack, so we had to be ready. We would be assigned to fighting positions along the perimeter in preparation for the attack.

We mounted an open flatbed truck and rode to the perimeter. Interestingly, we were very close to the tent mess hall where we were usually fed. It seemed strange that we were being delivered to the perimeter in a large, loud truck with its headlights blazing. Charlie probably knew where the fighting positions and bunkers were located anyway, so we weren't sneaking into place.

I was teamed with another 370th mechanic, Jim Purvis from Syracuse, New York. We had come over together.

The fighting position was a two-man structure made of sandbags and a piece of PSP, or portable steel plating, commonly used to construct aircraft runways. The sandbags were stacked about thirty inches high on three sides, with the rear being open. A portion of the front, just below the PSP roof, was open to serve as a firing port. A layer of sandbags was placed on the roof.

The position was not high enough to allow us to sit. The firing port was a height that required firing from the prone position. When lying prone and firing, your legs protruded from the rear of the structure.

Along the perimeter were several larger bunkers, regularly used by the perimeter guards who manned them on a nightly basis. They were approximately seventy-five yards apart, with the two-man fighting positions located about twenty-five yards apart.

Upon entering the position, both of us noticed that the swamp grass growing outside the perimeter came right up the position, blocking the firing port. We could see nothing from the port. The grass ran out from the perimeter about seventy-five yards before entering a tree line that bordered a canal. Horizontal barbed wire about a foot above the ground covered the ten yards closest to the perimeter. We were convinced that the VC could crawl right up to the port and drop a grenade on us and we would never see him.

As it became dark, our visibility declined. It was cloudy, so there was little moonlight. We could barely make out the silhouette of the tree line against a slightly lighter sky. The trees formed an uninterrupted black mass with no detail. The ground was equally dark. As we tried to look out of the position and survey our fire zone, anything below the top of the tree line was invisible.

It certainly was not the kind of setting one would choose for their first direct combat experience.

Jim and I alternated sleeping and guarding in two-hour shifts, beginning around 10 p.m. Around midnight a truck came down the perimeter road, stopping at each of the fighting positions for a few minutes. When it stopped at ours, a sergeant from the rifle platoon got out and approached us. He gave us about a dozen hand grenades, asking if we knew how to use them. Of course we did. After all, both of us had thrown them in basic training, only ten short months ago!

As the sergeant turned to walk away, he stepped back toward us and said, "Remember, zero-two-hundred. You might want to fix your bayonets."

That statement about bayonets really got our attention. There was no way we would be falling asleep now.

As we got closer to 2 a.m., both Jim and I were wide awake and as nervous as newborn kittens. No matter how hard we stared at that tree line, we could not see anything at all: no shapes, no movement, nothing. We figured we should be able to see or hear *something*. But we couldn't, and that made the waiting even worse. We did not want the first thing we saw or heard to be one of us being shot!

At some point before 2 a.m., the sky to our right lit up with tracers, and the guys in the next fighting position started screaming at the top of their lungs. They were still inside the position and firing out the back and into the sky.

After they had each gone through eighteen rounds of ammo, I duckwalked over to see what was going on. One of the guys had been lying on his back to light a cigarette, trying to hide the glow. When he fired up his lighter, he was looking straight into the eyes of a snake hanging down from the roof, less than a foot from his face. He freaked out, grabbed his M-16, and started firing at the snake. His partner had opened up as well, so it turned into a light show, tracers bouncing all over the place. I came back to tell Jim about it. We had a quick laugh, checked out the inside of our position, and went back to staring into the darkness.

Two a.m. came and went. Dead silence. No movement. No gunfire. No mortars being fired or exploding inside the perimeter. Besides the ever-present sound of popping Huey blades from the ship above us, the only sound was our breathing.

The sergeant came by again around 3 a.m. and said nothing was happening, but they would leave us "out here, just in case." We later learned that there was something about 2 a.m. In the remaining twelve months in Vinh Long, *all* of the mortar attacks started between 1:45 and 2:15 a.m. It never changed. Apparently, our sergeant and the other decision-makers were aware of this pattern and assumed it was now safe.

The rest of the night was uneventful, just as predicted. The truck picked us up at around 7 a.m. and returned us to the barracks, but not to sleep. We simply stored our gear, then walked back to the maintenance area to resume the day's work. SFC Smith seemed to take great satisfaction in having us work the full day on just a few hours of partial sleep. He loved it. Of course, he spent the night in his bunk.

The next morning, at exactly 2 a.m., the mortar attack took place. It was our first time experiencing this type of attack, and it was terrifying to us rookies. The first indication of the attack was the nearly simultaneous explosions of several mortar rounds inside the perimeter. No whistling or sound would tip you off that something bad was on the way. The explosions simply happened with absolutely no warning, shattering your sleep and jolting you into total confusion. There was no friendly, prestrike whine like we heard in war movies. Because mortar rounds were low-velocity projectiles, they fell silently. Since we were sleeping on the top floor of the hooch, I found this disturbing.

First, we had to wake up and realize what was happening and where we were. Next, we had to find our way out of bed and into our designated bunkers. Then we just hoped that the bunker did not suffer a direct hit.

Getting out of the bunk was not easy. Because it was so dark, the net was invisible, and it was easy to become entangled in it. If panic set in, you could ruin the net by thrashing around and tearing holes in it. We later learned to tuck three sides of the net well under the mattress while leaving the fourth side only slightly under the edge. You would use this side as your exit when the explosions started.

Once out of the bunk, you had to find your way to the proper bunker. These were located at the bottom of the stairs on either side of the barracks. Each troop had its own designated bunker, so it was considered bad form to enter the bunker of the wrong troop. The bunkers were pretty small and not very strong. I was barely able to get into the one belonging to A-Troop, but I did.

The attack was over twenty minutes later. The air seemed filled with helicopters as Huey gunships attacked the suspected location of the mortars. Because they were directly overhead when firing their rockets and miniguns, the noise was terribly loud. We rookies mistook this for more incoming rocket fire and dropped to the floor of the bunker. The more experienced troops got a big laugh from that and let us hear it.

We experienced "bunker boner." Being woken suddenly causes a strong urge to urinate, an urge so strong that it causes an immediate erection. We had about fifty guys standing around with bulges in their underwear. As soon as the all clear sounded, we ran for the piss tubes.

The restroom facilities at Vinh Long were definitely not four-star. Because we were located at sea level and close to the river, we could not use traditional hole-in-the-ground latrines. We constructed four-hole shitters made of wood. They were small sheds with a door on each end and an ingenious toilet setup. The four-man toilet was a plywood cabinet with the top surface about eighteen inches above the plywood floor. The plywood top had four oblong holes cut out, forming something like a toilet seat. Well, you could sit on it anyway.

Inside the cabinet sat four fifty-gallon steel drums that sat on the ground under the structure. The barrels were cut down to about eighteen inches in height to fit under the toilet/cabinet. Each drum was about half-full of diesel fuel that served as a solvent for the excrement.

Once the barrels were full, someone had the unpleasant duty of burning the contents of each barrel. This took a long, long time because you weren't really burning the stuff; you were boiling it away. It was not unusual to take all day to dispose of the crap.

Urination needs were met with the use of a piss tube or pisser, with the tube being the most civilized. A cutoff helicopter skid was stuck into the ground, protruding up at a forty-five-degree angle. These were usually located near the perimeter barbed wire, away from work areas, and in the sandiest soil in the area.

The pissers were fifty-five-gallon drums, buried about three quarters of the way into the ground. They had holes in the bottom, allowing the urine to seep into the soil. Because they were open on top, the contents were always visible and always stinking. Using one was not pleasant.

The worst thing about the shitters was using them at night, especially in the wet season. First, the interior was pitch-dark. Second, the wind always seemed to blow sand onto the surface, which in the wet season was always damp. Pulling down your trousers and sitting on that thing took real courage!

On another occasion, the mortar attack began just after our infantry platoon had completed building a bigger and much stronger bunker for A-Troop. The new bunker had a three-foot thick PSP and sandbag roof and was reinforced with a layer of six-by-six timbers. The outside walls were of typical sandbag construction but were covered with thick wood paneling and two-by-fours to make them more rigid. It was also large enough to accommodate all of the Apache enlisted men, including the 370th.

My bunk was located on the same end of the barracks as the bunker, but on the opposite wall. The exit door leading down the stairs and directly into the bunker entrance was no more than ten feet from the foot of my bunk. I could be in the bunker in seconds.

We soon experienced another mortar attack. When the mortar rounds started exploding, I rolled out of my bunk and onto the floor. I lay there for about five seconds as I gathered my thoughts and oriented myself. When I stood up and began heading for the exit door, there must have been twenty men ahead of me, yelling to the others to get moving.

The line of waiting soldiers stretched in two directions from the door. It looked like it might take ten minutes to get to the bunker.

As I observed this, I could hear the mortar rounds getting closer to our hooch. Charlie was very proficient at walking the mortar rounds across a target area for maximum effect.

I looked to my right and saw the other exit door was open. This led to the C-Troop bunker, but I didn't really care.

I decided to use that exit and take refuge with C-Troop. As I was stepping into the door, a motor round struck the ground about fifty feet away and sprayed shrapnel and rock all over the wooden stairs. I was lucky none of the shrapnel penetrated the wall.

Rather than walk down the stairs, I decided to crawl. Because the only clothing I was wearing was my boxer skivvies, this was not the best of moves. As I wiggled down the stairs, putting my low-crawl skills to use for the first time since basic training, I picked up about thirty splinters in my legs, feet, forearms, and hands. When I arrived at the bottom of the stairs, I slid onto the three-by-three concrete pad that prevented the formation of a hole where everyone walked.

I did not realize it at the time, but the pad was a new addition and had received a thorough roughing-up of the top layer, making it skid-proof.

I jumped into the last available spot in the bunker: standing in the doorway. When I turned around to look outside, I saw another mortar round explode about thirty feet away at the opposite end of the bunker. I was lucky again. No shrapnel found its way to the doorway, and I was at least momentarily safe.

When the all-clear alarm sounded, we exited the bunker and started heading for the piss tubes. When I stepped out of the shadows and into the light of a small electric bulb hanging above the door, one of the C-Troopers said, "My God! You're hit. Are you OK?"

I looked down and saw that I was bleeding from lots of small wounds on my forearms, knees, and chest. Flesh that wasn't displaying a splinter appeared to have been forcibly removed by the concrete pad.

The adrenaline rush had kept me from feeling the superficial wounds, even though there were dozens of them. I did not realize I was bleeding until it was pointed out to me.

I removed as many splinters as I could, then went to find Pat Fuller, the

Apache medic. He helped remove the more embedded ones and applied methylate to the patches of missing flesh.

He then surprised me by asking if I was going to apply for a Purple Heart. I said, "No. Of course not." I would have been laughed out of A-Troop had I applied for the PH because of splinter wounds.

After these experiences, receiving fire during guard duty, chasing the rat, and using our four-star dining and sanitary facilities, I felt pretty well acclimated to my surroundings. The future looked gloomy.

GROUND CREW

"The Beatles saved the world from boredom."

George Harrison

Within a few days, we had the maintenance area set up and all of our gear unpacked and ready to go. The Loach work area was a small (twenty-foot by thirty-foot) Quonset hut-shaped tent into which we built a workbench and shelves for our toolboxes and placed PSP down as a floor. The Huey and Cobra crews also had several tents, but they were significantly larger. The radio technicians had the best environment: air-conditioned containers. Yes. AC! The containers were trailer-mounted and only eight feet by ten feet, making them very cramped. There was a strict NO VISITORS policy, preventing us from hanging around in the cool air.

The Loach repair crew consisted of Oliver Granville (Gloucester, Virginia), Jim Reed (Texas), Craig Schmidt (St. Louis), Dave Raymond (California), Vernon Summerell (Virginia Beach), and me.

Our ability to work together and get things done was pretty remarkable. That three of us were E-5s and the other three were E-4s never entered the conversation. When a Loach came in for repair, we knew what to do and when to do it. We were self-directed, which was fine with me. Depending on the workload, we would divide the tasks and make sure everyone had enough help to get the job done. When a ship needed a special repair like fixing bullet holes or the engine, we would get help from the sheet metal specialist or an engine specialist. During the six months of service in the maintenance platoon, I never experienced anything short of total cooperation from everyone in the platoon.

Lt. Camp had long since departed for Headquarters Troop, and we rarely saw him again. The A-Troop maintenance officer was Captain Bill Sholtz, one of the best officers I came to know during my three years in the army.

Snake Hunter

One evening while preparing a Huey to be towed into the maintenance area, I accidently stepped on a poisonous snake. I was lifting a heavy tow bar to slip the hook into a tow ring on the end of the Huey's skid. I grabbed the bar, but I was not close enough to the end of the bar to get the leverage I needed to pick it up. When I stepped closer to the end and bent down to grab the bar again, I felt something wiggle under my right foot. It was pitch-dark, so I reached into the Huey and switched on the landing light to see what I had stepped on. It was a coiled snake, directly under the bar where I had just placed my hands. My buddy, a country boy from Arkansas, jumped off the tug and took a look. He said it looked like a "step-and-a-half" to him. So named because once bitten, the victim only survived long enough to take a step and a half. He grabbed a stick, slid it under the snake's belly, and picked it up. We then jumped on the tug and sped back to the maintenance shack so we could check it out under decent lights. Cpt. Sholtz, still working in the shack, came over to take a look. We could not figure out why the snake failed to bite me until my friend carefully picked it up. The snake seemed lethargic, so he grabbed it right behind the head and lifted it up, letting its tail dangle. A few seconds later the mystery was solved. Two dozen or more baby snakes fell out and landed on the plywood floor. She was pregnant and just about to bring her litter into the world when I stepped on her. The baby snakes started crawling off under the desks and cabinets. They were much faster than one would think, so the three of us started running around, stomping on them with our combat boots. Juvenile snakes can be extra deadly, and we did not want to take any chances with these.

When it was all over, the three of us had a great laugh and scraped up the remains. Even Cpt. Sholtz pitched in. We killed the mother and went out to retrieve the Huey.

Later that evening, while I was fulfilling my guard duties in the shack, Cpt. Sholtz noticed I was reading a copy of *The Bridges at Toko-Ri,* a novel about navy aviators in the Korean War. He asked me if I had seen the movie and gave it a strong endorsement. This led to a longer conversation in which he told me he had started his military career as an enlisted man, serving as a helicopter crew chief. In fact, when President Kennedy switched to a Huey as his helicopter of choice, then Spec-5 Sholtz served as his crew chief. I was more than a little awestruck as I thought about the pressure of serving in that capacity. Sholtz commented that it was dicey because the Huey was a single-engine aircraft, and the White House staff frowned upon putting the president into one of those.

We talked about other books we'd read and a small bond was established between us. I noticed later that Cpt. Sholtz treated me a little differently from that point on, even after I transferred to the Scout platoon.

Life in the maintenance platoon was monotonous drudgery. We worked seven days per week and had guard duty every fourth night. Days off were limited to two hours on Sunday morning, *if* you attended chapel, and the day after pulling guard duty. Either of these could be cancelled if things became too busy in maintenance.

We were typically awake by six in the morning and at the maintenance area by seven. It was approximately a half-mile walk to the area, and in the wet season the road was often covered with six inches of mud.

Lunch was served around midday in our new squadron mess hall, requiring another round trip – on foot – to the barracks area. During the first few months, we typically stopped work around five o'clock, returned to the barracks, retrieved our mail from the orderly room, and tried to get a shower. Even during the monsoon season the water was often depleted, causing us to go without a shower. After working and sweating all day, and often being covered in rotor-wash-driven sand and dirt, missing a shower was not fun.

Many of the troopers did not have day jobs if they were not in the field, so they had first crack at the showers and often used all of the water before we returned. They seemed to get a big kick out of watching us enter the shower and be disappointed by the empty taps.

While we certainly lived a much more comfortable life than the infantrymen and artillerymen in the field, SFC Smith made it his personal mission to ensure that we each received our fair share of misery. Smith took a perverse pleasure in abusing us. After a couple of months, A-Troop experienced a lot of combat activity, resulting in many helicopters being damaged by gunfire. They also racked up an unusually large number of flight hours over this month-long period, accelerating the need for periodic inspections and preventive maintenance. The nine-hour workday was not sufficient, so we began returning to the maintenance area after supper and working until 11 p.m.

For some reason, Smith loved this. While we were all dragging ass around the area, Smith acted like he'd been given a new pony. He enjoyed reminding us that we were working overtime and not being paid. He would make jokes about us not being able to "write letters to our mommies" because we were working so much, or how bad we smelled after not showering for a week or more. His taunts were endless.

The work wasn't so bad as long as we had legitimate work to do. But when the work slowed to a normal pace, the late hours continued. Smith would pick out one ship and demand that the work on it be completed that day, not carried over to the following day, as was normal. If you were on the crew repairing that particular ship, you faced a long night. To add to the pressure, Smith insisted that the entire platoon remain in the maintenance area until the job was done. This meant thirty to thirty-five men sitting there for hours waiting for four or five guys to finish their work.

Depending on the job, these sessions could go well beyond midnight. Our misery was multiplied by the monsoon season. During the day, we would usually stop working when the rainstorms blew through on their regular 10 a.m., 2 p.m., and 4 p.m schedule. But if it rained while we were working on one

Byron Hoyt
Best sheet metal tech in the 'Nam
(Iowa).

Tom "Mixed Drink" Collins
Huey & Cobra mechanic
(California).

Rich Ward
Huey & Cobra mechanic
(Baltimore, MD).

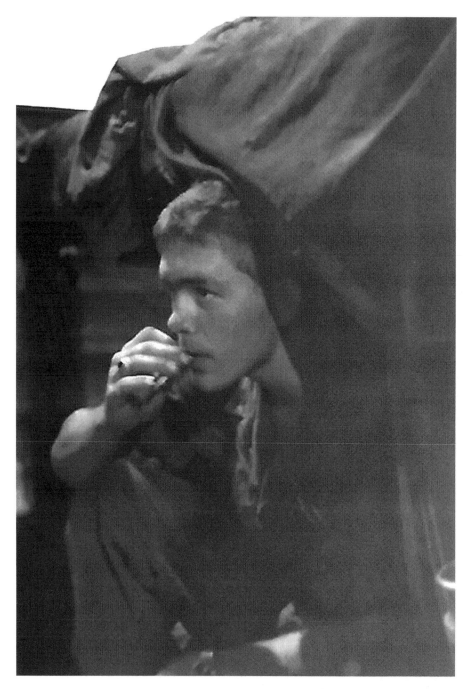

Mike Wells
Huey & Cobra mechanic
(Baltimore, MD).

of Smith's special projects, we would work straight through the rain, hoping to shorten the night. It was not unusual to return to one of the tents with a toolbox and our boots full of water. We would often pour out the water in front of Smith in a little ceremony in which we could announce the completion of the job. The others, waiting around for as many as six or seven hours, would give the returning crew a standing ovation and hurl anonymous, veiled insults in Smith's direction.

SFC Smith insisted on completing the work, so we were forced to work under floodlights, out in the open. Many ships were repaired on the flight line within yards of the perimeter wire. The mechanics were working in plain view, under brilliant lights, exposing themselves to sniper fire. While a few shots came our way during these absurdities, no one was ever hit.

This continued for about a month until Smith finally put a halt to it. Someone had mentioned it to Cpt. Sholtz, and he privately directed Smith to "call off the horseshit!" Smith was fulfilling my expectations.

Guard duty became an every-fourth-night affair, with the maintenance people alternating among the three bunkers and one guard tower that were A-Troop responsibilities.

The guard tower was a part-bad, part-good assignment, mostly bad. The bad things were its elevation above the ground and that it had to be manned twenty-four hours a day. This meant the four people assigned to the tower had to draw straws to see who would remain in the tower all of the following day. The elevation was problematic because it made the tower, and everyone in it, an easy target for an RPG. In addition, anyone in the tower was exposed to the wind and rain.

The only advantages to being in the tower were the presence of a large Starlight scope. This was as high-tech a piece of equipment as existed in 1968. I never understood how it worked.

The scope resembled a large telescope with a very large objective lens – maybe ten inches in diameter. An appendage on the side of the scope held the electronics that enabled the scope to magnify light. It must have been based on some type of TV-like circuitry. However, when looking through the scope, you did not get the impression that you were viewing a screen. The image appeared as though you were looking through a regular telescope, except the scene was tinted green.

When I eventually drew the tower assignment, the Starlight scope caused me quite a problem.

While looking through the scope, I noticed what looked like a gravestone had shifted positions and was now at least ten feet closer than it was on my earlier look.

Without the scope, the gravestones were barely visible. However, with the scope, they were clearly visible, even in the limited moonlight of that night. If a flare was up, the scope made it look like daylight.

In the back of my mind was a story we'd heard when we first arrived. During the previous dry season, the VC had rolled a barrel over the low-lying barbed wire and up to the perimeter wire, directly in front of the tower.

They detonated the explosive-filled barrel, killing all four Americans in the tower.

I didn't want that happening to us, so I shared my observations with the other three men in the tower.

They all took a look, and when I pointed out the stone's previous position relative to the tree line, they agreed that the stone had moved.

We got on the radio and reported it to the officer of the guard, who dispatched a flare ship to illuminate the area.

When the flare lit up, we could see that the stone had relocated to its original position. We all saw it and now wondered what was going on.

This movement went on throughout the night, but nothing else happened.

When the sun came up, we saw that there were actually two gravestones in two different spots. What we had observed was an optical illusion caused by the alternating light sources. The dim moonlight illuminated only one stone. When a flare was up, it illuminated the other gravestone, making it appear that the two identical stones were moving back and forth.

At least we had not requested an air strike!

Vung Tau

In early September, I was told that I was going to Vung Tau for a refresher course on the OH-6A. I believe this was some kind of reward, because only two of us went. Vung Tau had been an in-country R&R center until the Tet Offensive. According to rumor, US and other allied forces took R&R on one side of the town and VC took R&R on the other side. This arrangement was broken when the VC attacked the allied side during their Tet attacks.

It sat on the South China Sea and exhibited some beautiful French colonial architecture. Many of the buildings were painted white, creating a striking contrast between the tropical blue skies and dark blue South China Sea. During the French colonial period, Vung Tau was called Cape St. Jacques and was known by Europeans as the "Riviera of the Orient."

My travelling partner, Ron Toma, came over with us as part of the 370th TC. Ron was of Japanese heritage and stood about five feet tall. This was something that popped into my mind when barhopping downtown.

The base at Vung Tau was luxurious compared to Vinh Long. Hot water showers, flush toilets, paved streets, and bunks with sheets and real pillows. I could not help but compare it to the crappy conditions so many GIs endured during their tours.

Classes ended around 3:30 p.m. each day, leaving plenty of time for touring. Toma and I headed downtown as soon as our first day of classes ended.

Before we left, we asked one of the instructors which areas to check out and which to avoid. He told us where the VC section was and to stay away from "One hundred pi Alley," the nickname for a street where one could purchase the services of a hooker for 100 piasters, or about $1.00 US. We made note of that and took off – two truly naïve wanderers in the wicked world of a war zone.

Vung Tau was alive! The streets were packed with more people than I had seen in three months. Barkers stood in front of every bar and restaurant, trying to lure patrons to come inside. Temporary "restaurants," comprised of a cooking pot or grill, were all over the sidewalks. Motorbikes with up to four passengers flew up and down the street with all the caution of a thrill show. We had been warned about bike-riding bandits who would approach from behind and snatch your camera or anything else you carried, then speed off into the crowd. All this activity and noise, combined with the brightness of the buildings, made for a dazzling experience.

We had been walking around for about an hour when we saw two US Army officers enter a bar. We were thirsty and figured this must be a safe place. We quickly ducked in, with me entering first.

When the door closed behind us, we were completely blind! The bar was almost totally dark, with the only source of illumination being one bare light bulb at the far end of the bar, probably fifty feet away. That was the only thing visible because our eyes were still acclimated to the glaring scene outside. It was so dark, I became a little dizzy because there was no point of reference to tell up from down.

We had only taken about three steps inside when we stopped to get our bearings. As soon as I did, a strong hand grabbed my genitals and pulled me down onto a bench. As this happened, a woman's voice, obviously Vietnamese, said, "You sit with me, GI. OK?"

I had no choice. It was either sit down or forever lose the chance to have kids, so I sat. Toma was grabbed by another woman, but around the shoulders, and forced onto the bench across the table from me.

My first thought was that we were in trouble and I'm teamed up with a guy who probably weighed eighty-five pounds!

As far as I could tell, the bar was otherwise empty. The two officers had apparently disappeared. Of course, they could have been sitting next to us, but we couldn't see a thing.

A nearly invisible waiter came to our booth and Toma and I ordered beers. The two ladies ordered "Saigon Tea," actually watered-down Coke or Pepsi, for which the GI paid an exorbitant price. This was all part of the normal routine in Vietnam bars, so we weren't surprised.

After about fifteen minutes, our vision began to return. There was still very little light, so it remained difficult to see much beyond silhouettes.

A stream of small talk ensued, with the ladies asking all the questions. Most of these centered on where we were from in the States, what we did back home, did we have a Vietnamese girlfriend, etc.

A strange part of the conversation was their emphatic statement that they were *not* going upstairs with us. This seemed odd because I had assumed they were hookers and all the talk was just a prelude to the inevitable magic act that was going to happen upstairs.

Their preemptive refusal suited me just fine. I had no intention of hooking up with a Vietnamese prostitute. Frankly, I was too afraid of the potential consequences to even consider it.

This encounter led us to becoming regulars at this particular bar and getting to know the two ladies much better. As it turned out, they were not hookers at all. Both were from middle-class families in the Vung Tau area. The one I talked with was working in the bar to help her family make ends meet. Her dad had lost his business, and they were in scramble mode.

Both were strikingly beautiful and had much softer appearances than the women we saw around Vinh Long. Their faces were much rounder and their physiques were fuller. I attributed this to the likelihood that they had French ancestry somewhere in their family trees.

It was good to meet someone in the country who was not trying to swindle you out of your money.

Because Vung Tau was located on the South China Sea, the US established a secured beach where GIs could enjoy swimming, sunbathing, and surfing. Yes, surfing. Special Services, the army's recreation department, ran the beach and provided all types of beach gear rentals, including surfboards. They even provided a surfing instructor for those who wanted to take up the sport.

I found the instructor and introduced myself. I was curious about how he got this assignment. He told me that he surfed on the world tour, and when was drafted he let the army know. When he got to Nam, he talked them into a Special Services assignment.

Like everything in Vung Tau, the beach was very attractive. It had sharply defined hills that came right down to the beach, creating a bit of a West Coast look.

Unfortunately, I had not brought a swimsuit, so I could not take advantage of the surf.

After two weeks of relatively boring classes, Toma and I returned to Vinh Long. I finished as the top student again.

Earache

In late September, I began experiencing a strange popping noise in my left ear. It was intense and caused a few moments of deafness in that ear until it popped again. While it wasn't terribly painful, it was extremely uncomfortable, so I went to the flight surgeon.

He inspected my ears and told me that I had a severe growth of fungus in my left ear. He said it had to be treated right away to keep it from spreading to my right ear. He warned me that the treatment was not going to be pleasant, and I would be grounded for the two weeks of treatments.

I began visiting the squadron dispensary twice a day to have my ear flushed. He was right. It was not pleasant; it was downright painful. The medic would use a gigantic brass syringe to inject a waterborne antifungal agent into my ear. The syringe was approximately the size of an air pump one would use to inflate a football or basketball, and probably held about 250 cc of liquid. The business end held a narrow nozzle that increased the velocity of the solution when the medic pumped it into my ear canal. The pump handle was an ornate piece of brass with several curlicues and loops. Quite attractive, for a torture device.

The sensation was sheer pain. While I did not scream, I nearly passed out. A deep, dull pain seemed to come from the center of my skull. I clenched my teeth as hard as I possibly could and waited for it to stop. It probably took around thirty seconds to empty the syringe. The feeling of relief was tremendous. Then the medic said, "Only one more time" and repeated the process.

While he pumped, I held a kidney-shaped stainless steel bowl under my ear to catch the fluid. This gave me the chance to see what was being purged from my ear. It was not pretty. What I saw lying in the bottom of the bowl was a couple of dark green strands of fungus about an inch long and a little less than an eighth of an inch thick. They looked exactly like the algae I used to see while playing near a ditch when I was a kid. Only this time that smelly crap was coming out of my own ear. Of course, I had to return after lunch and go through the entire ordeal again. The prospect of two weeks of this was not a happy thought.

After the first week of treatment, a strange thing happened. The pain transformed into a pleasurable feeling. I could not explain it, but it simply stopped hurting.

Craig Schmidt, Dave Raymond, & Vernon Summerell (l to r) replace a main rotor blade.

Crotch Rot

The monsoon season was rough on me. Not long after recovering from the ear fungus, I came down with a bad case of crotch rot. It started out simple enough, an itchy rash in my groin area, reportedly from being wet all the time. However, it spread rapidly and the itch was intense. Before long, it covered the insides of both thighs, reaching from my crotch to my knees. The top layer of skin was completely gone, as if I had been skinned. Even being rubbed by the inside of my trousers was intensely painful. After a couple of weeks, I went to see the A-Troop medic.

He told me he could give me some salve that I could apply, but that it would only stop the itching, not get rid of the fungus. He said the only way to get rid of it for good was to rub alcohol on it a couple of times a day, "If you've got the balls to do it." It was going to be extremely painful because of the raw skin. I said I would try it, so he gave me a bottle of alcohol and said, "Good luck, man. You'll need it!"

Oh, how right he was. That night I sat on the edge of my bunk with my trousers around my ankles. I took the quart of alcohol and doused a handkerchief until it dripped. Then I placed it high up on the inside of my thigh. HOLY HELL! It burned as hot as fire. It was probably the most pain I had ever felt up to that time. Moreover, it wasn't going to end any time soon. I had two legs to do, and I had barely started.

It took nearly an hour to complete the treatment. Other guys came by to see what was causing all the grunting and snorting. Most took one look at by blood-red legs, mumbled something like, "Oh my God," and walked away.

The medic was also right about the effectiveness of the treatment. After a couple of weeks or so, the raw area started to heal. It was gone after a month. Fortunately, it never came back. To say I did not miss it would be a major understatement.

In November, Summerell was transferred to the Scout platoon. I was furious. I went to SFC Smith to demand an explanation. He said he had forgotten about my request for a transfer and promised to send me over as soon as they needed another crew chief. I was temporarily satisfied and reminded him not to forget me.

Trash Runs

One break in the monotony was the trash run. Because we were restricted to the base, this was the only opportunity to get outside the wire for some entertainment. The restriction was the result of the local VC activity and that the army considered the area to be unsecured. Wandering around, even in small groups, could get you killed.

The trash run occurred every two weeks or so. A long-bed deuce-and-a-half truck was used to collect all the trash in the squadron area and bring it to the local dump in Vinh Long. Three GIs typically made the trip: a driver, an assistant driver, and an armed guard riding in the bed of the truck. In most cases, the guard carried an M-16 or CAR-15, while the two drivers carried .45 ACP pistols. I served as the guard during my trip.

The ride to the dump was an experience. Before leaving the compound, I was told that I was not there to protect us from an ambush. That would be hopeless with only three men and one automatic weapon. I was there to keep the locals from jumping on the truck while we were moving. I thought this was a joke but soon found it to be true.

We drove down a narrow dirt road as fast as the driver could go without losing control. His constant beeping of the horn gave the pedestrians, scooter riders, and small vehicles a warning before they were forced off the road. Even at forty-five miles per hour, people were trying to jump on the moving truck. It was brutal and amazing that no one was killed – that we knew of.

When we slowed and turned into the dump, keeping people off the truck became hopeless. Both adults and children clamored up the sides and started pulling through the trash. Many were barefoot, and no one wore gloves. The trash they were walking on and sorting through was full of dangerous stuff: sharp, rusty metal, broken pallets with nails exposed, old building materials, tin cans, splintered wood – all kinds of stuff that most Americans would never let their kids get near.

They were in a frenzy. Everyone wanted the best junk. Pushing and shoving was everywhere, and a few fights broke out. I leaned against the back of the cab, observing the disgusting scene. These people were so poor they had to resort to this.

The truck, which had been piled three or four feet high with trash, was completely empty in less than five minutes! There was not one scrap of paper left on the truck. We drove away, leaving me to ponder what I had just seen.

But not for long. One of the benefits of making the trash run was the opportunity to hit the town for a little relaxation. The driver knew the location of a bar with a steam bath. We were able to get a hot shower, steam bath, and massage for about $3. It was the first time any of us had been really clean in about four months, so it was much appreciated.

The Scramble for Trash.

Thanksgiving

Thanksgiving arrived and we were treated to a turkey dinner. I was surprised to see that it was pretty well prepared and tasted decent – not as good as my grandmother's, but still a treat. The gravy was disgusting though and impossible to eat. The squadron mess sergeant made it a point to walk around the mess hall, asking everyone how they liked it. He was as proud as a new father and grinned his way around the whole place.

He needed an opportunity to gloat because what he fed us most of the time sucked. For some reason, we would eat the same thing, three meals per day, for a month at a time. Do you like fried chicken? Great. Because that is all you are going to eat this month. Like pork chops? Get used to them, because you will see them about ninety times over the next month. Of course, we always had rice with every meal, so it was not the only thing we ate. However, we never got an explanation, and this phenomenon repeated itself four or five times throughout the year.

Then there were his experiments. One I will never forget was the batch of sheet cakes he baked for one of the holidays. Unfortunately, he did not have any frosting on hand, but he did not let that stop him. Instead, he took packs of Kool-Aid, mixed in some water to create a colorful paste, and spread it across the cakes. He must have forgotten that Kool-Aid with no sugar is about as tart as anything you could put into your mouth. One bite of the cake and guys started spitting it out like poison. It was pretty humorous, but he was insulted and pissed.

Monsoons

We had arrived during the monsoon season. It was hard to believe just how hard it could rain. One minute it would be a sunny, beautiful tropical day. Then it would cloud up and begin pouring like I had never seen in the States. Visibility would drop to less than a hundred yards. When it stopped, there might be four inches of new rain on the ground.

They were as predictable as anything in nature, occurring at 10 a.m., 2 p.m., and 4 p.m. If Charlie ever wanted to get away from his 2 a.m. routine, a mortar attack at one of these times would have caught us all huddling in our maintenance tents, trying to stay dry.

It rained at night, too. One of the worst things about being outside during monsoon season was mosquitos swarming during the rain. The bunkers were unusable because the bugs would be so thick in there, you could not breathe. If you stepped in there, you would have dozens of bites before you could turn around and get out. If you were outside wearing a hat or helmet, the bugs would fly under the brim in huge swarms. They were often so thick that you had to be careful not to inhale them when you took a breath. You had to be adaptable.

In December, Dave Raymond went to the Scout platoon, taking a slot that I considered mine. Again, I went to Smith and received a partially intelligible explanation about it not being the right time. Again, he promised to send me next time. Regardless of my anger, there was not much I could do about it.

Entertainment

In addition to the trash run, reading our mail, and the small camp library, the occasional USO show would come around. Because Vinh Long had been overrun during the Tet Offensive and the entire Delta was considered insecure, these shows were rare. We had two. The first was an Asian rock 'n' roll band that played covers of American hits. They may have been Vietnamese. Performing in the squadron mess hall, they provided a lasting memory with their rendition of Jimi Hendrix's "Purple Haze." Their inability to pronounce the "L" sound made the chorus especially entertaining: "Puppa Haze, ah in your eyes."

The other show was a group of singing and dancing white girls, what we lovingly objectified as "round eyes." It was the typical variety act: song, dance, and occasional jokes. Nothing even close to risqué. My grandmother would have loved them.

Just before Christmas, Bob Hope announced that he was bringing his show to the Delta for the first time, visiting Can Tho, the capital city of the neighboring province and headquarters to the Special Forces group and the Sixty-Fourth Aviation Group, of which the Seventh/First was a component. His first visit was promoted as a big deal, again because of the security concerns in the Delta. A-Troop loaded a group of Hueys with about thirty guys and lifted them to Can Tho. I did not go because I had guard duty that night. When I got home in 1969, I was able to watch a replay of the show, hoping to catch a glimpse of one or two of my friends. Impossible. The portion of the crowd that made it into a camera shot was a huge sea of green, indistinguishable figures. The notable feature of the show was the sound of artillery or rocket fire in the background. Bob Hope made many humorous comments every time an explosion went off. He questioned the decision to visit the Delta.

Our most popular entertainment was drinking beer. Each troop had a Gedunk bar in their area. The bar opened at five p.m. and sold beer, sodas, and various snacks, when they were available. It closed around eight or nine p.m.. Many of us in the maintenance platoon rarely had the chance to take advantage of it. Beers were twenty-five cents; soft drinks were ten cents; cigarettes were twenty-five cents per pack.

We went through a couple of periods when we could not get American products, so the supply folks substituted Australian and New Zealand products.

These took some getting used to. The sodas were incredibly sweet and lacked the burn we typically associated with our carbonated drinks, like Coke. They were closer to fruit punch than soda. Drinking more than one in a short time could turn your stomach.

But they were nothing compared to the Kiwi beer. It was extremely heavy and dark. To me, it appeared much thicker than American beer and was hard to drink. If it was cold, I could tolerate it. But if it was warm, forget it. I used to swear that it came out of the can in lumps, and you had to stir it to get it into liquid form!

Ping-Pong

The most frequent mode of entertainment in maintenance was ping-pong. A couple of guys made a table out of a piece of plywood, bought a ping-pong set from somewhere, and set it up in one of the tents. During breaks, we would rush to the tent and play a couple of games. Playing priorities were arranged according to who held the table and who was next in line for the challenge.

During the ping-pong events we discovered we had a sports star in our midst. Bob Bauman, a Huey mechanic from Minnesota, revealed that he was the reigning state champion before entering the army. He was not bragging about it and only let us know of his success after he beat about ten guys in a row, all by crushing margins. It was quite a feat to score ten points on Bob. This was more remarkable since we were playing on a nonregulation-sized table. Instead of the official ten-by-five-foot table, ours was eight-by-four, a lot smaller than regulation.

On many days, Bob would not even play because even the best of us could not give him a real game. After a while, we got accustomed to his shots and several of us got within five or six points of his winning twenty-one. When we returned to work after the breaks, our individual scores were usually a topic of discussion, with the conversation going something like, "How'd you do? I got fourteen off him." No one was ever asked if they had beat him.

One day we were able to leverage the ping-pong scores into a longer-running joke.

A new PFC transferred into the maintenance platoon in late November. His name was Tweet. First, it was unusual that he was only an E-3. Most guys coming out of AIT were promoted to Spec-4 upon graduation. We learned that he had not been to any aviation-related training. Instead, he was drafted into the infantry and then reenlisted while in Vietnam. Signing up for a new six years entitled him to select a new MOS, so he chose 67N20, the designation for a UH-1 mechanic. He was transferred to us for on-the-job training, rather than being sent back to the States for the five months of mechanic's training. PFC Tweet did not take any steps to blend in; he did just the opposite.

He had a high-pitched voice with an extreme hillbilly accent. He used it to tease the other guys over stupid things. For instance, when we were working on a ship with the engine running and blades spinning, he would make it a point to ask us why we were trying to avoid the windblown sand and pebbles. He would stand there bare-chested and let the crap blow all over him and into his face and then say something about how tough he was.

He never missed an opportunity to throw a cutting comment in someone's direction. He routinely acted as if he *wanted* to get beat up.

The ping-pong scores gave us an opportunity to get even.

While standing in our tent after a couple of intense games and discussing our scores, he walked up and asked what we were talking about. Jack Morgan started the conversation.

Jack: Oh, we were just sharing our bunker codes to see who got which numbers. *(I had no idea what Bob was talking about!)*

Tweet: Bunker codes? What are they?

Jack: You know. Sergeant Smith gave them to us this morning.

Tweet: I didn't get one. What are they?

Jack: They're pass codes to get into the bunker when we're mortared. They'll check you in at the door, but you have to give them your name and code. Remember? VC got into the bunkers during Tet and killed a bunch of guys when they came in.

Me: Yeah. I can't believe you didn't get one.

Tweet: Man, I need to see Sergeant Smith.

Jack: Yep, I wouldn't wait if I were you.

Of course, this was all BS. We quickly told the guys in the neighboring tents about the joke. Everyone he asked gave him the same story. This sent Tweet into a full-fledged panic when he could not find Sergeant Smith. As luck would have it, Smith had caught a flight to the finance center in Can Tho and was not coming back until the next day. It was easy to stoke the fire by simply mentioning how much we hoped we would not be mortared that night, "because you'll be out of luck, Tweet!"

The joke was finally spoiled when Tweet caught up with Sergeant Smith the next afternoon. We got over twenty-four hours of laughs out of it and enjoyed the small amount of revenge it provided.

Door Gunner

On November 5th, I finally had a chance to fly a combat mission, instead of the routine test flights we made after repairs. One of the door gunners in the Lift platoon was ill, so I replaced him for the day.

We flew out to an area along the Cambodian border called Chi Lang. It sat at the base of one of the Seven Sisters Mountains, Nui Coto. This mountain would become the site of a bitter battle in 1969. It housed an ARVN basic training camp and a Special Forces (Green Beret) A-Team. Also on the little base was a group of Cambodian mercenaries I would later see in action.

We sat on the ground all day. When lunchtime came, we broke out a couple of boxes of C rations and heated them up with a jet stove. We made these by taking an empty tin can, punching a few holes around the top rim, and filling it with sand. We then drained some JP-4 from the Huey's fuel tanks into the can: Voilà! Instant stove.

While the crew chief and I sat in the Huey and ate, all the pilots went up the hill to the Special Forces dining hall: a small, one-room building with a long table inside. I also noticed that the Scout crew chiefs and observers were invited along for the hot meal. None of the other enlisted aircrew members attended.

Late in the day, with no actual troop insertions or extractions under my belt, we took off for the return trip to Vinh Long. I had not even fired the M-60. In retrospect, I didn't have to clean it either, and that was a good thing.

For some unknown reason, our ship flew back alone. This was not a big deal – until the pilot became lost. It was monsoon season and we had climbed to around 5,000 feet to dodge a storm. When we came down out of the clouds, neither of the two pilots knew where we were. They pulled out a map and began searching for something familiar. It was getting dark and it was getting cold in the back of the Huey. I was concerned, especially when after twenty minutes of comparing the map to the terrain, the pilots still could not determine our position.

The sun was almost down to the horizon when the pilots recognized a bend in the river and determined what we had to do to get back to base. Fortunately, we had plenty of fuel and touched down at Vinh Long about ten minutes after sunset. We were the last ones back after being the first to depart Chi Lang. I am sure the aircraft commander (AC) "had some 'splaining to do" when he ran into Apache-Six, the troop CO.

Just as the dry season was getting started, I was selected to help fill sandbags for a new bunker the rifle platoon was building. I spent that morning filling sandbags with two other guys. This too was memorable because we were driven to the middle of a Sahara-like sandbank and dropped next to a pallet of new sandbags and three entrenching tools. The driver threw three canteens of warm water to us and said, "Have fun, boys!" and drove off, laughing. It was hot. Working there was like being baked in an oven. I was dry for the first time in two days because the sand flats reflected the sun's heat back on me. Our skin dried out, and the skin on our hands began to crack open. Four hours later another truck picked us up and returned us to the squadron. I think they had it timed, knowing we'd be dead if we stayed out there a couple more hours.

Christmas

The Christmas season brought us lots of gifts from The World: all of them some type of food. Because we had no refrigerator and could not store anything, everyone shared everything they had. The one exception for me was a large pack of Oreo cookies.

My parents had sent them a month early, so they arrived around Thanksgiving. I wanted to save them for Christmas and thought that leaving them sealed would prevent them from going stale. I stored them in the bottom of my footlocker to keep them out of sight. I would share them all at Christmas.

I got so much food I could not use it all. Particularly popular were canned Cheese Whiz and Kool-Aid. Evidently, someone had told the folks back home that we needed them. Everyone in the platoon had tons of the stuff. I had so much they practically filled my footlocker, so I began making periodic trips to the local orphanage and giving these to them. The children and nuns loved it.

While in the maintenance platoon, I made it a practice to stay sober. I was afraid to get drunk and not be able to find my way into a bunker if a mortar attack occurred. I would drink a beer or two at night, but I was never out of control.

Enlisted men below the rank of E-6 were limited to drinking beer. We could not even possess hard liquor or wine. Getting caught doing so could result in an Article 15 hearing and a demotion.

I did fine maintaining my sobriety until December 24th, 1968 – Christmas Eve. For some reason, I took a headlong dive off the wagon. It started in the afternoon when we had a cookout in the maintenance area. We had chilled several cases of beer and got our hands on some hot dogs and rolls. The party began.

Within a couple of hours, practically everyone was stumbling drunk. As a practical joke, I took a hand flare out of one of the helicopters, aimed it over the fence toward the Thirty-Fourth engineers' area and fired it. Everyone got a big laugh out of it, even though it started a small fire in one of their tents.

Craig and I downed a couple of beers and then heard that one of the engineer officers was asking around for the guy who launched the flare. Craig and I decided it would be a good time to go back to the barracks and rest.

About ten minutes after we got to the hooch, I heard Lt. Rob Lytle, one of our maintenance officers, yelling my name. My first thought was that someone had ratted us out and he was bringing the engineer over to arrest me. WRONG.

Lt. Lytle was carrying two bottles of liquor, one in each hand, and he was pretty relaxed. Because he was originally from Newport News, Virginia, he wanted to bring Christmas in with a fellow Virginian! He, Craig, and I sat on our footlockers and emptied both bottles, straight. One was a fifth of vodka and the other a fifth of "brown." After a few shots, I could not taste the difference anyway.

That much liquor, on top of five or six beers, had a weird effect on me. It made me hyper, and I started bolting around the barracks, greeting the other guys as they returned from the party. Lt. Lytle left at some point, but I did not notice. After an hour, it was time for me to lie down. As soon as I did, the barracks started spinning like a tornado, with me lying on my back, looking straight up the funnel. Having heard that touching one foot to the floor would stop the spinning, I dangled my right leg over the edge of the bunk and tried to find the floor. It felt like it was ten feet below me and I was scared I was going to fall off the bunk! I touched the floor and must have passed out, because I remembered nothing beyond that point.

There were two memorable aspects of my fall from grace. First, I never got sick. After downing that much mixed alcohol and greasy hot dogs, I never experienced any nausea. It was unbelievable.

Second was the absolute debilitating nature of the hangover.

Christmas Day was a workday, and Sgt. Smith woke us up bright and early. I felt like about 20 percent of my brain was operating, with the rest in sleep mode. The walk to the maintenance area was torture. When I arrived, I saw that everyone else was in the same sad state. It was going to be a long day.

We had plenty of work to do, but we were in no shape to do it. We shuffled between the ships, carrying our toolboxes and walking like zombies. It was a bizarre scene. The NCOs and officers would come out of the shack and try to roust us into action, but it was no use. Everyone just sat there or made up a reason to go to the supply room, anything to escape the gaze of the leaders. Doing any work on an aircraft probably would have been unsafe, so it was just as well that the leaders did not put much effort into putting us to work.

Christmas 1968 came and went, like any other workday. We had a nice turkey for lunch and went back to work. That evening, I bought a Coke and got ready for the opening of the coveted Oreos. I dug to the bottom of my locker, and the Oreos were gone! I could not believe it. No one started joking me, which they would have done if they had taken them. I figured one of the hooch maids had liberated them. Oh well.

In 1995, I learned that Lieutenant Lytle, later promoted to captain, was killed in a midair collision near Vinh Long.

TRANSFER

"Only the dead have seen the end of the war."

George Santayana

Early in January, Craig Schmidt told me that he was transferring to the Scout platoon, making him the third friend to get the assignment before me. I was livid.

I ran down Sgt. Smith and asked him what in the hell was going on. I reminded him that he had promised to move me to the Scout platoon on three occasions, and I kept getting bypassed. I respectfully informed him that if Craig went to the Scouts and I did not, I was not lifting another wrench to repair another helicopter, that I was beyond putting up with this crap.

It was a desperate and risky move, but I had no other choice. It was January, and I had only seven more months in-country. I did not want to miss this opportunity because there was no telling when another crew chief spot would open up. He could have had me disciplined or even court-martialed for failing to follow orders. But I was so enraged, I did not think about those consequences. I *had* to get into the Scouts in order to fulfill my desire to experience combat. I felt that I could not leave the war without that test.

I moved to the Scouts the next day, and Craig remained in the maintenance platoon. He was angry at me. But when I explained that I had been waiting since the day we arrived and about Sgt. Smith's promises, he understood.

Twenty years later, I received an explanation for Smith's consistent refusals to let me transfer. At one of our earliest Blackhawk reunions, I met an E-7 who worked in squadron personnel. He told me that Smith wanted to hang on to me because of my AIT results. Finishing first in both UH-1 school and OH-6A school made me a hot property with promising career implications. Smith wanted to keep all of his top guys under his control. In effect, I was being punished for my strong performance!

The Scout Platoon

When I checked in, Sgt. Howard, the original platoon sergeant from Ft. Knox, was in the process of heading home. Howard was a hard-core guy with a reputation as a hard-working and hard-drinking warrior. I had already heard the story about him trying to get some sleep before an early mission. When his tentmates refused to end a poker game, he sat up, pulled out his .45, and shot the light bulbs out!

Howard was being replaced by Master Sergeant Bosworth, a roly-poly guy who was way over 250 pounds – the exact opposite of Howard, who at six feet and about 135 pounds personified the army term lean-and-mean. While Howard sported a dark tan and weathered face, Bosworth was fair-skinned and pasty. Howard had a tall V silhouette. Bosworth resembled a bowling pin. He was way too polite, and it was obvious that the other Scouts took maximum advantage of him.

My first day was a stand-down day, meaning no combat missions. We were to spend the day working on our ships (we *never* referred to them as choppers), doing the little maintenance things that you never had time to accomplish.

Master Sergeant (MSgt.) Bosworth decided that we were going to spend the day building a bunker beside the flight line hooch. It was obvious from the moment I walked up that things were not going well.

Bosworth was personally directing the placement of each and every sandbag. Most of the Scouts were standing around, cracking vicious jokes at Bosworth's expense.

Personally directing the work was a big mistake. Some of these guys had been in-country for nearly a year and knew exactly how to build a bunker. From the looks of things, Bosworth had never *seen* a bunker, much less built one.

The basic footprint of the structure had already taken shape, and it was a mess. From what I could overhear, it was supposed to accommodate two individuals who would be on flight line guard duty overnight. If we were mortared, the guards could take shelter in the bunker. Unfortunately, the interior size of the bunker, which had reached a height of about three feet, was only about two feet wide and six feet long. It also looked as if it might collapse at any moment. Evidently, Bosworth had extra sandbags placed on the inside for extra protection. This consumed all the space. It also had no opening through which the guards could enter. They would have to stand up and dive over the walls to get in, exposing themselves to shrapnel from the mortar rounds and small arms fire.

A major debate about the bunker started. Most of the guys wanted to take it down and start over. Bosworth and a few guys wanted to keep going. I believed for a long time that the guys who supported Bosworth were doing so to embarrass him. Anyone who saw this mess would want to know who was in charge of such a screwed-up project.

While these guys egged Bosworth on, one wall of the bunker started to fall over. Within a minute or two, the wall was down and everyone stood there making more jokes and teasing Bosworth. He walked off, head down, toward his jeep.

Mysteriously, Bosworth disappeared two days later, transferred to God knows where. While no one would admit it, one or more of the senior guys probably went to the platoon leader and reported on how poorly Bosworth was performing.

We suspected an E-4 crew chief named Johnson. He was older than the rest of us, probably twenty-four or twenty-five. He regularly played poker with the pilots, most of whom were closer to his age than we were. Because he had this frequent access and was probably perceived as a peer by many of the officers, he had a perfect opening to blow the whistle on Bosworth.

In any event, Bosworth left and was replaced by another E-7, MSgt. Saunders. He also turned out to be a piece of work, but we will address that later.

The other crew chiefs when I arrived were:

- Vernon Summerell and Dave Raymond, both came from the maintenance platoon and the 370th. All three of us had attended Huey and Loach school together.
- E-4 Johnson, the poker player.
- E-4 Dietrich, who had a small, black-and-white TV on which we would later watch a replay of the July '69 moon landing. He did not volunteer for combat flight duty.
- E-4 John Orebaugh, a nice guy. Always upbeat and eager to help. Wounded in '69.
- E-4 Jim Lucido, who would become a close friend and hearts partner with Vernon. Jim was married and also chose not to fly combat missions.
- E-4 Masters, a "Baby Huey" guy who stood about six four and weighed in at 250-plus, so heavy that he was not allowed to fly.
- E-4 Seale, from Baltimore. He was leaving as I was joining the platoon. One of the best marksmen I ever saw. He had reportedly fired an M-79 from a moving Loach at a running VC and hit him squarely in the middle of the back.
- Spec-5 Mike Jones, the line chief when I arrived.

The observers were:

- E-6 Conley – a National Guardsman who volunteered for Nam when he thought his Guard unit was going to be activated and sent to Nam. It never was. He was A-Troop's reenlistment NCO. He was teased constantly. He flew about three times.
- E-5 Mike Pounds.
- E-5 Jim Banlow, my previous guard duty mentor.

- E-4 Steve Holmes.
- E-4 John Tillery.
- E-4 Cotton, a general's son.
- E-4 "Frenchie" LeMoyne, a French Canadian who took great pride in living up to his country's reputation as hard fighters and harder partiers.
- A couple of months after my arrival, an additional observer came in:
- E-4 Mark Hansen – we would become close friends.

A month after that, two new observers joined:

- E-4 Tom Gery.
- E-4 Jim Heller, a mortar man from D-Troop.

All three were great guys, and Tom often flew in the wing ship when I was flying lead.

This mix of guys provided many humorous stories and memories that I will never forget.

The first thing to know about the Scout platoon was the aggressive manner in which we executed our missions. VC and NVA (North Vietnamese [regular] Army) body count was the primary measure of success, as it was for every combat unit in Nam. While capturing enemy weapons was a good thing, Confirmed Kills, KBA (Killed by Air) was the real measure. For this reason, guys who had not racked up their first kill were occasionally called "cherry boy." This did not happen all the time, but when the topic of experience or killing came up, that term could be thrown into the conversation without warning.

The Scout missions and how they were completed stood out from the rest of the squadron.

Each of the three aviation troops, a unit equivalent to an infantry company, had a Scout platoon. In the 7/1 Cav, three of the five troops were aviation units. The other two, D-Troop and Headquarters (HHQ) Troop, were not. HHQ Troop was primarily administrative, and the only members of HHQ Troop who took part in combat missions were a few of the senior officers and a couple of crew chiefs. They typically orbited the area of operations (AO) at 3,000 feet and watched the missions unfold. Command of the actual mission was left to the troop CO.

D-Troop ("Powder Valley") was a mounted unit, using jeeps in the place of horses or tanks. They operated independently, often conducting patrols that lasted a month or more. Their jeeps were equipped with mounted machine guns, belt-fed M2 .50 calibers, and M60 7.62mm machine guns. Several of their jeeps carried 106mm recoilless rifles, capable of firing high-explosive 106mm anti-tank shells. Originally designed as an anti-tank weapon, these were devastating when used against bunkers or enemy troops at close range.

The aviation troops were:

A, nicknamed "Apache"
B, nicknamed "Dutch Master," and
C, nicknamed "Comanche."

D-Troop Jeep with 106mm Recoilless Rifle.

Each of these troops had five platoons:

- **HHQ** – a small platoon that included the troop CO, Executive Officer (XO), Supply Officer, Intelligence Officer, troop first sergeant, company clerk, and a few others; the maintenance platoon was attached to the HHQ platoon in a loose manner.
- **Rifle platoon** – comprised of infantrymen who were responsible for security when we were in camp; they rarely went outside of the base while I was there.
- **Scout platoon** – of which I was a member.
- **Lift platoon** – comprised of about eight UH-1H model Huey helicopters used for inserting infantrymen into an LZ or extracting them from an LZ after a mission. The platoon also included about eight crew chiefs, eight door gunners, and maybe fifteen to twenty pilots. Depending on the nature of the troops, US or Vietnamese, the H-Model could carry ten to fifteen troops at a time.
- **Guns platoon** - comprised of about nine AH-1G "Cobra" model gunship helicopters. The platoon included about a dozen pilots and a like number of weapons officers, as well as nine crew chiefs. These crew chiefs did not fly combat missions and had an unappealing life. In addition to the natural first-echelon maintenance for which crew chiefs were responsible, Cobra crew chiefs were often dropped off at a refueling and rearming point near the AO. They stayed there alone until two Cobras would return for fuel and ammo. Then the crew chief had to work like mad to get them refueled, load the minigun ammo, the rockets, and the 40mm ammo to bring each ship back to fully loaded status. This could easily take over an hour. Just about the time this was complete, the other two Cobras would return. The crew chiefs were usually armed with an M-16 and a radio, so they could call for help if any military-age males – meaning possible VC – showed up on the scene. I would have hated this assignment.

Scout Operations

The Scout platoon was the essential element in the execution of reconnaissance missions. We had two types of missions, either of which could become awfully exciting.

The first type, which we flew most often, was search-and-destroy. The CO would pick an area to search, and we would go out and see if we could find any VC or NVA, depending on the location. If so, either the Scout or Guns platoon would engage them. This depended on the specific circumstances of the discovery, number of VC, types of weapons they possessed, and who fired first. If the VC fired at the Scout, the observer would drop a red smoke grenade to mark the spot. The Cobras would then make gun runs on the area marked by the red smoke. If the Scout saw the VC first, he would usually fire on them, using either the pilot-controlled minigun or the observer's CAR-15.

The second type of mission, which we flew about a third of the time, was to clear predefined landing zones (LZ). This was done whenever the slicks were either inserting troops or retrieving troops from the AO. Slicks were UH-1H Hueys specifically designed as troop carriers. They did not carry the heavy armaments of the Huey gunships, which often appeared to have short wings. When viewed from the front, their profile appeared "slick." Closely related to the LZ clearing was flying ahead of an advancing infantry unit, looking for booby traps, ambushes, etc.

The search team consisted of five ships: the command and control (C&C) ship in which the troop CO (Apache-Six) flew. These were UH-1H models with a crew of four. At times, they would carry interpreters or possibly the local Vietnamese province chief. They flew at about 2,000 feet, out of range for most VC weapons.

The next group in the stack were two Cobra gunships, flying at about 1,500 feet. They would orbit the AO and provide supporting fire if the Scouts received fire or located something too dangerous to handle themselves.

To bring ground troops into a fight or search, four UH-1H models ("slicks") would land at a staging area, where the troops were. The troops would board the slicks for the ride to the AO when necessary.

Flying at very low levels were the two Scout ships, one flying lead and the other flying wing. Each carried a two-man crew. In the right seat was the pilot, who was an officer or warrant officer. In the left seat was the observer or crew chief. For brevity, I will refer to this person as the observer, regardless of the person's actual training. On most days, we liked to have a crew chief in one ship and an observer in the other. This enabled us to take care of minor repairs in the field, whether the problem was with the aircraft or the minigun.

The experiences of the wing ship and the lead ship were quite different.

When clearing an LZ, the lead ship typically flew low and slow, looking for things that might indicate the presence of VC. The lead ship hovered around the LZ at three feet above the ground to determine if the slicks would be exposed to enemy fire when they came in with the troops. This could take a while. The more experienced Scout pilots rarely actually hovered.

To present a moving target, they kept the Loach moving from side to side, forward and backward, and up and down. However, these tiny maneuvers were done at only three to ten mph, giving both the pilot and observer plenty of time to inspect the ground.

The wing ship had a more sickening ride. While the lead ship hovered around in search mode, the wing ship orbited above in a constant right turn. This enabled the pilot to look out his door and keep a watchful eye on the lead ship.

The orbits were flown in an elliptical pattern in which the pilot was constantly diving or climbing while turning to the right. The low point would be about twenty feet above the ground, while the highest point might be two hundred or three hundred feet above the ground. This was done by diving at a high speed, doing a hard right turn at the bottom, and then climbing hard to two hundred feet, then repeating the pattern. The pilot constantly shifted the orbit to avoid flying over the same spot twice and allowing the VC to get a bead on the Loach. This was unbelievably demanding because of the G's experienced at the bottom and the negative G's at the top. At the bottom, you could feel your stomach and throat sag hard. At the top, everything inside wanted to come out through your mouth. The pilot kept the ship in a constant right turn so that he could keep the lead ship in sight at all times. If the lead ship took fire, the wing ship would dive and make a gun run on the area marked by the red smoke.

Flying wing was the way all new Scouts were introduced to the job, including the pilots. They started flying a couple of missions as observers on the wing ship, then moved to the observer seat in the lead ship for a couple of missions. When it came time for them to begin flying the ship, they spent a significant amount of time in the wing ship before taking on the responsibilities associated with the lead role.

Crew chiefs and observers followed the same path.

The embarrassing part of this indoctrination was what we referred to as "Calling Ralph." This was Cav jargon for vomiting out the door because of motion sickness. Everyone did it, often more than once, until they became accustomed to the physical strain.

When this happened, the person doing the puking was responsible for cleaning the helicopter. No exceptions. The vomit was usually on the outside of the ship. Puking inside the ship was a big no-no. When the ships would return to Vinh Long after a day of flying, everyone could see the yellow stripes streaming down the left side of the ship. We could all tell that someone had been Calling Ralph a lot that day. Out came the buckets and sponges. The perpetrator was busy for a while.

When pulling our usual search and destroy missions, with no planned LZ to clear, the lead ship would sometimes use more airspeed. This was required to cover more ground than when clearing an LZ. We might fly at twenty to fifty knots, zigzagging around the area to see what we could stir up.

When flying lead, both the pilot and the observer were looking for signs of VC activity. This could be anything: footprints, trash, discarded equipment, spider holes (a camouflaged foxhole), trip wires, booby traps, tunnel entrances, remnants of cooking fires, etc.

A key skill in these searches was the ability to judge how old the signs might be.

If we found many fresh signs, or if we received fire from a VC or NVA, the troop CO might decide to insert troops to intensify the search. In that case,

Apache-Six would locate an open field of a suitable size to serve as an LZ. Then the Scouts would clear it for the incoming slicks.

In addition to searching, the obvious role of the Scouts was to entice an enemy soldier into firing on the Loach before any slicks came onto the scene. Two men and a $50,000 helicopter were a more affordable loss than fifteen men and a million-dollar Huey. We would often fly around an area where we knew Charlie was present so that they would expose their positions by firing at us. If this happened, the observer would drop a red smoke grenade to mark the spot, and the wing ship and Cobras would unleash a brutal rocket and minigun attack.

In addition to the sometimes overwhelming airsickness that often struck rookie observers was the physical sensation associated with a Loach takeoff.

To take off, the pilot would bring the engine up to the proper operating RPM by twisting the motorcycle-like throttle on the "collective" control stick, located left of his seat. The stick was called "collective" because when the stick was pulled up, it placed an equal amount of pitch into all four main rotor blades simultaneously and at all points of their rotation. This pitch changed the angle of the rotor blades and allowed them to achieve more bite into the air, creating lift. This is the opposite of what we might know as "feathering" a propeller, in which the angle of attack is lessened and the prop provides no bite into the air. Simultaneously with the pulling up on the collective, two things must happen. First, the engine's fuel injection system senses the additional strain that the pitched blades are putting on the engine, then it automatically adds fuel. This allows the engine to maintain the proper RPM, even though it is under more strain.

Second, the pilot must press the left control pedal to prevent the torque of the rotor from twisting the ship to the right. The more heavily he pulls up on the collective stick, the more the helicopter will rise vertically and the more left pedal he must apply. This balance between the collective stick and use of the pedals is the most difficult process for a new pilot to learn. It is strictly a matter of feel, and it can take hours to develop. Good coordination is a must.

While the pilot's left hand and left foot have been executing this brief dance

– we're talking about two to three seconds – his right hand has a gentle grip on the "cyclic" control stick, the one affixed to the floor, directly between his knees. While the collective stick can only move straight up and straight down, the cyclic mimics the joysticks we find on video games. It can move 360 degrees.

Once the helicopter is hovering, the cyclic stick controls direction. Push the stick to the right, and the controls tilt the rotor disc by increasing the pitch of the blades as they rotate past the left side of the ship. The ship then slowly slides to the right. The same thing applies as the pilot pushes the cyclic forward, backward, or to the left. When he centers the cyclic stick, the ship stops moving.

During takeoff maneuvers in Vietnam, where the air is hot and far less dense than it is in more temperate climates, the pilot has to exercise great care to get the ship into the air and heading in the right direction. More often than not, this provides the observer with a bit of a thrill.

Once the pilot has the ship clear of its protective revetment, and the other ships in the formation are ready to go, he pulls up on the collective stick, placing the ship "light on the skids." This means it is still in temporary contact with but not fully resting on the ground. The pilot can then check his engine instruments one last time to make sure everything is still green while the engine is under a load.

He will then continue to pull up on the collective, bringing the ship to a hover about five or six feet above the ground. Because the ship has not moved forward at this point, it is resting on a column of air that has been compressed by the rotor blades, between those blades and the ground.

To transition the ship from hover into forward flight, the pilot must achieve about fifty to sixty knots of forward airspeed. At that speed, the aerodynamic forces will hold the ship straight and the pilot can ease off of the left pedal. He will no longer be hovering – he'll be flying.

The trick is getting up to the desired speed.

When flying a Loach, the way to gain that airspeed is to push the ship off its cushion of air, go into a slight dive, then pull back on the cyclic stick to avoid colliding with the ground.

Again, all of this is done by feel. The pilot pushes the cyclic stick forward, causing the nose to drop and the ship to begin moving forward. As the ship moves forward it falls off of the air cushion and starts heading for the ground. The pilot pushes the stick forward some more as the fall causes the ship to gain a little speed.

As the ship is making this short dive toward the ground, the observer is looking out through the front of the bubble as the ground rushes up to meet him. A crash always appears imminent.

When the pilot feels he is going fast enough, he pulls back on the cyclic, pulls up on the collective to get a little more power, and hopes that the ship climbs away. When he does so, he and the observer feel a couple of extra G's as the ship tries to climb. As soon as he is sure he has cleared the ground in front of the ship, he stops the climb by pushing forward on the stick. Both he and the observer became weightless for a couple of seconds.

It's a thrill I remember clearly.

The OH-6A Cayuse

The OH-6A Cayuse, built by Hughes Aircraft in California, was the ideal aircraft for low-level reconnaissance. The army designated the OH-6A a Light Observation Helicopter or LOH. GIs quickly bastardized LOH into Loach, and that name was used throughout the service. Like Huey (UH-1), the word Loach described the type of helicopter. Highly maneuverable and quick, the OH-6A also had several design features that enhanced the crew's survivability in the event of a crash.

First, the frame incorporated an integral roll bar. The frame members created an elliptical cocoon that formed a rigid sphere when the ship hit the ground and rolled over. This shape enabled other parts of the ship to tear away while the cockpit remained intact. The frame also prevented the detached rotor blades from piercing the cockpit and decapitating the crew, a major problem in the Hueys and Cobras.

The gas turbine engine was mounted low in the frame, several feet behind the cockpit, making it highly unlikely the engine would fall into the cockpit and injure the crew.

The OH-6A also had features that could help prevent a crash. The ship had two self-sealing fuel tanks under the passenger compartment floor. If a bullet passed through one or both of the tanks, a special compound embedded into the rubber walls would seal the hole after the bullet passed through. This helped prevent fires that would otherwise occur when the leaking fuel contacted something hot – like the jet turbine engine located about two feet aft of the tanks! Of course, the self-sealant did not help if a tracer bullet penetrated the fuel tank. In that case, the Loach and crew were likely to disappear in a smoky flash.

Another feature that reduced fatalities was the design of the rotor head and how it attached to the helicopter. In most helicopters at that time, the rotor head was attached to the mast, a hollow steel tube that also served as the driveshaft for the rotor head. It was directly attached to the transmission, with no other supporting structure. This older design brought two significant risks. First, a high-caliber round could sever the mast, separating the rotor from the aircraft.

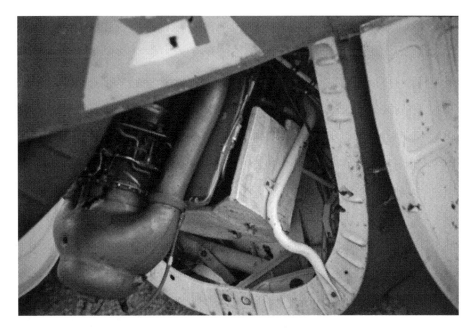

Loach turbine engine and armor plate, with bullet holes.

The second risk in the traditional design was the possibility of a transmission failure, either from gunfire or another anomaly. If the transmission locked up, the rotor would continue rotating, wringing the mast off the ship. When either of these misfortunes occurred, the aircraft assumed the aerodynamic characteristics of a brick.

Loach rotor heads had two safety features. First, the rotor head was attached directly to the airframe and was not dependent on the mast for support. The driveshaft served no purpose in connecting the rotor to the frame of the ship. Also, the driveshaft incorporated a breakaway spot in the tube. If the transmission locked up, this weak spot would snap the shaft in half, freeing the rotor to continue spinning and allowing the pilot to autorotate to a safe landing, an option far better than impacting the planet at terminal velocity.

Perhaps the most important safety feature of the Loach was its silence. AN OH-6 had four short rotor blades that rotated at 400 RPM. The combination created a buzzing sound completely different from the "wop-wop-wop" sound of a Huey, Cobra, or any other helicopter with two rotor blades. While those ships could be heard from miles away, the OH-6 had the ability to sneak up on the enemy, especially if approaching from downwind. We used this ability to surprise VC and NVA.

Another safety feature was the installation of ceramic armor plates beside and under the front seats and around the engine. I never knew what the design parameters were; which bullets fired at what distance would it stop? I also never saw one stop a bullet! Every bullet hole I saw in a piece of armor plate passed clean through and into whatever object was behind the plate. Moreover, I saw tons of them. I think the armor was there for morale purposes only.

In addition to sitting in partially armored seats, both the pilot and observer wore frontal body armor commonly called chicken plates. These nylon vests contained a thick ceramic and steel mesh plate in the front. You pulled them over your head and secured them with Velcro straps that ran from front to back under your arms. Because of the close ranges at which we engaged the VC, they would not stop a bullet. The best to be expected was for it to slow the bullet and reduce its destructive power.

For me, the chicken plates presented a mixed blessing. Because we often operated around water and canals, the prospect of crashing in water deep enough to cause drowning was a reality. I could imagine trying to remove both a flight helmet and a chicken plate while under water. It would not be pretty.

The OH-6 first flew in 1963, and the army selected it for use in 1966 as a replacement for the fixed-wing O-1 Bird Dog, famous for its role as an artillery fire spotter. The OH-6 arrived in Vietnam that same year, along with a strong reputation as a performance aircraft. Prior to action in Vietnam, the OH-6 set twenty-three world records for speed, endurance, and rate of climb. With a top speed of 152 knots and a cruising speed of 135 knots, the Loach could keep up with any army helicopter of the day.

The OH-6 only weighed 1,965 pounds but could lift 1,594 pounds of cargo and crew, an important capability when Loaches were called upon to rescue wounded soldiers or downed aircrew and carry them to safety.

Key to the Scout's mission was the OH-6 price tag. The army initially bought 714 Loaches at the bargain price of $19,900 each, plus the cost of the radios. When compared to the cost of its nearest competitor, the Fairchild-Hiller at $29,400 per ship, or a UH-1B at $585,000, the economics of using a Loach to draw enemy fire was obvious.

The Minigun

In 1969, A-Troop Scouts utilized a two-man crew with a minigun mounted on the port side of the aircraft. This pilot-fired weapon was the main armament on the OH-6, backed up by the Colt CAR-15, carried by the observer.

The minigun was an electrically powered Gatling gun with six barrels. Rather than use the gas from the fired rounds to operate the mechanism, a small electric motor drove the gun. As the barrels rotated, each barrel's bolt travelled along a track that would move the bolt backward from the breech to expel the empty shell casing, then move forward to load a fresh round into the barrel's chamber. When the bolt reached the point at which it was locked into place, the bolt would release the firing pin, firing the round.

The gun was attached to a short pylon that was part of the assembly containing the ammo box. The assembly was securely mounted to the floor of the passenger compartment. The box held 2,000 rounds of NATO 7.62mm, belted ammunition. Because of the gun's rate of fire, the linked ammo was specially assembled for minigun use. Linked ammo used in the M-60 machine gun would immediately jam a minigun, so the crew chief and observers had to make sure that they were loading the appropriate ammo.

The pylon holding the minigun could be elevated or lowered by the pilot. His control stick had a positioning button that would raise or lower the gun. The stick also had a trigger switch that fired the gun. Pulling the trigger to the first click caused the gun to fire at 2,000 rounds per minute. The second click brought 4,000 rounds per minute. The third click fired at 6,000 rounds per minute. The use of this rate was prohibited because the resulting vibrations would shake the rivets out of the tail boom! Most of the firing was done at the 2,000-rpm rate.

The XM-27 minigun, mounted on an OH-6A. (Image: Military-Today.com)

The elevation and depression of the gun was only done to make the gun safe when on the ground. At those times, the gun was always depressed so that it pointed down at the ground at about a forty-five-degree angle. Once airborne and beyond the perimeter of the airfield, the pilot would elevate the gun so that the barrels were parallel with the cockpit floor. Any aiming of the gun was done by the pilot adjusting the flight path or attitude of the ship, similar to what is done in a fighter plane.

The impact of the minigun cannot be overstated. Even when firing at the lowest rate, the bullets came out so fast that the tracer rounds made what looked like a solid laser beam. A flame exited the muzzles, reaching a distance of six feet, longer at night. The sound was incredible. The sound of individual rounds being fired was imperceptible. The gun made a loud growling sound and emitted a continuous pressure wave that was painful to the observer's ears. Sitting less than four feet from the muzzles, the observers felt the full force of the blast and could be partially deaf in the left ear for hours following long gun runs.

The impact on the target was even more impressive. When minigun rounds struck the ground, the earth appeared to boil because the rounds were hitting so close together. Even a short burst of fire could fell a tree or cut a person in half. The minigun was an awesome weapon. The Loach crews also carried various types of hand grenades, each with a particular purpose. Fragmentation grenades, which we called hardballs, were not carried in the Loach because of the likelihood of a grenade being struck by enemy fire and exploding in the cockpit.

Most of the grenades we carried were smoke grenades of various colors: red, green, yellow, white, and purple were the usual colors. We used red smoke to mark enemy targets. If we wanted the ground troops to move in a specific direction, we would pop a red smoke grenade and hold it out the door, trailing smoke to indicate the direction.

We also carried white phosphorous grenades for setting hooches on fire. We called these "Willie Peet." When they exploded, they threw grape-sized chunks of burning phosphorous in all directions. Because the burning phosphorous created dense white smoke, the explosions were very pretty: bright red burning pieces of phosphorous, trailing pure white smoke. They were also deadly. If the burning phosphorous struck a person's skin, you could not snuff it out unless you submerged the wound in water and kept it there. This deprived the phosphorous of oxygen. If the wound was removed from the water, it would ignite again. In the case of a phosphorous wound in the arm or leg, it was common for the phosphorous to burn all the way through the limb. If struck in the torso, the phosphorous would burn its way into vital organs, killing the individual.

One problem with carrying Willie Pete grenades in the Loach cockpit was the likelihood of them being hit by enemy fire. When this happened, the bullet would pierce the grenade, making a small hole. The chemicals, stored under pressure within the grenade, would then fly out of the grenade in a pressurized spray. It resembled a flaming aerosol spray. Anything touched by the semisolid, flaming spray would suffer the same fate as being hit with a larger, flying piece of burning phosphorous.

If this happened, the observer was responsible for grabbing the grenade and tossing it out the door. For this reason, we stored the WP grenades in a small net pouch mounted between the seats at about shoulder height, our bodies partially shielding the grenades from direct fire.

In the monsoon season, we used thermite grenades to set fires because the dampness would prevent the Willie Pete from setting anything on fire. While thermite did not explode and spread the fire, it burned at temperatures around 4,000 degrees Fahrenheit. Initially intended for use in disabling cannons and tanks by melting steel, a thermite grenade could start a fire in even the wettest conditions. They were also a little safer if hit by enemy fire.

Scout Guard Duty

One day I learned that I had guard duty and that it would be different from the guard duty we pulled as members of the maintenance platoon.

Members of the Scout platoon had a standing assignment on Bunker 9, well known for being attacked by snipers and sappers carrying grenades.

When we went out for guard duty, no one wanted to be assigned to Bunker 9. I had experienced Bunker 9 once or twice before, so I knew what to expect. In maintenance, we had an equal opportunity to pull duty on any one of three bunkers and the guard tower. Not so in the Scouts.

Because the Scout platoon crew chiefs and observers were the only enlisted men to have frequent combat experience, our leaders felt that we would be better adapted to handling any situation that might arise on Bunker 9. We were to provide the steady hand if the bunker came under attack.

This theory somehow made sense to the people in charge: "Someone has a lot of combat experience? Great! Let's expose them to even more of it on their day off!"

During one assignment, the army tried using guard dogs on the perimeter. The belief was that the dogs could easily smell VC trying to penetrate the perimeter long before we could see them.

Dogs and their handlers became the norm. We would sit on top of the bunkers, even in the wet season, because the mosquitos owned the inside of the bunker. You simply could not stand to be in there for more than a minute or two. The bugs were so thick in the air that you would inhale them when you breathed.

Most of the handlers would come over to the bunker to chat and let us meet the dogs. They were all German shepherds and were friendly toward GIs. They hated Vietnamese people and would try anything to get at one. We often saw them during Guard Mount, standing on their hind legs and pulling on their chain if a Vietnamese person walked by.

During one stint of guard duty, a handler approached the bunker. His dog was huge. When he reached the bunker, the dog stood up and put both front paws on the bunker roof – more than six feet high! I was lying on the roof, and his head was right in my face. It was tremendous, more like the head of a tiger than any shepherd I had ever seen. I asked the handler how big the dog was. He said it weighed 125 pounds and was the biggest guard dog he had ever seen too.

Guard duty often provided some entertaining moments.

One night soon after my transfer, I pulled flight line guard with a Scout named Steve Holmes. Flight line guard duty meant you spent the night guarding your helicopters against thieves from a neighboring troop. It was relatively risk-free and a pleasant respite from Bunker 9.

About an hour after sundown, Steve started pulling at one of the sandbags on our small bunker. He dislodged that bag and retrieved a grenade can, typically used when grenades were in storage or being transported in a case. He reached into the can and pulled out a plastic bag full of something I did not recognize. It was marijuana – pot – ganga, whatever you wanted to call it. I had never tried it.

He asked if I wanted some and rolled a joint. The evening sky, with Puff the Magic Dragon, an armed C-47 cargo plane, lighting up a VC position a few miles west, never looked so good.

In '69 pot was plentiful. We often smelled it burning when we started grass fires or burned hooches in the AO. The purchase price was unbelievably low. In the Delta, one could buy a sandbag full for around $15, a pillowcase full for $25. If you preferred some degree of refinement, you could get twenty rolled joints in a plastic-wrapped Marlboro box for fifty cents.

Studs & Duds, Even in the Scout Platoon

Most of the people I met in the Blackhawks were intelligent, mature, and easy to live with. Even those who fell a little short in certain areas were generally bright individuals who tried to do the right thing. Those who failed in these areas were usually transferred out of the unit or harassed consistently.

Vernon Summerell was the first member of the 370th to transfer to the Scout platoon. Vern and I had been in AIT together at Ft. Eustis. Like me, he had finished high in the class and was promoted to Spec-5 upon graduation. His parents and my parents had attended Norview High School together and had known each other for years. Vern was disciplined and tough and could hold his own in any situation. Before I joined the Scouts, Vern's pilot was hit in the leg, shattering his femur and preventing him from flying the Loach, so Vern flew them to a hospital and successfully landed the ship. Vern never

Steve Holmes, A-Troop Scout
(Cocoa Beach, Florida).

Jim Lucido, OH-6A crew chief.
(California).

saw the pilot again. However, that pilot did show up at one of the Blackhawk reunions. Vern did not attend the reunions, so he missed the opportunity to link up with his former crewmate.

Spec-4 Jim Lucido was a crew chief and a couple of years older than me. He was from California and was married, so he did not volunteer to fly combat missions. Jim was an absolutely great guy. He and Vern became close friends and eventual hearts partners against Dave Raymond and me.

Jim saved my ass from being busted just before I returned home in July. I had come in from guard duty and was exhausted. I mistakenly left my .45 pistol on the foot of my bed when I lay down to catch some sleep. When I woke up that afternoon, I could not find my weapon. I knew the penalty for failing to secure a weapon – one stripe – and I appeared to be on that path. I could not locate the pistol anywhere. I knew that I did not have enough time left in-country to earn that stipe back. I was near panic.

Jim came into the barracks about an hour later and saw me pacing the floor and cussing. After I told him, he joined in the search, but there was no weapon to be found. After about thirty more minutes of this torture, I decided to report my crime to the first sergeant and prepare for my fate.

Just as I stood up, Jim said, "I don't think you need to do that, Al." He reached into his locker, retrieved my pistol, and handed it to me. I wanted to kiss him but did not. Fortunately for me, Jim had come back to the barracks at midmorning, spotted my unsecured pistol, and stowed it into his locker.

Dave Raymond was another of the Spec-4 crew chiefs who had gone to AIT with Vern and me and had come over with the 370th TC Detachment. We would later become close friends and were assigned to Ft. Knox when we returned from Nam.

Spec-4 Dietrich was another crew chief who did not fly. Dietrich and I never became close. He had a small, ten-inch black-and-white TV, which he watched constantly – when his antenna worked. He kept to himself virtually all the time, never participating in the nightly hearts games or heavy drinking that occurred almost every night.

John Orebaugh was another Spec-4 crew chief who stuck to himself. He often came off as a know-it-all, never missing a chance to tell you the "right" way to do something. He had a way of getting under my skin, so we did not become close friends. I rarely hung out with him and only pulled guard duty with him once, on our favorite Bunker 9.

Vern, Jim, Dave, and I played hearts during most of our spare time. This included mass quantities of twenty-five-cent beers and sometimes led to weird experiences. One such occurrence happened when Dave went down to the gedunk shack to retrieve another round of beers. The attendant was gone and the shack was locked up. Dave probably did not need another beer. He got pissed off and took a swing at the shack wall. When his hand was still swollen the next day, he reported to the flight surgeon and learned that he had broken his right hand. He returned to Ft. Apache with a cast reaching from his fingers to his elbow. Grounded! He could not fly again for about a month.

However, there were a couple of guys who would not make anyone's list of all-stars.

One such case was a crew chief named Masters. He was present in the platoon when I arrived. Spec-4 Masters was not allowed to fly combat missions because he was significantly overweight. Standing about six four, his comfort and mobility in the aircraft were limited.

The most irritating characteristic he brought to the platoon was his obnoxious personality. He was an unrepentant know-it-all. He interjected himself into conversations, often making negative comments to get people upset.

He never knew when to shut up. On one occasion, when I was getting a flying lesson from one of our pilots, Masters came up on the radio and suggested that we bring the ship back because it was raining! He then cited some obscure rule about flying the ship with no doors in the rain, something we did routinely during the monsoons. We never flew with the doors on. He actually read to us from the manual. Oakley, the pilot, did not appreciate it and asked, "Who in the hell is that individual?" I told him it was Specialist Masters. When we landed, he gave Masters a good chewing out and directed him to never do such a thing again. Everyone got a big kick out of it because nothing we said ever had an impact on Masters.

One person Masters really annoyed was Dave Raymond. For some reason, Masters loved to needle Dave. Unfortunately for Masters, Dave had an imaginative sense of humor and decided to exercise it at Masters' expense.

One afternoon while we were hanging around the Scout shack, Dave decided to get some revenge. While Masters was outside tinkering with his ship, Dave took the buckshot out of a 10-gauge shotgun shell and repacked the cotton wad, turning the shell into a blank – plenty of powder, but no projectiles.

One of us kept watch for Masters' return to the shack and gave Dave the high sign when Masters approached. Dave picked up the shotgun, and as Masters walked in, Dave shouted, "Goddammit, Masters, I'm fed up with your bullshit and I'm going to stop it right now!" Dave pointed the shotgun at Masters for a hip shot. As Masters cried, "No! Don't, Dave. Please!" Dave said, "Go to hell," and pulled the trigger. The blast was so loud we all went momentarily deaf. Among the sparks and smoke from the shotgun, the cotton wad flew out and struck Masters in the center of his chest.

Masters's knees buckled and he dropped to the floor in a heap. Masters let out a noise like nothing I had ever heard before, a long, deep moan that seemed to take ten seconds to complete. He then started sobbing uncontrollably. He had pissed his pants and sat there in a small puddle of urine.

I stopped laughing for a moment because I thought something had gone wrong and he had actually been shot.

Dave was laughing so hard he could not breathe. Jim Lucido, who could not stand Masters, was bent over at the waist laughing so hard no sound came out. He looked up and said, "Jesus Christ, Masters! Stand up, you big pussy! Look what you've done."

Like an old man who had fallen out of bed, Masters pulled himself up to lean on the wall, still with his face in his hands. When asked if he was OK, he just shook his head no.

Someone volunteered to drive him back to the barracks so he could change clothes. Once they left, all of us retold the story and described the scene several times, bringing about unrestrained fits of laughter. We probably scarred

Masters for life. His behavior changed and he became mostly silent on items that were not his business. Dave had done us all a great service.

Another individual who suffered from self-inflicted wounds was Spec-4 Cotton. He was an observer who came over from the rifle platoon. When I arrived, he was midway through a period of being grounded. I was told he kept falling asleep in the ship, and the pilots demanded that he be removed from the flight rotation.

Cotton was a nice enough guy but a bit immature, doing and saying many inappropriate things. I found out that he was also the son of an in-country army general, so he did not receive the level of harassment that the rest of us received. He was scheduled to get another chance to fly to determine if his sleepiness was the result of a medical condition.

His chance came just a few days after I joined the platoon. The evening before his flight, he was playing with his CAR-15 when a shot rang out, scaring the hell out of everyone in the barracks. Following the shot, we could hear Cotton say, "Oh shit."

For some unknown reason, he had loaded the weapon and accidently fired it. People came streaming upstairs from the first floor, demanding to know who had discharged the weapon. They told us that the bullet had passed through the floor, through the mattress of an upper bunk, and through the pillow on a lower bunk. Someone was in that bunk, laying on his back with his hands clasped behind his head. The round had passed between his head and his elbow, just a couple of inches away from his head. He was incredibly lucky.

Cotton was also lucky. Loading a weapon in the barracks was strictly prohibited. It was about as big a no-no as someone could commit. Cotton was lucky that he did not kill the guy on the first floor. He was in enough trouble as it was.

When we went to the flight line the next morning, Cotton was ordered to remain in the barracks. When we returned for lunch, all of Cotton's belongings were gone. His lockers were empty. He was nowhere to be found. The squadron commander had transferred him to a noncombat unit where he would not have to handle weapons. I'm sure his dad was proud.

Unfortunately for the platoon, another individual who turned out to be more of a dud than a stud was our new platoon sergeant, E-7 First Sergeant Saunders.

Sgt. Saunders was a piece of work. He had spent his entire fourteen-year army career in Germany, assigned to one armor unit or another. Prior to his Vietnam assignment, he was a member of a Scout platoon. Regrettably, US Army Scouts in Germany did not use helicopters. They used tracked vehicles called armored personnel carriers, or APCs. They were deathtraps in Vietnam because of the terrain and the popularity of RPGs among the VC and NVA.

Sgt. Saunders had never ridden in a helicopter of any type. He knew absolutely nothing about their operation or maintenance. He knew nothing about the responsibilities of the crew chiefs and observers within his platoon. He was now the Apache equivalent of the proverbial tits on a boar hog. He simply did not fit.

As a committed lifer, he turned to what he knew best: antagonizing, harassing, and generally abusing the enlisted men in his charge.

It was impossible to relax when Saunders was around. He found an endless list of meaningless make-work tasks for us. It was obvious to all that he resented us because we knew more about the helicopters and the combat situations than he did. He could not effectively direct our daily activities because he had no idea what we were doing or why. We resented his presence because he did nothing to earn real respect. He also waited months before volunteering for flight duty. When he did so, he openly admitted that he volunteered only to get a confirmed kill. When he eventually got that kill, he refused to fly again. He lorded over us and frequently gave us erroneous directions, which we would then try to politely explain away.

First Mission

Unlike my later missions, my first Scout mission did not go well. I was flying in the wing position while we undertook a search and destroy mission south of Can To. The area was not secure and included many free-fire zones, which meant we could fire on anyone we found without asking permission.

When we dropped into the AO to relieve the previous team, just about everything was a blur. It was hard for me to detect much of anything on the ground because it seemed that things were zooming by. Combined with the nausea and Calling Ralph, it was disorienting.

As we were looping around the AO, a horrendous stench was sucked into the cabin by the rotor wash. Looking out the left door, I could see a dead body sitting at the bottom of a tree, only twenty feet away. It was a VC. He had been wounded and sat down against the tree to die.

The sight of my first dead body transfixed me. While I was staring at it, a shot rang out, startling the hell out of me. Two American soldiers had approached the body and fired a make-sure shot into it. I was not expecting it because the body had started to decompose and all of the flesh had already turned black. He was obviously dead. More disturbing than the shot was that I had not even seen the GIs before they fired. If they had been VC, I would have probably been dead too.

We soon found a large hooch in a free-fire zone. It was closer to being a house than a hooch. It was probably 700 square feet in size and contained more substantial framing than I was expecting.

Apache-Six decided to burn it, something the lead ship would usually do. For some reason, we were directed to drop a white phosphorous (Willie Pete) grenade on the structure. My pilot, Sewell, lined up the Loach about a hundred meters away and dove toward the house at a speed of a hundred knots. As we approached the hooch, I leaned out the door and dropped the grenade. At this speed and dive angle, the grenade seemed to hang just outside the door for what seemed like thirty seconds. I was concerned that it might explode before dropping away from the ship.

Finally, it did descend toward the hooch. Unfortunately, it overshot the hooch by about fifty feet, exploding on the ground beyond the target. I had not considered our airspeed when I dropped the grenade, causing it to go long. My mistake. Sewell threw out a couple of curse words and we circled to make another run.

This time I dropped it correctly, hitting the hooch wall about a foot below the roofline. Perfect shot! I thought. To my embarrassment, the grenade went straight through the hooch and exploded about twenty-five feet beyond it. A longer string of curse words came over the intercom. Sewell could not see the grenade strike the hooch, so he thought I had missed again.

We made a third run, and I finally destroyed the hooch. My heart was about to leap out of my chest. I was humiliated.

We cruised away and found another hooch surrounded by South Vietnamese Soldiers, or ARVNs. There were over fifty of them, so I suspected it was close to a full company. In front of the hooch another thirty or so ARVNs surrounded an adult woman with an infant in her arms.

The ARVNs took the baby away from her, then proceeded to beat the mother and push her around inside a circle of men. She fell to the ground several times, and the ARVNs repeatedly knocked her down as soon as she would stand. Being caught in a free-fire zone was a big no-no, and the ARVNs probably had justification for killing her.

After a couple of orbits around this scene, Sewell said, "Let's get the hell out of here before it gets ugly." That sounded like a great idea to me. I was already thoroughly disgusted with the way the ARVNs were treating her, and I certainly did not want to see what might happen next.

My naiveté was shattered. The ARVNs were brutal. This would be the first step in my realization that the good guys were rarely as good as we hoped.

We continued our patrol, with our ship doing its best to mimic the roughest roller coaster in the world. After about thirty minutes of this thrill ride, the lead ship discovered a VC crawling in the grass. The pilot attempted to kill the VC, but his minigun jammed. We dove on the VC, and the pilot pulled the trigger of the minigun. Nothing happened. No firing, no spinning barrels, no jam. "Arm the goddamn gun!" came screaming out of the intercom. I reached down and flipped the switch, arming the gun. We dove again, this time the minigun worked. We spun around and went in to make sure the VC was indeed dead. The minigun had virtually liquefied the man's chest. We had a confirmed kill, despite my bungling.

The pilot did not speak again for the next hour. I had never been told that arming the gun was my responsibility. I was totally mortified.

We flew back to Vinh Long in silence. I did not know it at the time, but the combination of this particular pilot and me was never going to be a successful partnership.

HUNTING CHUCK

"There is no hunting like the hunting of man, and those who have hunted armed men long enough and liked it, never care for anything else thereafter."

Ernest Hemingway

Between January and July 1969, I was able to fly enough combat missions to log 147 hours of combat flight time, enough for five Air Medals. Compared to some of my friends who crewed slicks or medevac ships, this was not a great deal of hours. However, the intense nature of our flights more than made up for it. Any individual observer flew about every three or four days. Because of the high casualty rate, commissioned officers were not allowed to remain in the Scout platoon for more than six months. Among all helicopter aircrew, the Loach crews had the highest casualty rates. That is remarkable, because helicopter crews had the second-highest casualty rate of all army and marine jobs, second only to armored personnel carrier (APC) crewmen.

This level of participation and the constant exposure to other close friends, who were also flying, provided many unforgettable experiences.

One of my earliest missions involved one of our instructor pilots (IPs), Coakley. He was a great guy and, as an IP, genuinely liked teaching people to fly. He gave me many lessons and took interest in my development.

On this particular day, we were flying wing, working out of Chi Lang and patrolling an area we called the "Tram." I never knew why it carried that and was never able to find it on a map.

When we arrived at the AO, ARVN troops were already on the ground and had encountered several VC. They had also detected several weapons caches, which they planned to remove later in the day.

Agent Orange had been used to defoliate this portion of the AO. All of the vegetation was the color of cigarette ashes: flat gray. We flew over a small group of ARVNs attempting to make their way to the top of a small hill. As they walked over the gray grass and among the small gray trees, the contrast between their new green uniforms and the gray surroundings was stunning. The bright sun brought out the deep, rich green of their uniforms against the flat gray.

The group consisted of about fifteen men, accompanied by their US Special Forces Advisor. They were not receiving any fire but would not advance on the hill. Every few moments, one or two of them would go down to their knees in what resembled a kneeling fetal position. They pressed their helmeted heads to the ground and would only stand up and move when their American advisor struck them on the back with his pistol belt. I thought this was pretty weird, given the absence of hostile fire and that our lead ship was scouting the ground in front of them.

I learned that this lack of aggressiveness was common among the ARVN. My illusions about our ally continued to fade. Confusion crept into my thoughts. Why are we here fighting for them, when they refuse to fight?

They finally made it to the top of the hill, and we departed for Chi Lang to refuel. We did not need any ammo because we had found no VC to engage.

Post-Mission Receptions

When the Scouts returned from a mission, all of the enlisted men went to the flight line to greet them. This was not just a social gathering. There was plenty of work to be done. The crew chiefs inspected each ship, checking for combat damage or anything else that might need repair. Oil levels were checked. Exhaust pipes were checked for cracks, a sign that the pilot had not let the turbine engine cool sufficiently before shutting it down. The windshields were cleaned and the blades tied down. Basically, the ships were made ready for the next day's mission.

The observers removed the miniguns for cleaning. This was a somewhat tricky task that often resulted in accidental discharge if the firing action was rotated the wrong way when unloading. To prevent the bullet from hitting anyone, a 105mm shell casing was slipped over the muzzles. Any rounds escaping the gun would strike the old artillery casing and be deflected.

The pilots were driven back to the barracks in our truck, a five-quarter-ton pickup belonging to our platoon.

Once the pilots departed, the party began. All of the crew chiefs and observers who flew that day recounted their missions and answered questions. This provided a way to let off some steam and decompress after a challenging day.

Beer and pot were retrieved from the line shack, and the serious relaxation commenced. Generally, this was a harmless routine and an effective way to self-medicate after traumatic experiences.

Of course, that was not always the case. One evening after a mission, John Orebaugh started horsing around, drew his revolver, and pretended to fire a shot. Unfortunately, he had forgotten to unload the weapon! The bullet struck the Loach tail boom on the port side and passed through the starboard side before disappearing into the twilight.

Everyone started yelling and asking what the fuck he was thinking. We looked through the bullet hole and determined that the round had not struck the tail rotor driveshaft. If it had, there would be no way to keep the accident from becoming known to the NCOs and officers. Orebaugh would surely have been busted if his stunt was detected.

Vernon and I jumped in the truck and drove to the maintenance platoon to grab Byron Hoyt, our sheet metal man. He agreed to come out and fix the bullet holes ASAP.

It took Hoyt only a little over one hour to patch the holes, including the paint job. Hoyt was extremely talented and it always showed. Working by flashlight, he was able to make the bullet hole patches look like they'd been there for months. Orebaugh escaped and we all had a great laugh.

Another memorable incident occurred one evening after we had returned from a mission. As the pot and beer were being passed around, Frenchy Lemoyne reached into his shirt pocket and retrieved something wrapped in a handkerchief. When he unwrapped it, we could see that it was a huge, black joint. The thing was over a half-inch in diameter and much darker than marijuana. Frenchy said it was hashish and he'd bought it during one of his trips to the dump. He wanted to share.

He placed it into his mouth, lit it, and took a long draw. He then pulled it out of his mouth, held it out in front of him, and asked if anyone else wanted a hit.

The words had just crossed his lips when his eyes rolled back and he collapsed to the ground! He was out cold.

A couple of people grabbed two canteens and began pouring water on his face. "What the hell happened?" Frenchy asked when he came to.

Frenchy was not a small man. He was about five ten and a solid stack of muscle with the build of a linebacker: broad shoulders, thick legs, and huge arms. We knew from the way he went down that whatever the joint was, it was some strong stuff. Every single person rejected his offer of a hit.

We later speculated that the joint was probably laced with heroin, explaining Frenchy's collapse.

While not particularly admirable, pot was part of our culture when we were not flying. Steve Holmes carried a joint in his chicken plate when he flew. He intended to light up if he was shot down and badly wounded.

When the Scout platoon was removed from Bunker 9 duty, we pulled guard on the flight line. This was done to keep personnel from B- and C-Troop from stealing Loach and minigun parts. This was low-stress duty, so burning a joint was standard procedure. We would sit outside the line shack and watch Puff the Magic Dragon unleash streams of tracers from three miniguns it carried on each side of the aircraft. Lots of flares always accompanied this, and the gunship runs we could see became an entertaining light show.

One night while Mark Hansen and I were enjoying the show, a jeep roared around the revetment and slid to a halt about six feet in front of us. The bright lights were on, blinding us. We could see the Blackhawk 6 placard on the jeep bumper, meaning this was the squadron commander's jeep and this was the officer of the day. We had no idea who was in the jeep or from which troop he may have come. Seriously bad stuff was about to happen.

A man of small stature stepped from the right side of the jeep. We could barely see him. When he stepped in front of the jeep, he asked, "OK, where is it? I know you two have some pot out here."

We stammered our denial as he kept walking past us and into the shack. He pulled an ammo box from against the wall, stepped onto it, and reached into the rafters of the small shack. As he was doing this, he mumbled about someone saying it was on the sixth or eighth rafter.

We had a propane lantern inside the shack and could see that the raider was one of our A-Troop Scout pilots, Borders, a twenty-year-old warrant officer we all loved. He pulled the grenade can from atop the rafter, inspected the baggie of pot, and said, "Ah, yes. This is what I've been looking for."

He headed back to the jeep and said, "Hey, thanks for the pot. You boys have a good time tonight. See you tomorrow."

We were in shock. It had all happened so fast, and we were a little high from our earlier party. We weren't going to be busted after all.

Forty-nine years later, I can still see that jeep, with its Blackhawk 6 placard, sliding to a halt. Then the image of a man walking slowly through the glare of headlights streaming through the cloud of dust.

On one occasion, after Cpt. Stark and I had a particularly successful day, the party was winding up just before sundown. The sunset was brilliant, displaying all the shades of blue, yellow, and red that a tropical sunset can provide. Four of us jumped into the back of the truck for the trip back to Fort Apache.

As we pulled away from the flight line, one of the guys cranked up his transistor radio. The song that spilled out struck me like a slap in the face. It was "The Age of Aquarius," by the Fifth Dimension. The song was a popular anthem for peace, love, and kindness to our fellow man. However, here were four individuals who were responsible for killing several people and leaving them rotting in a field.

A chill came over me as I let the irony of the scene sink in. It perfectly represented the contradiction most of us felt about the war and our participation in it. Many of us were coming to realize that the ARVNs' hearts were not into the effort. Without that, we could not see how they were going to defeat the VC. Antiwar protests filled the news reports from home, making it painfully obvious that we were losing support on the home front. We talked about all this during our nightly games. Yet each morning we would climb into our ships and go out to chase and kill those we considered the enemy. I was never able to reconcile this paradox to my satisfaction.

Saunders Gets a Just Reward

I was assigned to fly a "last-light/first-light recon" along the Cambodian border one evening and the next morning. This required us to fly to the border late in the afternoon, fly a low-level search and destroy mission at sunset, staying with it until it became totally dark. We would then spend the night in our Loaches and do the same thing at sunrise. These missions frequently resulted in enemy contact.

My assigned pilot that day was Lt. Tucker, an officer I would come to like and respect as a result of one of these missions.

As I was loading Willie-Pete grenades into the ship, Lt. Tucker was performing his preflight inspection of the aircraft. Out of nowhere, Saunders sprang on me and started yelling that I was not authorized to carry WP grenades in the Loach. When I attempted to explain that carrying WP was part of our standard routine, he elevated his attack by screaming that the OH-6A was a recon aircraft and that we were not supposed to directly engage the enemy. Evidently, he had been reading some old documentation somewhere. He was in fantasyland.

While he went on screaming and I stood there with my arms folded across my chest, Lt. Tucker stepped around the ship and asked what was going on. I did not get a chance to say anything before Saunders started explaining that he was "straightening the specialist out" about our mission and what I was authorized to carry in my aircraft and what I was not to carry. Saunders restated his opinion that our role was reconnaissance and we were not supposed to be engaging the enemy.

Tucker listened patiently, then asked Saunders to join him on the other side of the revetment. They both walked around the revetment. When they came to a stop facing each other, Lt. Tucker stepped up to Saunders, pointed his index finger at Saunders's nose and started dressing him down in one of the most rewarding verbal assaults I had ever heard. Tucker explained our procedures, then referred to my level of combat experience. He asked Saunders if he had ever flown a Scout mission. He answered, "No, sir." It continued for a couple of minutes, at which time Lt. Tucker asked First Sergeant Saunders if he understood what had been explained to him, did he need to repeat it, or if there was any confusion about the issue. He closed by telling Saunders that he never wanted to see that happen again or hear of it happening again. I could hear Saunders's repetition of "Yes, sir. Yes, sir. No, sir."

The humor of this scene was Tucker's request for Saunders to join him on the other side of the revetment, obviously so they could speak in private. The revetment was only twenty-four inches thick and forty-eight inches high, so I was standing about three feet away, hearing and seeing everything. If Tucker had wanted to speak to Saunders privately, all he had to do was ask me to excuse myself from the scene. He obviously wanted me to hear the whole thing.

When the two men returned to my side of the revetment, I slowly asked, "Sgt. Saunders. Is . . . it . . . OK for me . . . to load . . . the grenades . . . now?" Saunders growled something I could not understand and walked away.

Saunders seemed to have remembered this dressing down. We never got along very well after that.

Body Snatches and Bad Vibes

Body snatches, a common practice for the gathering of local intelligence, were frequent, and the Scouts spent a great deal of time participating in them.

The lead Scout ship would approach an individual or a group of military-age males, then extract one person at gunpoint. The ship would hover near the individual, and the observer would motion the man in the direction Apache-Six wanted him to go. The suspect was kept directly outside the Loach's left door, no more than six feet away, where the observer could cover him. When the "snatch-ee" was a safe distance from the group, the Scout would hold him there until the C&C ship would land and pick up the detainee for questioning. This distance could be as much two or three hundred yards away and take a considerable amount of time to cover. It exposed the Loach to a great deal of risk because of the length of time the ship was hovering in an open field. Success depended on the C&C ship landing within a few seconds of the prisoner reaching the designated spot.

When the suspect was in the required location, the C&C ship, usually containing an interpreter and sometimes a Vietnamese province official, would land and retrieve the man. C&C would take off and return to 1,500 or 2,000 feet, where the man would be interrogated. If they found or heard no suspicious evidence, the C&C ship would land at a different site, also a safe distance from the group of people awaiting the man's return, and turn him loose.

One of my early snatches was with Sewell.

As we approached an open paddy we could see a military-aged male trying to make his way back to a group of men working beside a canal. Because he was in a hurry and the paddy was flooded, he kept falling down. By the time we got to him, he was soaked from head to toe.

When we pulled to a hover in front of him, cutting him off from the group, I gave him the hands-up sign and signaled for him to show me his identity papers.

As soon as he reached for his papers, Apache-Six exploded, yelling at me to make him keep his hands up.

This was not easy. His loose-fitting pajama pants were soaking wet. As soon as he lifted his hands above his head, his pants would fall to his ankles.

This spooked Apache-Six and he yelled at me again. Sewell said to fire a couple of rounds between the guy's feet to get his attention. I did so.

After about four rounds came out, I realized that I had the CAR-15 on full auto! Fortunately, I had a tight grip on the weapon. Otherwise, it could have recoiled up and I would have accidently killed the man.

Sewell got a big kick out of this and began laughing. The suspect did not. He dove to the ground and lay facedown in the water. For a moment, I thought I had killed him.

He jumped to his feet and turned to face me. His eyes were the size of golf balls and he was trembling.

We then began moving him about 150 yards to a spot where the C&C ship could pick him up. As he tried to walk with his hands up, his pants kept falling down. He would trip and fall back into the water and Apache-Six would go nuts on the radio.

When we finally reached the designated pickup point, we held the man at gunpoint as the C&C ship descended. It seemed to take about three minutes for him to get to us, rather than the normal thirty seconds. We were exposed to gunfire from four sides as we hovered about two feet above the ground.

Sewell began to cuss. He knew that we were in danger, being in the same vicinity so long. Any VC within 1,000 meters were probably heading our way.

The suspect was still standing just outside our door, trembling like an abused puppy. He was probably scared to death. His ID papers were OK, but he knew they were no guarantee of safety.

Finally, Apache-Six landed about fifty meters away, and we herded the man toward the ship.

When we reached a point about twenty-five meters from the C&C ship, the man tripped and fell facedown into the water. Apache-Six released a long string of curses over the radio. I looked up from our suspect and saw the C&C ship lift off and climb for altitude. My heart sank.

We now had to move the man to another spot and repeat the whole drill.

We finally reached a spot where Apache-Six felt secure enough to land and make the snatch. They did so, and both Sewell and I let out a "Hoo fucking ray" when we took off.

Later that night I ran into the C&C crew chief. He then told me what had taken so long. Every time the suspect dropped his hands or fell down, Apache-Six would abort his descent and climb back to 2,500 feet. Evidently, he was terrified of being ambushed while executing the snatch. He kept initiating his approach, then pulling out every time the guy went down.

On another snatch, not long after, I saw the impact of sheer terror.

We cut out a young man from a work party on the edge of a flooded paddy and began herding him toward the pickup point.

When we were about two hundred feet from the group, an older woman began running after him. She was struggling because of the depth of the water and she was trying to run with her hands clasped in a praying grip. It appeared that she was his mother and was begging us not to take her son.

It was sickening to watch. It also took a long time, making my guilt last even longer. She would run, fall to her knees, and begin bobbing up and down as if she were doing a prayer chant. She would then stand up, run a few more steps, and fall down again.

Apache-Six did not like this, so he directed us to make her stop trying to reach her son. We hovered in front of her, where she could see me shake my head and direct her back to the group.

She would drop to her knees and begin begging me again.

While this was going on, the suspect would stop walking toward the C&C ship and turn around to see what was happening to his mother. We would then fly back to him and get him moving.

As soon as he was moving, Apache-Six was back on the radio, yelling at us to, "Stop. That. Goddamn. Woman!"

We would slip back to her, whereupon she would drop and begin begging again. She was hysterical. Tears were flowing down her cheeks. I felt like a complete asshole, more like an SS stormtrooper than an American GI.

After a few repetitions of this cycle, the man finally reached the pickup point and Apache-Six took him away. As we left the paddy, we flew right by the mother, only feet away. She sprang to her feet, looked me right in the eyes, and shook both fists at me. I'm sure she put a curse on me. That image stayed with me for the next fifty years.

Another body snatch may have been the most dangerous of all.

I was flying with Cort Stark, working just south of the infamous Parrot's Beak. It was known to be a bad area because the Beak was a section of the Cambodian border that protruded dozens of miles into South Vietnam. It was a major jumping-off point from the Ho Chi Minh Trail, and several significant battles had occurred there over the years.

We happened across a group of men crossing a dry paddy, with no tools or weapons in sight. Apache-Six wanted to detain a man for interrogation, so we flew over to the group, selected one of the older men, and started moving him toward a tree line, the designated pickup point.

As Apache-Six began his descent, late and slow as usual, he directed Cort to hover above a dirt road that ran parallel to the tree line and a small canal. He wanted to make sure that no VC snuck up on us by using the tree line and canal as cover.

As soon as Cort pulled to a hover a few feet above the road, we were enveloped in a white dust cloud blown up by our rotor wash. The only thing we could see was the surface of the road directly below us, with the dirt being sucked off it, and it was only visible through the chin bubbles.

Cort reported the situation to Six, telling him that our position was untenable. Surprisingly, he told Cort to stay where we were until he gave us the OK to move.

Cort could only maintain position by looking down through the chin bubble to ensure that we were still over the road. Looking through the bubble or side doors was impossible because of the dust racing up and through the rotor blades before being blown down on top of us.

It was quite a scene. The dust blowing off the road would travel horizontally until it reached a point about ten to twelve feet away from the ship. It would then be caught by the rotor wash that was bouncing off the ground and go straight up for about twelve feet. When the dust reached the twelve-foot level, it would be sucked down to the ground, near the rotor head, and begin the cycle again. Visually, the dust cloud formed a sphere, with us in the middle, through which we could see nothing. It felt like we were floating inside a gray basketball that was about twenty-five feet in diameter. We were blind to anything happening outside that sphere of dust.

We remained there for about two minutes. It felt like twenty. When Six gave us the OK to depart, Cort slid the Loach to the right, away from the tree line, across the canal, and over the paddy.

Before he executed a right pedal turn to climb away, I looked back at the tree line and spotted about fifteen males walking through the tree line, approaching us. None of them appeared to have weapons, but I still reported them to Cort. He replied, "Not a minute too soon," before he pulled away in a full power climb.

Muc Hoa

Muc Hoa (*muck-wah*) was a small village in western Vietnam, just south of the Parrot's Beak. It was considered a hot area. On this particular day, Vernon Summerell was flying lead and I was in the wing ship with Jones.

Our entire group of nine ships landed in a small clearing just outside and out of sight from the village. Apache-Six instructed us to remain there until he returned and would then give us the signal to follow him. We shut down the engines and relaxed.

He returned in about ten minutes. As he passed over our parked ships, the crew chief leaned out the left door and gave us the crank-up signal. As he did so, he trailed red smoke, the signal to follow him.

We strapped in and everyone in the four Cobras and four Loaches cranked up – except us. As Jones hit the starter button and pressed the ignition switch, the rotors didn't move. The engine did not whine. All we could hear was the rapid popping sound of the ignitor plugs firing in an attempt to ignite the jet fuel. We had either a dead battery or a broken starter/generator. On a Loach, the starter and generator are actually the same unit. Once the engine starts, the starter switches to the generator mode and charges the 12-volt nickel-cadmium battery.

We were motionless. Vernon ran back to our ship to see what was going on. Jones told him, and Vernon ran back to his ship to deliver the news. Just a few seconds later, the pilot of the lead ship announced they were leaving us there and would send for help. We sat there and watched the three Loaches lift off and disappear beyond the tree line.

Jones and I decided to get out of our seats and sit in the cargo area, each facing an opposite direction. This allowed us to see anyone approaching the clearing or the ship. After a few minutes, young Vietnamese men started to appear in the tree lines. The trees were only about a hundred feet away from the Loach on either side of the ship. We were in an exposed position and only armed with one CAR-15, a .45 caliber automatic pistol, and Jones's .38 revolver. Not exactly overwhelming firepower.

After about ten minutes, the size of the military-age male gathering had tripled in size, and there now appeared to be about thirty men milling around in the trees.

Jones said, "I don't like this a damned bit. Not a damned bit."

I said, "Neither do I. Let's try something."

From some unreachable portion of my brain came the idea that the starter might be stuck. How and why it might be stuck did not occur to me.

I asked Jones to get strapped in, and that when he heard a banging noise, to try the starter again. I told him I was going to see if I could strike the starter with the muzzle of my CAR-15 and jar it loose.

I opened the right-side engine door, stuck the CAR-15 muzzle between the armor plate and the engine, and began banging the muzzle against the starter in an abbreviated stabbing motion.

Right on cue, Jones hit the starter button. I began stabbing a little harder, and the thing started turning! As the ignition plugs began popping, the fuel ignited and the engine was running. I was as happy as I could possibly be, in light of my still being in the Nam.

I closed and secured the engine door, walked back up the port side of the ship, and jumped into my seat. Jones pulled pitch, and we lifted off before I even had a chance to strap in.

By the time we were airborne, the others had been gone at least fifteen minutes, meaning they had a huge head start on us. We had no idea where they were.

To find them, Jones turned on the RDF – radio direction finder – so we could locate their radio transmissions and make our way to them.

The RDF was an incredibly crude piece of electronic gear. Two thirty-six-inch wires were taped to the front bubble, one on the left and one on the right edge of the Plexiglas. These antennas were supposed to pick up radio signals, determine the direction of the source, and actuate a gauge on the instrument panel. That gauge had a thin pointer/wire anchored in the center-bottom of the gauge. When the signals came through, the wire would peg itself against the side of the gauge from which the signals originated. It was then up to the pilot to turn in the direction to which the needle pointed and keep turning in that direction until the needle was centered and pointing straight up in the gauge. Unfortunately, the gauge could guide you in exactly the wrong direction because it could not tell if the radio signals were straight ahead or dead astern! You had to be a little lucky.

We knew we were just southeast of the Cambodian border, so there was little risk of us heading in the wrong direction and that the RDF would likely lead us back to the troop.

After about five minutes, we spotted the C&C ship and the Cobras orbiting above the AO. Jones radioed to tell them we were back on station and would join the search in the wing position.

We flew our nauseating loops for about thirty minutes when I noticed that I had not heard any radio traffic in several minutes. This was odd. The various aircraft were usually exchanging information constantly, and ten minutes of dead air was highly unusual. I glanced down at the instrument panel and saw that the fuel gauge was showing empty. I knew we were not out of fuel. I checked a couple of other gauges and saw that they were all dead. We had an electrical failure. Apparently, the starter/generator that I had given CPR to was now legally dead and no longer generating any juice.

I tapped Jones on the leg and then touched several gauges on the instrument panel, pointing out their inop condition. We could not speak to each other because the intercom was also dead.

I made a hand signal, indicating we needed to get back to Vinh Long.

Jones then dove the Loach to the center of the AO and did a couple of rapid pedal turns, simulating a tail rotor failure. We then headed back to Vinh Long, about twenty minutes away. We could not hear anything the other ships were saying about our weird departure, but I'm confident we were being cursed.

Two fuel pumps fed the turbine engine, one electrical and a mechanical one driven by the engine. The electrical pump was not required at altitudes under 15,000 feet. Hopefully, the mechanical pump would take us home. Going down in this area, with no radio on which to send an SOS, would be fatal. A-Troop would never find us.

As we arrived and entered the Vinh Long approach pattern, I popped red smoke and held the grenade out the door, trailing smoke. This let the control tower know that we had a serious problem. Again, we could not hear what was being said to us or about us.

My ship "892" between sorties at Rach Gia.

When we were on the final approach, I pointed to the maintenance area, indicating to Jones that we should land there, not in our normal spot on the flight line. This would put the Loach on the electricians' doorstep and prevent us from having to push the ship to maintenance, about 400 yards from the flight line.

Other members of the Scout platoon saw us land, so they came over with the truck to retrieve the minigun, ammo, all the grenades, and us. Leaving that equipment mounted in the maintenance area was strictly verboten.

No post-mission party this time. I was just glad to be back.

Last-Light Patrols

One of the predictably scary missions we flew were the so-called "last-light patrols" or "last-lights."

We would execute them anywhere, including Vinh Long and Chi Lang.

Last-lights in Chi Lang required an overnight stay on the Cambodian border. Not an attractive prospect. We would fly to Chi Lang and arrive right at sunset. We would then patrol a section of the border until it became dark, return to Chi Lang, warm some C rations for dinner, and spend the night on the ground.

The next morning we would be up before sunrise and execute a "first-light," again trying to catch Charlie on the move.

On one particular mission, I was flying with Lt. Tucker. We flew a completely ineffectual last-light, finding nothing. We returned to Chi Lang, cooked supper on a jet stove, and hunkered down for the night.

We did not have sleeping bags, so we rolled up into our ponchos to avoid the bugs and escape the rain. Because we were lying on cheap, sandy, and broken asphalt, it made for a miserable night's sleep. We got as close as we could to the tin and sand revetments to shield the wind.

What we did not know that night was that the recently relocated 155mm howitzer battery just across the runway would receive a fire mission.

A 155 is a monstrous cannon; much more powerful than the more common 105mm guns used by the majority of artillery units.

This particular fire mission required the guns to fire directly over our sleeping heads. We would have greatly appreciated a heads-up, warning us what was about to happen.

When the first 155 went off, we got the full effect of the muzzle blast and concussion. I was deafened, so it didn't sound that loud. However, the concussion shook the ground so violently that it tossed me about a foot into the air. As I landed, not really knowing what had happened, I was covered with a shower of sand. Then the second 155 cut loose, again bouncing me into the air and repeating the sand shower. I asked Lt. Tucker if he was OK because I thought it was incoming rocket fire that had just missed us. He said, "Yes," waited a few seconds, and said, "I think it was those 155s just across the runway," when another round went out.

This time we could see the muzzle flash coming from the direction of the 155s, so we knew what it was. We covered up again and tried to go back to sleep. It was not easy.

The next morning we awakened to a steady rain and near zero visibility. We were socked in and certainly would not be flying our first-light recon.

Apache-Six decided to keep us on station until the weather cleared. When that would be was impossible to know.

Tucker and I got into the Loach and tried to rig our ponchos over the doors to keep the rain out. It was nearly impossible because we had no rope to secure the ponchos to the ship. Every ten minutes or so we would jump out and reset the ponchos as best we could.

After a while I noticed that Tucker was reading a very thick book called *The Arms of Krupp*. I recognized the name but not the story, so he gave me the three-minute summary. I read it later when I returned to the States.

After a few minutes Tucker asked, "What do you think, Moore? Can we ever win this thing?" I replied that I hoped so but did not think the South Vietnamese had it in them, that they showed no enthusiasm for the war and tried to avoid every fight. I admitted my confusion. I also mentioned that virtually all the enlisted men felt the same way. I told him that we would often sit around the barracks and have deep discussions about the war and the unlikely probab ity that the South Vietnamese could win. I told him of my personal amaze ent that we would have these talks, but not hesitate to strap ourselves into a oach and undertake some wildly dangerous mission the next day. I was baffle

He agreed ar said that most of the population was indifferent to the war because they sir ply did not care who ran the country. They were busy trying to scratch out a l ing and did not care who collected the taxes. They were more interested in th affairs of their villages. He then went on to ask me how we were going to e iblish a democratic, capitalist society in a country that had two products: fi and rice.

What he said made sense. I now had another piece of evidence supporting my belief that e South would not make it. We then entered into a long conversation ab it the war being a lost cause and the US needing to get out. He had obvious done much more research on the topic, and I had a lot of catching up to d

Life on the Flig t Line

Only four enlist d men flew on any given day. More of us hung around the flight line than f w in the air.

The second ost popular activity was helping the other crew chiefs perform minor naintenance tasks on the ships. This could be taking oil samples, changi g an oil or air filter, or repairing cracked exhaust pipes. Most of the heavier r untenance tasks, such as replacing rotor blades or engines, were performed y the maintenance platoon. The OH-6A had no hydraulics or complex tail rot drive systems. The normal amount of time one would spend tracking down le ks, tightening fittings, or lubricating bearings on a Huey was not required on e Loach.

The most p ular flight line activity was reading while listening to the radio. Our smal ase PX sold paperback books and magazines, and the base had a small libra y. It was unusual to see a crew chief or observer without some form of reading aterial in their hand.

In several ca s, we spent spare time simply watching the activities around the airstrip. There always seemed to be something going on.

On one such occasion, we heard that an air force jet was about to make an emergency landing on our runway. This got our attention, so we jogged over to the main runway so we could watch the fun.

The airplane had lost hydraulic pressure, making the craft almost impossible to fly. The pilot needed to get to the ground quickly. The loss of hydraulic pressure also meant the landing gear would not go down. The pilot would have to make a belly landing on a runway comprised of steel plating. The odds of pulling this off without starting a fire were not in his favor.

Evidently, Vinh Long did not have very sophisticated fire equipment because they did not spray the runway with foam. Doing so would have greatly reduced the creation of sparks and the chance of fire, but it was not to be.

Within a couple of seconds of our arrival at the runway, we spotted the jet on final approach. The pilot was struggling to steer the plane. It veered from side to side and rolled back and forth. I began to think that he might not be able to execute the belly landing because he was going to crash first!

Another danger was that our runway was only about 5,000 feet long, typically too short for heavy jet fighters. To bring the plane to a stop before running off the end of the runway, the pilot needed to touch down at a point very close to the leeward end. Without hydraulics, this would not be easy.

As we watched, the jet hit the end of the runway. Being nearly a mile away at the opposite end of the strip, we had no depth perception and could not tell how far up the runway the touchdown had occurred. We could only tell he had landed because a small dust cloud came up among a shower of sparks. The long slide had begun.

Because he could not steer the plane into a perfect alignment with the runway, the pilot had to rely on luck to avoid sliding off the side of the strip and hitting something dangerous.

The slide and continuous shower of sparks emanating from the belly of the plane appeared to last forever. In reality, it was probably ten or fifteen seconds, but we expected the plane to burst into flames at any moment and kill the pilot.

Remarkably, the pilot hit the right spot on the runway and at the correct angle. The plane id to a stop, with a small spin to the left, right in the center of the runway and ss than a hundred feet from where we were standing. The fire trucks and med s were on site before the pilot had unstrapped and stepped out of the plane. No fire was present.

We approach l and showered him with praise and pats on the back. He had a huge smile on is face as he jumped into the back of a truck and sped away, waving.

On another c casion, we watched good ole Cpt. Sholtz pull off a MacGyver-like rescue of a C Model gunship.

The Huey C- Iodel served as the first gunships in the war, before Cobras partially replace them. The Charlie model was based on the original airframe first put into ser ce in Vietnam, the A-Model. When the Charlie model came out, it had a sligh ly more powerful engine and a modified main rotor system, giving it higher ft capacity, which made them excellent gunships, but only up to a certain oint. It was easy to overload a gunship, so the crews took extra measures > reduce their weight as much as possible. This included removing all the loors, removing the sound insulation from the entire cabin, and removing a extra seats.

With a maxi ium payload of rockets and minigun ammo, the gunships could barely tak ff. Most Hueys would lift off the ground into a hover a couple of feet above th ground. Gunships could not achieve a hover, so the pilot would get the sh light on the skids, then slide the ship down the runway until it achieved enou h airspeed to lift off. Unfortunately, this was rarely, if ever, a one-bounce a mpt. In every case I saw, the gunship would bounce down the runway, son times four or five times, before getting the speed required to achieve flight.

It was a sight o behold. The pilot would be at full power. As the ship began sliding, he woul put the control stick all the way forward, forcing the ship into a nose-dov attitude. The tail would lift up as the ship began to bounce forward. The on portion of the skids contacting the ground were the extreme front sections, here the skid turns up into a ski-like shape. Eventually, the ship would be fl ng, hopefully before bouncing off the end of the runway.

Gunships from other units routinely used Vinh Long as a rearm/refueling point. The refueling point, or Petrol, Oil, and Lubrication (POL) point, at Vinh Long was just to the north of the Scout shack, about fifty or sixty yards away. The POL point was a row of slightly elevated steel plate pads sitting atop small sand hills about twenty feet square and eighteen inches above the surrounding ground. Next to each pad was a fuel bladder, hand pump, and a three-inch hose. There were about six or eight of them in the row. Our line shack was beside the westernmost of the pads.

On a day when the wind was blowing from the west, two gunships landed to refuel, both landing at the eastern end of the POL point. As they were about to take off, four or five of us walked around to the back of the Scout shack to watch them.

The first ship took off with no problem and zoomed past us at about six knots and in a shallow climb.

The second ship was not as lucky. While attempting a bouncing takeoff, the ship hooked the front of both skids under one of the PSP pads. This could have resulted in the Huey crashing into one of the fuel bladders, with horrendous consequences for the crew and even us onlookers.

Fortunately, the forward motion of the ship pulled the two skids away from the front cross tube to which both were attached. Once loose from the front mount, the skids rotated down and to the rear of the ship. Both skids were still attached to the rear cross tube, making the Huey appear like a flying bug or ski jumper, trailing his skis.

All of us jumped up and started waving and pointing toward the rear of the ship, signaling the crew chief that he needed to look to the rear.

He noticed us as he flew by, looked to the rear, and then turned back to face us. His eyes looked like they were going to pop out of this helmet. He was surprised, to say the least.

We put in a call to the A-Troop maintenance platoon so they could arrange a fix. Unfortunately, the skids were hanging at about a forty-five-degree angle, back toward the tail rotor. This made it impossible to land the Huey.

Cpt. Sholtz came up with the idea of building a stack of mattresses and having the gunship land on the mattresses while some A-Troop mechanics removed the skids. Otherwise, the skids could have made their way to the tail rotor, causing the ship to go into an uncontrollable spin just two feet above the ground. This would certainly lead to an ugly crash of a helicopter full of fuel and rockets.

The only problem with Sholtz's plan was that the Huey was now too heavy to land. It would be impossible for the ship to come to a hover, meaning it would just plow into the ground when the pilot attempted to slow down.

Sholtz directed the pilot to fly circles around the Vinh Long perimeter until he was down to about one quarter of his fuel load, then try to land.

The risk in staying airborne for another ninety minutes was the possibility of the skids tearing loose and striking the tail rotor.

As the gunship began circling, a bunch of guys headed back to the A-Troop barracks to retrieve as many mattresses as they could fit into the two trucks we had available, one from maintenance and one from the Scout platoon.

Once they returned to our line shack, the construction began. It did not take long to realize that a simple stack of mattresses would not suffice; once the weight of the Huey began to settle onto the stack, the stack would fall apart.

We dispatched a truck to fetch some strong rope to lash the stack together and give it some rigidity. Because the gunship still had many laps to complete to burn off the excess fuel, we had plenty of time to get ready.

After an hour and a half, the pilot said he wanted to attempt a landing. The first step was to determine whether the gunship was light enough to hover. Unfortunately, this would be a one-time-only test. If the ship was still too heavy to hover, it would simply crash on his first attempt. It was time for the crew to break out their crucifixes and rosaries. There wasn't anything else we could do but wait.

The pilot began his approach, trying to maintain flight while he went as slowly as he dared. He was about three hundred feet away, a safe distance from the fuel bladders and us.

The Huey came to a hover.

When he was about fifty feet from the mattress stack, the ship was about four feet off the ground. At that point, the crew chief and door gunner should have jumped out to further lighten the ship, but they did not. No one thought of it at the time.

The pilot gently crept up to the mattresses as one of the Scouts guided him onto the stack. As soon as the belly of the Huey touched the mattresses, four guys from our maintenance platoon jumped under the ship and began removing the skids.

Within minutes, the skids were off and the pilot was signaled to reduce power until the full weight of the ship rested on the mattresses.

This was the final risky step of the process. Helicopters are inherently unstable. Once the power was cut and the blades continued to spin, a puff of wind could easily roll the ship onto its side.

To counter this, Sholtz had us fill a bunch of sandbags and place them on top of the cross tubes.

Finally, the blades came to a stop and the gunship was fully at rest. Needless to say, the crew appreciated that the Scouts had emphatically pointed out the situation, preventing them from flying into a more dangerous situation.

Our VC Flag

I was not scheduled to fly this particular day, and certainly not as the lead observer in a hot area. I had only been a member of the A-Troop Scout platoon for two months. I was one of the newest Scouts in the platoon and still learning the ropes. Apache Troop took the role of the lead observer seriously, having the new observers spend weeks flying in the wing position to gain experience before moving into the lead ship.

A-Troop was operating in an AO very close to our home base of Vinh Long. The AO was so close that we were using Vinh Long as the staging area, where we would come to rearm, refuel, grab some food, and stretch our legs. Typically, the staging areas were an hour or so away from Vinh Long but very close to the AO.

Around noon, two Loaches and two Cobra gunships returned to base to rearm and refuel. The crews were trucked into the troop area. The rest of the platoon, who were not flying, had already returned to the squadron mess hall to get lunch. I had stayed at the flight line to assist the flight crews when it was time for them to return to the AO and relieve the two Loaches still operating there.

With nothing important to do, I was reading a book when a jeep slid to a halt in front of our line shack. Capt. Stark came in and said that one of the Loaches had been shot down and we had to get a ship to the AO ASAP. There was only one problem, his assigned observer, Steve Holmes, was still back at the troop area. He was having some stomach issues and was stuck in the latrine.

Cort looked at me and asked, "Moore, you fly, don't you?" I said, "Yes, sir, I do." "Grab a helmet and let's go," he said.

We cranked the Loach and away we went. I did not mention that I had never flown lead before.

It seemed that we got to the AO instantly. As we dropped down to the deck, it was an ugly scene. In the middle of a dry rice paddy lay one of our ships, a brand-new one that had only a few hours of flight time on it. It was on its side, with the main rotor wrapped around the mast, a fractured and detached tail boom, and the tail rotor nowhere in sight. To the left of the ship was a dead VC, faceup in the grass stubble and dust.

How the Loach got into that position was a story in itself. The lead ship, with a new Scout pilot flying in the observer seat, had caught a VC crawling across the paddy trying to escape the ARVN troops sweeping the area. As the Loach hovered above the VC, the observer attempted to shoot him with his CAR-15, but the gun jammed. Rather than backing off and letting the wing ship come down for the kill, the observer pulled his sidearm and shot the VC. The VC, probably surprised at being shot at with an underpowered .38 revolver, rolled over onto this back, revealing that he had an AK-47. He fired a burst of automatic fire into the Loach's engine, dropping it on the spot. Because the Loach was hovering about five feet off the ground, it was a quick trip to the ground. Luckily for the observer, the VC had aimed at the engine and not into the cockpit, where he could have easily killed both men.

He was not the only dead VC on the ground. Several others were scattered around the paddy, a few creating some pretty gruesome and memorable scenes. As we circled the paddy at about ten feet high to make sure no VC were approaching, we noticed one VC lying facedown, with his arms fully extended and perpendicular to his body. His neck was slightly extended with his chin on the ground and his face tilted skyward. His entire forehead was missing, from the top of his eyebrows, back to the middle of his head. The interior of his skull was visible. His head looked like a blown egg. His mostly intact brain was on the ground in front of him. He had been struck in the back of the head with a high-power bullet, blowing out the front of his head and ejecting his brain. His eyes were still open.

We then saw four ARVNs kneeling on a wounded VC, lying on his back and close to the canal that bordered that side of the paddy. He was struggling, and it took a few orbits of the paddy to figure out what was happening.

Two ARVNs were holding his arms while a third was lying across his legs. The fourth ARVN was in the process of removing his heart while he was still alive. After a couple of minutes, they jumped up in celebration while the "surgeon" triumphantly held the heart high in the air.

I saw this repeated in the movie *The Last of the Mohicans*.

A feeling of utter disgust swept over me and I thought, *These are the guys we're fighting for?*

With the paddy secured, we began sweeping the area at low level. This carried us a mile to the northeast. After a few minutes of this, I spotted a flag and banner flying in the corner of a rice paddy. The flag was attached to a thin bamboo pole, and the banner appeared to be attached to trees that came together in a ninety-degree angle, forming the corner of the paddy. The banner was white and about six feet long and a foot wide. A long phrase was written in Vietnamese.

We reported the find to Apache-Six, who told us to ignore it. We went back to checking a canal that ran off to the northeast. We flew a slow slalom pattern from one bank to the other, looking for VC who might be hiding in the long grass that grew out of the water and hid the banks from view.

After a couple of minutes of flying this pattern, I spotted a VC on the left side of the canal. He was trying to pull the grass over his head and shoulders to stay out of sight.

I stepped on the floor switch and yelled into my mic, "I got a man! Break left and get over the canal!"

We did a quick circle to the left as I kept an eye on the guy to make sure he did not slip out of sight. Cort reported to Apache-Six that we had found a VC and he had a gun.

It only took about twenty seconds to complete the 360-degree turn and arrive at a spot across the canal, directly in front of the VC. I was elated as we swung around. I had found my first VC! However, I did not feel scared. I was wondering what was going to happen next when Cort pulled to a stop and hovered about four feet above the ground and about twenty-five feet away from the VC.

Cort requested permission to kill the VC. Apache-Six asked if he had a gun. Cort said he definitely did. I had not seen a gun and was wondering how Cort saw it. I stepped on my floor mic and told Cort that I had not seen a gun. I repeated it twice. While I was doing so, Cort and Apache-Six were also talking, and it was a bit confusing. Cort may not have heard me.

Suddenly, Apache-Six said, "Burn him!" That was my queue, so I opened up with my CAR 15 and shot the man. It took quite a few rounds to kill him.

Cort took off and we continued our search of the area.

Just a few minutes later, Apache-Six called us back to the spot. A couple of Special Forces advisors were wading around in the canal trying to find the weapon. Apache Six had landed his Huey next to the canal and had his crew chief looking for the weapon as well.

We landed, and Cort asked me where the weapon was and did I want to get into the canal and help with the search. I told him again that I did not see a weapon. He asked if the VC had been holding it in his left hand. I just said, "Yeah, I guess . . . his left side."

Six asked Cort if he was sure about the weapon. Then Cort said something that stunned me. "Damn right I'm sure. He took a shot at us!"

My stomach started heading for my throat. Everyone would have known if

Charlie had fired on us. I would have dropped the red smoke grenade and Cort would have reported that we were receiving fire. Our wingman and the Cobras would have initiated gun runs and unloaded their ordinance on the red smoke. None of that happened.

Much to my surprise and relief, Six dropped the subject and directed us to resume our search. He must have been suspicious. If so, he kept his thoughts to himself.

Now I was completely confused. Prior to Cort's statement that we had been fired upon, I believed Cort had seen a weapon when we were making the turn. I thought I had probably just missed it. Now I had serious doubts.

Neither of us let the confusion about the weapon dampen our joy over having scored our first confirmed kill. I would just have to live with it.

We had now been on the AO nearly two hours, and our relief ship came in. We climbed out of the AO and Cort thumbed his mic, saying, "Which way to that flag?" I said, "I think we go southwest to the third canal and turn right." I have no idea how I remembered that because I had forgotten about the flag once we left it behind.

Because we were cruising and not zigzagging down the canal, the flag and banner came into sight in about three minutes. I pointed it out to Cort. He said, "What do you think?"

I said, "Just hover as close as you can get to the trees and I'll step out and grab it."

The idea of doing the right thing and leaving it alone barely entered my mind. I did recall that every war movie I had ever seen included a dead GI who stupidly picked up a booby-trapped souvenir. Were we about to join that club?

As we descended, I placed my CAR-15 into the space between the side of my seat and the armor plate, where we stored the weapon when we were not in the AO. I unbuckled my harness and prepared to snatch the flag.

I noticed the grass in the corner of the paddy was unusually high but thought nothing of it. I should have. Cort flared the Loach into a hover at what we thought was four feet above the ground. However, the Loach slammed to a stop and we were now on the ground. Worse, my CAR-15 flew out the door!

Surprisingly, rather than going down into the tall grass, the muzzle stuck into the mud, with the carbine stock sticking straight up in the air and allowing me to simply step onto the skid and grab the weapon by the butt and put it back in the Loach.

With that crisis averted, I reached for the flag. The corners of the flag were twisted into rubber bands on the bamboo.

Just as I was close enough to grab it, the rotor wash blew it off the bamboo and about four feet into the tree line! Fortunately, it hung on a branch at about the same height. All I had to do was guide Cort to hover closer to the trees.

It was obvious that I would never reach it if I stayed in my seat, so I stepped out, placing my foot on the port-side skid. I could hear the rotor blades snipping the small branches and twigs as I called out the distance to Cort. He gradually slid the ship to the left with the touch of a brain surgeon. We hovered as steady as a rock. Amazing.

With my right hand gripping the small grab handle mounted on the doorframe, I stretched out as far as I could and snagged the flag with my left. When I finally had it in hand, I yelled, "Got it, let's go!" Cort gently slid the Loach to the right to clear the trees, did a quick pedal turn and climbed quickly away from the tree line. I grabbed the doorframe with my left hand as I swung back into my seat, waving the flag so Cort could see it.

As we headed back to Vinh Long, Cort asked, "OK, now who's going to keep it?" I said, "Why don't you take it and we'll both own it. You be the caretaker." Cort agreed and said, "Yes. We'll co-own it, and I'll take care of it for both of us." Later, I realized that I had been too rank-conscious and should have claimed it as mine.

We flew a couple more sorties that day as the maintenance crew came out and airlifted the broken Loach back to the base. We realized later that we had each scored our first confirmed kill.

When we landed back at Vinh Long at the close of the day and Cort shut down the engine, he pulled off his helmet, looked at me and said, "Apache-Six doesn't need to know anything about this, right?"

"No, sir," I said.

Later, we realized that the flag was probably set up as a trap, and our surprise landing placed us on top of a recently built bunker, with transplanted grass for camouflage. That would explain the wet mud in which my CAR-15 was stuck. March was the dry season in the Delta, and fresh mud should not have been there.

That night, I experienced my first of many nightmares to come. I kept waking up after seeing a slow-motion vision of our rotor wash blowing the long grass, like a field of wheat in a Kansas breeze. As the blades of grass swayed in the wind, dozens of AK-47 barrels began poking out, pointing straight at me. I did not know that I would have this same nightmare hundreds of times in the future.

Pilot Assignments

Now that I had my first confirmed KBA while flying lead, Kenny Jones, our line chief and squad leader, approved my moving from a wing observer to a lead observer. This was a step up. While I would still fly in the wing ship on occasion, this promotion would allow me to escape those nauseating circular orbits.

Shortly after capturing the flag with Cort Stark, our platoon leader decided to assign pilots to specific ships. This meant that the pilot would most often fly the same ship, building familiarity. Hopefully, this would lead to better flying. I always wondered why this had not been the practice previously, because I thought this was the way the Air Corps did things in WWII and Korea.

I wasn't so eager to implement this practice once I found out who was assigned to my ship: Lt. Tanner, a National Guard officer who had volunteered for active service.

Lt. Tanner was not a confidence builder. He was nervous and a little depressed. He worried about everything, imagining strange noises in the helicopter. You had the impression that he was a little shaky and lacked confidence in himself, not a trait you wanted to see in a Scout pilot.

On one occasion, as were taking a down day to catch up on our ship maintenance, Lt. Tanner was assigned to fly down to Can Tho on what we called an Ash & Trash mission. These were noncombat missions to fly someone somewhere, pick up or deliver repair parts, or complete other tasks that were too far away to be done with a truck. In this case, Can Tho was quite a distance away. Flying was quicker and much safer than driving.

I assisted Lt. Tanner preflight the ship. He strapped in and cranked up. I did not go with him, so he was alone in the ship. The ship was also unarmed, carrying no minigun.

While Lt. Tanner was warming the engine and going through his pretakeoff checklist, Cpt. Wrenn, the A-Troop executive officer, drove up in his jeep and asked to use the PRC-25 radio we had in the line shack.

Cpt. Wrenn was a hardcore cav officer who never smiled. He was tough, as all execs are required to be. An executive officer is typically the troop disciplinarian, responsible for enforcement of all the rules and regulations that governed our daily lives. As such, Cpt. Wrenn perfectly fit the role.

It became painfully obvious that Lt. Tanner had not seen Wrenn's arrival, despite Tanner's ship being parked right next to the line shack. Wrenn was standing in the door of our shack, less than twenty-five feet from Tanner. He had the radio handset to his ear, and I was standing next to him, waiting for Tanner to come to a hover, back the Loach out of the revetment, face into the wind, then move forward in the typical takeoff maneuver. This was the approved method.

Unfortunately, Lt. Tanner must have been feeling a bit spunky that morning. Undoubtedly, the Loach probably felt very light and maneuverable when he came up to a partial hover, what we called "light on the skids." He carried no observer, no minigun, and none of the ammo that usually accompanied both. He must have been inspired.

Rather than back out of the revetment as described earlier, Tanner looked around and pulled up on the collective control stick, launching the Loach straight up to a height of about thirty feet. He was directly above the revetment. He snapped the ship left with a pedal turn and screamed down the runway in a full power takeoff! It was spectacular.

My jaw dropped. I thought, *Uh-oh, Wrenn won't like that.*

I was right. I looked at Wrenn as he stood to my left.

He had removed the handset from his ear and watched in disbelief as Tanner zoomed down the runway, finally pulling up into an excessively steep climb and turning southwest toward Can Tho.

It felt like ten minutes before Wrenn spoke, and I knew it was not going to be pleasant. He turned to me and asked, "Specialist, who in the hell is that son of a bitch?"

I replied, "That, sir, is Lieutenant Tanner," and gave him Tanner's call sign.

"Well, Specialist Moore, I would greatly appreciate it if you would tell Tanner that when he returns, I want to see him in my office before those blades stop spinning, and please tell him to bring a change of underwear."

Those of us who were standing around got away from Wrenn, trying to look busy. We did not want any of his anger to spill onto us. As soon as he drove away in his jeep, we all laughed like crazy, knowing Tanner was going to get a serious ass-chewing.

While I still flew in other ships with other pilots, I flew with Tanner almost as often as I would fly with Cort Stark. At first, Tanner was relegated to fly wing, lots of wing before he moved up to the lead position. Those observers who had flown with him wondered why he was ever promoted to fly lead, having watched him in action.

I witnessed a couple of instances when he demonstrated a trait I often heard about him: the tendency to be overcome by "target fixation," which caused the pilot to fixate on the target during a gun run. If not corrected, the pilot would fly the ship straight into the target, failing to pull up in time to avoid a crash.

During one gun run, while we were reconning-by-fire along a tree line, I noticed that Tanner was continuing to fire a very long burst on the minigun. When I turned from the door to look to the front, I saw what was happening. Tanner was staring straight ahead at the tree line as we dove toward a large tree at the end of the line.

It was apparent he was not going to pull up, so I kicked my mic switch and yelled, "Watch out! Pull up!" at the top of my lungs.

It must have stunned him, because he snapped out of his trance, pulled back on the stick and we scraped along the very top of the tree.

When I was able to breathe again, I asked if he was OK. He said he was and asked me if I would keep this near miss between us. I agreed but said it probably would not matter. Apache-Six had probably seen the whole thing. I found out later that I was wrong.

When Tanner started flying lead, he also had the habit of flying too close to the trees, often striking the smaller branches and twigs with the rotor blades. This was a very bad habit. It showed his depth perception was a little weak. If he made this mistake with the tail rotor, he would probably kill himself and his observer: me.

On another occasion, when we were low-leveling across a large paddy to get to a tree line on the other side, we noticed several peasant women gathering rice. They were making the rice fronds into bamboo contraptions to separate the rice grains from the plants.

By "low-leveling," I mean flying at about five or six feet above the ground at eighty-five or ninety knots. This was required in situations where the terrain was wide open and Charlie could get a good, clear shot at you from 500 or 600 yards. You never wanted to fly slowly in such conditions, unless you were searching for signs, as when clearing an LZ.

While looking out the left door and to the rear (as usual) to ensure that a VC did not pop up and take a shot as we sped by, I noticed that our skids were zipping through the rice plants. We were gradually getting lower and about to fly into the ground at a fatal speed.

I turned to check Tanner. Incredibly, he was looking back over his right shoulder at a group of women we had just passed, watching them work.

I yelled, "Goddammit, pull up!" He again came out of his trance and righted the ship.

When we returned to base and were crawling out of the ship, Lt. Tanner attempted to stand up in the cockpit, a physical impossibility. He planted his feet on the portion of the deck that covered the radio. As soon as he did so, the cover broke, emitting a loud crack. The cover was comprised of a nelsonite-like material and clearly marked as a No Step surface. Why was now obvious.

Why Tanner did it was completely unknown to me and everyone else. *Nobody* exited a Loach by attempting to stand on the radio cover. I had no idea what he was thinking. Now I had to repair the cover and hope that the fix would be good enough to avoid a dreaded Red-X, a mark in the ship's log saying the ship was not airworthy. That is, grounded.

As Tanner struggled to extricate himself (his foot was now stuck in the small radio compartment!), I looked him in the eye and said nothing. I had my head tilted to the right and my mouth was open, in an obvious gesture of: What the fuck are you doing, you idiot?

My disgust was quite evident, and I wanted it to be.

Later, I regretted not reporting his incompetence to Apache-Six and getting him out of the Scout platoon. Going straight to the platoon leader about another officer was not how things were done in the army. Therefore, I only repeated these stories to my fellow enlisted men. Unfortunately, most of them had similar stories but did not know what to do about them. This would later turn out to be a tragic mistake.

Once Tanner was cleared for lead duty, he also became eligible for one of our most hated missions: Firefly. We flew these missions at night with three ships in a team: the command-and-control (C&C) ship, a Cobra, and a Loach. In each door the C&C ship carried a large rack comprised of about twenty-four vertical tubes into which large flares were stored and readied for use. These flares, which were four or five inches in diameter and about thirty inches long, would be dropped over the search area, illuminating the ground in a weird, high-contrast scene. Because the flares were so bright, the AO would look like a moonscape: extreme brightness and extreme black shadows. No grays or mid-tones. You could see or you couldn't. Absolutely no in-between.

While the flares were falling, the tiny Loach would be flying at treetop level, doing about fifty knots, zigzagging, and looking for Chuck. Because we were always mortared at night, the idea was to catch Charlie moving his mortars and rocket launchers into position.

I only flew a couple of Firefly missions, and those were enough for me. The possibility of going down into trees, at night, was not appealing; even though we were patrolling around the Vinh Long base, spending the night on the ground while your friends searched for you was not a good way to extend your career.

On my first such mission, I was paired with Lt. Tanner. I wanted to puke. The prospect of doing this for the first time with a pilot who had never done it was worrisome, to say the least. By now, Lt. Tanner was secretly referred to as "Shaky." Not something that filled me with confidence.

Once it was completely dark, we took off and began our search. It was an amazing, unforgettable experience. As we were skimming the treetops and zigzagging as we went, one or two flares would be descending under their parachutes. This caused a visual effect that probably matched the hallucinations of a bad acid trip.

Because the flares swung back and forth under their parachutes, the source of the intense light was shifting as well. This caused the shadows of the trees to swing from left to right and back again while the flare kept changing its position in relation to the trees.

While we were flying along, Tanner became obsessed with the anti-collision beacon, a flashing red beacon on top of the helicopter. Its function is obvious.

Tanner repeatedly asked me to turn the beacon on, then turn it off, then turn it on again. This was happening about once per minute or thirty seconds, based on what I do not know.

One of the four Loach rotor blades is painted white on top, making them appear to flash when viewed from above. The vertical and horizontal stabilizers are painted International Rescue Orange, for visibility. We have a mega-megawatt light above us in the flares. Why he wanted the anti-collision light on and then off completely baffled me. Besides the craziness, his constant requests were causing me to direct my attention at the beacon switch on the console panel and ignore what was going on below us.

He then entered a state wherein his mind was telling him that the beacon was not working. He began repeatedly asking me if it was operating or not. When it was on, you could easily see its red reflection blinking on the bottom of the rotor blades! He should have been able to see it as well.

After about thirty minutes of this nonsense, he became adamant about the beacon not working. He saw that I was taking my conclusion from the reflection on the rotor blades. This was not proof positive for him. He insisted that I turn around in my seat and look directly at the light to verify its operation. This was impossible because the beacon is sitting atop the body of the Loach. I would need X-ray vision to look directly at the light. All I could see was the light's reflection on the blades spinning about fifteen inches directly above where the beacon was mounted.

Anyone with any piloting experience can tell you that you should never, never, never look back over your shoulder while you are flying an aircraft. Doing so can cause a severe case of vertigo, a condition where you cannot tell up from down. This happens because turning into this particular position disturbs the fluid in your inner ear. What you feel in your ears does not match what your eyes see. Therefore, you cannot orient yourself. Gravity does not help.

I turned around, looked up and saw that, gee whiz, the beacon was operating properly.

I told Tanner, then spun around in my seat to face forward. When I looked out through the bubble, we were upside down!

Well, at least I *thought* we were upside down.

What I saw after I turned around was completely different from what I saw before I looked back at the beacon. I was now dizzy and thought we were falling into the trees, upside down. I let out a loud scream and had the urge to jump out of the ship!

Tanner said something to me and I calmed down. I now knew what had happened to cause me about five or six seconds of sheer, unmitigated panic.

When Tanner directed me to look at the beacon, we were banking sharply into a left-hand turn while the shadows were swinging around. When I turned back to the front, Tanner had already initiated a sharp right-hand turn, changing our vertical attitude by ninety degrees. The flare was also at a different point in its oscillation, throwing the shadows out of sync with my previous vision.

I was convinced that the Loach was upside down, causing me to momentarily lo   touch with reality. I felt weightless. And doomed. This disorientation c sed me to lose my poise, and I screamed. I was also soaked in sweat, probab   from an intense adrenaline rush. I felt like hell. I was eager to get back on th ground. I was again pissed off at Tanner because his paranoia about the beaco had caused a near catastrophe.

We found n VC or sign of their recent presence. Actually, I had never heard of *any* Fi fly mission ever finding anything. So, this was par for the course.

A similar ex   rience affected my close friend Dave Raymond while flying between Vinh L ng and Chi Lang.

It was what v   called a bluebird day, puffy white clouds against a deep blue, tropical sky. Cru sing along at 1,500 feet, the formation of four ships suddenly flew through a nall cloud. It resulted in a complete whiteout: no sun, no horizon. Flying   trough clouds was prohibited, but sometimes could not be avoided.

When the sh   s emerged from the cloud a few seconds later, Dave looked down through tl   clear chin bubble. He saw blue sky and clouds. He concluded the ship was ups le down and tried to jump out of the Loach in a panic. Before he could escape   is harness, the pilot grabbed him and pulled him back down into the seat. Da   regained his composure and started breathing again.

Dave then r   lized what had happened. When he looked down through the chin bubble   the ship was directly over a river. What Dave saw was the sky's *reflection* o   the surface of the river. He thought he was looking down at the sky and pan ked. Fortunately, he was slow clearing his seat belt harness. Otherwise, he n   y have jumped to his death. There were many ways to die in a Loach.

A few days a er our Firefly mission, the anti-collision light switch failed! I could only im   ine why. Duh. We probably gave it two years of use in that one night and it   st couldn't take it. I reported the failure to the maintenance electrical shop   d they dispatched one of the 370th guys, whose name was Pacquing. He w   a southern Californian who was obsessed with the Harley Davidson Sport   er. He wrote "XLCH" on everything he owned. That was the official Harley model number, and he wanted everyone to know what he was going to buy when he made it back to The World.

"Pack Rat," as we called him, was also one of the earliest discoverers of cheap pot in Nam. He burned one as often as he could and everyone knew it, apparently even the officers.

When he arrived at my ship, he was carrying a toggle switch. However, the switch did not look like the one in the console. I told him I wanted the correct switch, so we pulled the broken one, and he returned to the maintenance area to find a match.

About fifteen minutes later, he was back at my ship with the same incorrect switch. I asked him about it, and he told me that he had checked with the other electrician and this was an authorized replacement.

I was skeptical but allowed him to install the switch.

The next morning, Tanner and I climbed aboard for another mission. As soon as Tanner turned the anti-collision light on, the console started spewing smoke, and small flames shot out of the switch.

I asked him to report a fire and abort the mission, or at least our part in it. There was no way we could fly this ship today.

We switched to another Loach and completed the day's mission. As soon as we landed, I was told that Cpt. Sholtz wanted to see me. I knew this was not good.

I rode back to the maintenance area with the pilots and reported to the maintenance office. Sholtz was hot and wanted to know why I had installed an improper switch. When I told him that Pack Rat had installed it, he jumped up and said, "Goddammit! That's even worse! You know as well as I do that Pack Rat has peanut butter for brains, and you should never let him make any decisions about your ship."

I was struck by the humor of it and said, "Yes, sir!" We saluted each other, and he told me to go eat. I was off the hook and my mistake had no further consequences for me.

I was just glad the fire started *before* we took off.

A subtle but definite change took place following our scoring our first confirmed kill nd capturing the VC flag. It was not something that I consciously cha ged or made any effort to achieve. However, I noticed that when flying the Scout missions, a serene calm came over me. It was almost as though I was notionally detached from what was going on and what I was doing. My sense were on high alert and I noticed everything. If we were fired upon, I did not xperience the famous pucker factor that so many combat air crewmen spoke bout. I was not startled or confused and knew exactly what I was supposed to lo. My emotional state and muscle memory seemed to be in perfect sync.

This feeling as present in all my subsequent missions. I now believe it was a way my b in chose to react, to deal with the fear of doing something extremely dang ous, knowing that it was extremely dangerous. My mind found a way to s ppress anxiety.

Stick Time

As mentioned eviously, Scout observers got plenty of stick time. Most of the pilots were damant about making sure the observers could land the ship if they wer wounded. When watching the Scouts return to Vinh Long after a mission, ll four ships would make the ugliest of final approaches. Because it was ficult to get used to applying enough left pedal to hold the ship straight as e power declined, the ships would crab to the right as they descended. Som imes, too much pedal was applied, and the ship would slide to the left. Som observers overworked the pedals, causing the tail boom to swing violently f om left to right. The pilot would always take the controls and straighten it out t was not easy and took many attempts to get proficient at it.

On several c casions, the Scouts would return to Vinh Long alone. This gave us opportu ties to do something that would have upset Apache-Six. We would low-level ll the way back to base. When returning from Chi Lang or Rach Gia (rock- w), this could be an hour-long flight. It was thrilling.

We would b ak out of the normal trail formation and line up the ships with all four flyi g side by side, about fifty feet apart, at eighty to eighty knots. Because we wer nly five or six feet off the ground, we had to hop over the tree lines and rice paddy dikes. The scene was vividly etched into my brain.

When you looked from side to side, you could see your buddies' ships hopping over the trees and then returning to the deck. Each would disappear momentarily, hidden by the trees as they descended.

While this was going on, the radio was tuned to AFRN. We would be listening to late-'60s rock and roll as we zoomed over the landscape, usually giggling like schoolgirls! When "Born to Be Wild" was broadcast, it made the perfect soundtrack.

These were two-hour-long thrill rides and were truly exhilarating. I believe these experiences account for my later fascination with roller coasters, which I happily passed on to my children and grandchildren!

CS-Gas

Not long after the switch-fire incident, I flew another mission with Jones. The night before the mission, all four Loach crews were issued gas masks, which were nothing like the ones we had for ground. The mask itself resembled an oxygen mask, similar to what fighter pilots wore. The corrugated hose went over our shoulder to a filter canister hanging from the back of the seat bulkhead.

When we arrived at the AO, we were told to don our gas mask. We did so but did not know what to expect next.

We were circling a large stand of woods at a height of about fifty feet when the C&C ship flew to the windward side of the woods and slowed down at 200 feet. Apache-Six announced, "Gas away!" and we saw a canister roll out of the Huey's left-hand door. The canister looked to be about the size of a fifty-five-gallon drum cut in half.

After it fell for a few seconds, it burst. It did not explode in a technical sense, but something did cause it to burst open, spilling its contents.

Out came a couple of dozen CS grenades, trailing smoke. They flew away from the canister and fell to the ground in an upside-down tulip pattern. The gas started to spread out and blow through the woods.

CS gas is a very nasty concoction that will motivate anyone not wearing a gas mask to vacate the area. It attacks several of the body's systems, including the eyes, nose, digestive track, lungs, and sensitive areas that are prone to sweat, namely the armpits and crotch.

When the first sniff hits, you go blind and lose your ability to breathe. Your lungs lock up. The next sensation, which hits in less than ten seconds, is to gag and vomit. You become disoriented and run or stumble away, looking for clean air. I remember our gassing during basic training. Three hundred men broke into pure panic and tried to save themselves by running into the nearby woods. Many people were injured because they ran into trees.

It was an effective weapon.

We then received word to begin searching the woods. As we flew into the gas cloud, my armpits and groin began burning like mad. Soon, the entire boundary where the mask met my face began burning as well. The gas attacked any dampness on your skin. Jones and I were equally miserable.

We scooted along at treetop level, itching and scratching. Fortunately, none of the gas penetrated our masks and got to our eyes.

Just as we broke over the edge of the woods, we spotted a VC squatting in a spider hole. He was unarmed and had his hands covering his eyes. In the bottom of the spider hole was a CS grenade spewing out gas. It swirled up and around Charlie's head as he sat motionless on the hole.

I was amazed. For a moment I thought he might be dead. We got him out of the hole, and some ARVNs who were already on the ground came over and took him prisoner. How he withstood the effects of the CS gas was beyond me.

Recon by Fire

I drew another mission with Coakley, an instructor pilot who had recently joined the Scout

Coakley was one of the good guys and everyone liked him. His role as an IP only required him to give the other A-Troop pilots check rides to ensure they remained proficient in certain types of aircraft and in certain skills, like instrument navigation.

This was not very demanding, so Coakley loved giving flying lessons to the observers. This further endeared him to the observers and crew chiefs and allowed him to strengthen his relationship with the enlisted group.

One day while flying wing with Coakley, we were directed to recon a tree line that ran beside a canal. The lead ship had spotted a VC running through the trees but had lost sight of him.

We were hoping to draw fire from Charlie, so our gun run was a little out of the ordinary. Rather than flying a straight line down the tree line and firing the minigun straight ahead, we needed to expose ourselves to the VC so he would be tempted to shoot at us.

To accomplish this, Coakley put the Loach into a sideways slip to the right, with the tree line on the left. By flying parallel to the tree line, he could fire into the trees while still presenting the Loach as a clear target. My job was to spot the VC before he could take a shot at us. If he did not fire, I would provide covering fire when Coakley stopped firing and pulled out of the gun run.

As we neared the end of the tree line, I prepared to begin firing as soon as Coakley ceased fire. I would aim and fire my CAR-15 at the point in the trees where his fire had stopped, so I was aiming slightly forward of the ship, at the eleven o'clock position.

As soon as the minigun went quiet, I began firing bursts of automatic fire into the trees.

Just as I did so, Coakley opened up again with the minigun and threw the Loach slightly to the left. This created a problem for me.

When he threw the ship to the left and then quickly back to the right, the smoke grenades that were hanging on a wire loop beside the door swung into my line of fire. I hit three or four of the grenades with my CAR-15 rounds.

This was possible because of the way the grenades were stored. The wire loop was about ten inches in diameter and attached to the airframe by another wire of about six inches in length. With six or seven grenades on the loop, it was stretched into a long oval, with the grenades hanging by their safety spoons. So this mass of grenades easily swung into my line of fire without me noticing it.

A moment later, as were coming around for a second run, I noticed purple smoke blowing out of a hole in one of the grenades. I reached down and grabbed it so I could check it out. I turned it over to inspect the seal on the grenade's bottom. BOOM! The grenade popped in my hand, sending the burning powder into my face.

Fortunately, I had my visor down and saved my eyesight. I tossed the grenade out the door, then noticed two or three other grenades leaking smoke out of bullet holes that I had inadvertently shot into them.

I told Coakley what had happened and began throwing the rest of the grenades out of the ship. I had to be careful because dropping one of the smoke grenades down into the chin bubble and behind the pedals could be fatal. B-Troop had recently lost a Loach and crew when a mishandled smoke grenade fell into the chin bubble and filled the cabin with smoke. The observer could not reach the grenade. The pilot attempted to land but could not see. He crashed, killing himself and his observer.

Suddenly Apache-Six came up on the radio wanting to know, "What in the hell is going on down there? I'm seeing smoke all over the paddy!"

Coakley explained that we had a couple of accidental grenade ignitions and that everyone was fine.

When we completed our second gun run, I looked around and saw four or five different colored grenades spewing smoke into the air directly under where we had just flown. If Charlie was trying to decode our smoke signals, I am sure he was as confused as I was embarrassed.

On April 24, all of the people who came over with the 370th TC Detachment reached the ninety-day mark. That is, we had only ninety days to endure before we would go home, or DERO, the Date Enlistee Returns from Overseas. This was a major milestone and cause for great celebration. The party was on.

Dave, Vernon and I left the flight line and had someone drive us over to the maintenance area to join in. The 370th had done it right. They had all kinds of food, some of it prepared in the mess hall. They had two or three cases of steaks, and, of course, a virtually unlimited supply of beer!

A couple of radios were tuned to AFRN, and the music was flowing.

When the three of us crawled out of the jeep, we were greeted with a great deal of good-natured teasing for being chauffeured to the event. Shouts of "Big shots!" and "VIPs" came at us. This was followed by hugs and handshakes all around. It was good to be back in their company.

We saw a lot of new faces in the group. This resulted from the army's effort to diffuse the impact of having thirty-five guys leave the unit on the same day. It appeared that about half the people were strangers. They had replaced some of our original team, who had been transferred to other aviation units around the country. One of the diffused was Craig Schmidt, my former pinochle partner. He had gone to a unit in Can Tho, about thirty miles away.

All of us were officially "Double-Digit Midgets," meaning we had less than one hundred days to go.

Once the beer started taking effect, things got a little crazy. A group of us jumped onto one of the workbench serving tables and started dancing go-go style. Trying to get the potato salad off my boots was one of the last things I remembered.

I also remember being stuffed into the rear floor of the jeep for a ride back to the barracks. I think there were about six of us in the vehicle, taking up every cubic inch of available space.

The next day, one of the guys from the headquarters platoon returned my lighter and comb, telling me that he found it in Apache-Six's jeep. He wanted to know what I was doing in the jeep.

I would have loved to have been able to tell him, but I did not recall anything about the ride. I explained that I was merely cargo and had no recollection of the jeep.

While I did not remember much of it, I know it was a great party.

Captain Cannon

We lost our platoon leader, Cpt. Robert Cannon, on April 20th, when he and his observer, Kenny Jones, were shot down during a search and destroy mission.

Robert Cannon came to the platoon and took over as platoon leader about a month or so after I joined the Scouts. He came with a reputation.

He had been a Scout pilot in B-Troop and had served beyond the six-month limit imposed o officers. Rather than accept a transfer to a safer aviation job, he insisted on re aining a Scout. He made the switch to A-Troop and became heir apparent fo the Apache-Six position when it came open.

Cannon had reputation as a great Scout pilot, having never been shot down or had a ach take a small arms hit while he was at the controls. An incredible feat i '68 and '69.

He was also own for loving to start fires. He could often be seen loading twice the norm load of Willie Pete and thermite grenades into the ship he was about to fly. le would be spotted in a crouching walk, holding the shirttail of his blouse in ont of him, overflowing with grenades.

He was Apac e Troop's pyromaniac. I guess all troops had to have one.

I flew with h n often. This became the case after Tanner and I were flying on his wing one ay, and he wanted to burn a small footbridge that crossed a canal.

As luck wou have it, he and his observer had already used all of their thermite grenad and the small bridge was too damp for a Willie Pete. He told Tanner to come own and put a grenade on it.

Tanner dove at the footbridge from about a hundred yards away. The problem was th we were doing about one hundred knots when it came time for me to toss th grenade. A thermite grenade does not explode; it burns like a welding torch. is a precision weapon. You pull the pin, then set the grenade on whatever you vant to destroy. You don't try to drop one on a small, wooden bridge that is a out eighteen inches wide; especially when you're doing a hundred knots.

As we appro hed the bridge, I tossed the grenade. I held no hope that I would hit the br ge. I didn't.

When we sw ng around for another attempt, I suggested to Tanner that he hover above the ridge so I could simply drop the grenade on the bridge. He objected, asking e if I knew we were in a free-fire zone. We had not seen any VC all day, but t is didn't sway him.

When we st ted our second run, he said he was going to slow down – down to eighty ots! I said nothing.

I concentrated hard and dropped the grenade at what I hoped was somewhere near the bridge. To my surprise, the grenade hit the ground short of the bridge, took about a fifteen-foot bounce, then rolled about three feet directly onto the bridge. I could hardly believe it.

When the grenade ignited, everyone could see that it was about two feet onto the bridge and dead center on the wooden walkway. It was an incredibly lucky shot and one that I probably couldn't duplicate if I tried a hundred times.

Captain Cannon went nuts on the radio, congratulating me for the shot and asking the whole team if anyone had ever seen anything like it. Even the Cobra pilots got into the act, talking about what a shot it was.

When we returned to the POL point, Cannon was ecstatic. He couldn't believe it. I tried to shrug it off because I knew it was blind luck. He wouldn't have it, teasing Tanner about making it so hard on me and asking him if he could have done 150 knots, just to see what I could do! Of course, he worked into the conversation that Tanner was too scared to hover over the bridge, like any other Scout pilot would have done.

From that point on, Cannon would often ask to have me assigned to his ship on those days when we were both scheduled to fly.

Flying with Cpt. Cannon was not always this much fun. The first time I flew lead with him resulted in two very uncomfortable situations, one of which was extremely dangerous, for me.

Working with ARVNs on that first mission, I learned that Cannon had a grisly mindset. He reminded me of *The War Lover* novel, in which the lead character loved the bloodshed associated with being a B-17 pilot in Europe.

The ARVNs had uncovered a sizeable weapons cache and killed about six or eight VC. The VC bodies were in a tangled stack, placed there by the ARVNs while they waited to be extracted. As we circled the ten or twelve ARVNs and the stack of bodies, Cannon pulled a Kodak Instamatic camera from the pocket of his chicken plate, handed it to me, and told me to get about four or five shots of the dead VC.

I felt utter disgust and almost refused to do it. To me, this seemed very disrespectful of the dead men. I shut up and did as I was told. I can still remember the feeling of embarrassment as the onlooking ARVNs watched me snap the picture while the Loach flew around in small circles, ten feet above the ground. I felt like a tourist.

Another incident with Cannon taught me that I had to be very careful with him.

We were doing body snatches not far from Vinh Long

On one such occasion, we hovered around the designated drop spot and cleared it for Apache-Six's landing. After the suspect exited the ship, Apache-Six took off and headed out.

While this was occurring, we were orbiting the drop site at about a hundred feet above the ground. We could see that the suspect still had his hands tied behind his back. We didn't know why and we didn't ask. We continued to circle.

As soon as Apache-Six was about two hundred yards away, Cannon came up on the intercom, saying, "Let's go kill that guy as soon as Six is out of here."

I was beyond shocked. My pilot was asking me to commit murder. I nodded my head as we dove toward the victim. I turned to say something to Cannon. Looking through Cannon's door, I saw Apache-Six heading back in our direction. I pointed this out to Cannon and said we couldn't kill the guy now. Six would find a dead man with his hands tied behind his back less than five minutes after he turned him loose. That could not end well.

Why Six turned around was unknown to me. He radioed, telling us to follow him. He then did another 180 and headed back in the direction he was originally flying

Whatever the reason, Six had saved me from an untenable situation.

Cannon's shot-down and eventual death was quite a story.

Cannon was flying with Kenny Jones in the left seat as they reconned ahead of an ARVN unit sweeping the AO.

As they checked the area, a VC fired a couple of rounds, striking the Loach in the engine compartment and severing a fuel line. The ship was immediately engulfed in flame.

When he realized that his ship was on fire, Cannon turned the Loach and flew back to the ARVNs where he could land safely. He knew if he went down in the area where he had drawn fire; the ARVNs might not advance to rescue him and Kenny Jones, his observer on this mission.

Capt. Cannon crash-landed the burning ship and Jones jumped out. Within seconds, the wing ship, piloted by a young warrant officer named Ashworth, with Tom Gery in the observer seat, landed nearby.

When Gery reached the downed ship, Jones told him to return to his ship and retrieve the fire extinguisher. Cannon was on fire when Jones and Gery pulled him from the burning Loach. Jones sprayed a short burst from the extinguisher, dousing the flames on Cannon.

When they unbuckled his harness and extracted Cannon from the pilot seat, he attempted to stand but collapsed onto his back as soon as his feet touched the ground. Then they lifted him, draped his arms over their shoulders, and half walked, half dragged him to the starboard side of Gery's aircraft. He was still conscious and tried to assist with his short hike to the other Loach. He was still wearing his flight helmet.

They got him into the cargo space with great effort. He had stopped assisting at that point. They placed him in the horizontal position, laying on his side. It was obvious that he was in a life-threatening condition. Jones jumped into the cargo area from the starboard side, while Gery ran around to the port side of the ship and jumped into his front seat. They took off and flew Capt, Cannon to a nearby base for medical attention.

Cannon was transported to a hospital in Japan, where he succumbed to his wounds approximately one week later. Kenny Jones never flew another Scout mission.

Despite all he had been through, Kenny Jones walked away with only a gash on the bridge of his nose. No burns. No broken bones. The visor on his helmet slammed down on his nose and caused the gash.

Cannon's funeral, and the eulogy Maj. Schaeffer delivered, set up our expectations for another funeral one week later.

The major delivered a somewhat half-hearted speech. It sounded scripted, lacking warmth or personal recollections. It was a little too sanitary.

Mark Hansen

Our supply clerk, Mark Hansen, had joined the Scouts in mid-March. When he arrived, we hit it off right away. How could we not? We were about six months apart in age, surfed on opposite coasts, and talked about returning to The World and getting back to real life. Because we pulled guard duty together every four days, we had plenty of time to share aspirations and paint imaginary pictures of what civilian life would be like after a year in Vietnam.

I knew Mark well, even before he volunteered for the Scouts. He worked in the supply room and we saw each other often. He entered the army for the same reasons I had. Because our families shared a history of military service, sitting out the war was simply not an option. When Mark arrived in Vietnam, he was lucky enough to be assigned to the supply room – an unusual stroke of luck for a rifleman. This meant he did not participate in combat patrols, go to the boonies for weeks at a time, or take part in anything that would put him at great risk. Aside from the mortar attacks that hit the base several times per week, Mark did not have to worry about any direct threats. He was relatively safe. But he was bored.

The Scout platoon looked like a great way to escape the doldrums.

Being a member of the Scouts was a heady experience for a nineteen-year-old. Highly successful days, typically measured by the number of confirmed kills inflicted on the enemy, could result in free cases of beer brought to the barracks by senior NCOs and junior officers. When working with US Special Forces teams, Scout enlisted men often ate their meals with the officers in the SF camp dining room. Other crew chiefs and gunners ate C rations, sitting in their helicopters. The Scout platoon was where the glamour happened.

But that glory has a price, and young people have to pay it. Members of the Scout platoon were routinely reminded of that price. On April 27, 1969, we heard the radio report that Mark was killed by small arms fire. He was shot while clearing an LZ in Kien Giang Province in the Vietnam Delta. Mark became the Scouts' second fatality in less than two weeks. He wouldn't be coming back that evening and drinking a customary beer. We would pull guard duty together no more.

We looked forward to his memorial service with mixed emotions – eager to collectively remember the good man he was, sad to have to do so. Our recently assigned troop CO had provided a brief eulogy at Cpt. Cannon's service less than two weeks prior. We knew the real Mark and doubted that Major Schaeffer would be able to capture Mark's spirit with his words. When it was time to deliver Mark's eulogy, we all hoped Maj. Schaeffer would do a better job. He did, by far.

We were all surprised. Sitting in the second and third rows of the small chapel (the Scout pilots sat in the first) we listened attentively to Maj. Schaeffer's remarkable eulogy. He captured Mark perfectly, drawing on many of Mark's traits that made him so special to us.

The grieving period was short. We boxed up his personal belongings and sent them to his family in Reseda, California. I asked about escorting his body home, but that wasn't allowed at the time. The sadness was quickly replaced with the unspoken realization that it was better him than one of us. Within days, Mark wasn't mentioned anymore.

Mark Hansen sitting in an OH-6A.

What made Mark's death particularly galling was that he was flying lead with Lt. Tanner. I was told in 2014 by the wing pilot that Tanner might have left Mark in the ship when they went down, and many thought that Mark was still alive. When they recovered his body, there was no way to tell.

Another Mission with Sewell

I soon drew an assignment to fly a lead mission with Sewell. During the preflight, I could tell that he wasn't particularly enthused to fly with me. Frankly, I didn't care what he thought, as long as he flew the ship properly.

As soon as we dropped into the AO, he showed his attitude. As we were skimming the ground looking for signs, I spotted what looked like the remains of a cooking fire under a tree. I asked him to turn around so we could inspect it.

Sure enough, it was a campsite, and we saw several pieces of discarded mess gear lying around but no weapons. It did not look like it was a fresh site, so we moved on. As we pulled away, he mumbled into the intercom, "Well, that was a waste of time." Yeah, sure. It must have wasted at least sixty seconds. Besides, this was what we were supposed to do. He had not spotted it, and maybe that pissed him off.

We were soon ordered to fly a couple of miles ahead to provide some low-level recon for a company of the Ninth Infantry Division who were on a sweep. They were searching for a VC hospital, reported to have been set up in the area. We flew ahead of them as they advanced into the edge of a large paddy with relatively tall grass covering it. Small canals and tree lines surrounded it, possibly exposing the grunts to fire from four directions.

We started scouting around the edges, then headed for the center of the paddy, just in front of the grunts as they stepped out of the tree line into the paddy.

We were about a hundred yards in front of the grunts when I spotted two trip wires in the tall grass. They were only visible when our rotor wash separated the grass, revealing the deadly wires about ten inches off the ground. The rotor wash made them stand out in clear sight because the grass bent against the wires. They would have been nearly invisible to anyone approaching on foot.

I told Sewell what I had seen. He radioed Apache-Six, who told the grunts that the wires were directly below our hovering Loach. We recommended that they stay out of the middle of the paddy and walk closer to one of the tree lines, which we had already cleared.

For some unknown reason, they opted to walk right into the trip wires! We were about five hundred yards away when we heard the thump. We came back to the paddy, and two grunts lay on the ground, wounded. The remainder of the company was crouching down in the grass, trying to become smaller targets, but they were afraid to move.

We joined them and cleared a path for them to make it to the nearest tree line. I had no idea why they had ignored our advice, and two people were now paying the price. I wasn't impressed with their performance. We were ordered to relocate, so our five ships headed off in the same direction the grunts were heading. At that time, our relief team showed up, and we headed back to the POL point to refuel.

A little over an hour later, we rejoined A-Troop at the new AO, probably five miles ahead of where we had left the Ninth ID unit.

Unknown to us at the time, the company of grunts had swept through a wooded area just prior to reaching a large paddy that would serve as the LZ for their extraction. We had four slicks from our Lift platoon on the way to get them. The grunts had split into three columns and cleared the LZ in anticipation of the slicks' arrival.

While we were patrolling about five miles away, we could listen to the slicks as they approached the LZ. Suddenly, our commo channel was overwhelmed by so much traffic we could barely understand what we were hearing.

Just as the four slicks landed in the paddy, intense automatic weapon and mortar fire began raking the LZ from three sides. People were being wounded, and the grunts were pinned down. They needed help immediately. Apache-Six turned us around and we headed toward them. Sewell said to me, "There won't be anything for us to do. They've already found all the VC they want!"

As we approached the LZ, we could see plumes of smoke blowing across the paddy, but we did not see any actual explosions. As Sewell started to climb to an altitude where we could safely orbit the LZ, the Cobra's poured fire on the tree lines.

Sewell could not have been more wrong.

As we reached about three hundred feet, we heard Apache-Six tell the infantry CO, "Note the position of our Scouts and do not fire in their direction. I am going to send them in to scout your perimeter."

Sewell and I looked at each other in disbelief. The VC were obviously in the surrounding tree lines and woods. Why make us dive into the mess, instead of simply having the Cobras blast the tree lines?

Sewell dove the Loach toward the woods at a very high speed and said, "We're going in hot, so hang on."

As we screamed across the tops of the trees and canal, we could see about a dozen trails where Charlie had crawled into the canal, but we saw nobody. They had vanished. We turned toward the woods at the bottom of the horseshoe formed by the grunts' perimeter.

I did not have a chance to look at our airspeed indicator because I was leaning out the door, looking for Mr. Charles. However, we flew over the edge of the woods at the highest speed I believe I had ever seen in a Loach. Sewell was wisely taking no chances.

Again, no Charlie.

We were zigzagging across the trees, about a hundred yards into the woods, when I spotted something that startled me. It was a freshly built bunker about fifteen feet square and eight or nine feet high.

I told Sewell that I had a bunker and asked him to turn right until he saw it.

As soon as he did, he said something like, "Holy shit!" and reported it to Apache-Six. As we pulled away from the bunker, Six told us to hover in front of the bunker and attempt to draw fire from its occupants! I did not believe it.

Sewell simply said, "Say again, sir?" as though he did not understand the order. He was now looking at me with a confused look on his face.

Apache-Six repeated the order, showing a little frustration in his voice.

Sewell mumbled a few curse words and said, "If this doesn't get us killed, nothing will."

We dove to a position about twenty feet in front of the bunker and maybe three feet in the air. We remained there about three seconds before I dropped a red smoke grenade and we flew away.

With that, the Cobras had a clear target.

While we circled above the small clearing containing the bunker, the first Cobra rolled in. Remarkably, he put the first pair of rockets right on the bunker – direct hit! One of the rockets actually entered the bunker door and exploded inside. That was impressive.

The second Cobra rolled in, also firing 2.75 rockets and its miniguns.

When the smoke cleared, we went down to take a look.

The bunker was now a smoking pile of mud bricks. No VC to be found. Unbelievable.

What was even more unbelievable was that the infantry company had walked right past the bunker and failed to notice it.

Because the LZ now appeared to be void of any VC threats, three of our slicks returned to begin the extraction process. The fourth slick was taking a wounded crewman to the hospital and could not participate in the lift.

When we returned to Vinh Long at the end of the day, I learned that the wounded crewman was a friend from the 370th maintenance platoon I'd come to Nam with, Steve Strachan. A bullet had struck him above the knee, traveled up his femur, ricocheted off his pelvis, and stopped in his lung. That was a bad wound.

Chi Lang Again, and Again, and Again

Several weeks later we returned to Chi Lang for another mission supporting the ARVNs. Again, Coakley was my pilot in the wing ship. The lead ship was being flown by my old "friend" Mr. Sewell, with Steve Holmes in the observer seat.

On the way to the AO, I spotted two surprising scenes. The first was a bomb crater, with an ARVN soldier attempting to climb out of the deep hole. What surprised me was the sheer size of the crater. It must have been at least thirty feet wide and eighteen to twenty feet deep. The ARVN soldier was dwarfed by the size of it. I figured that he had ventured into the crater to take a dump and was only now realizing how far he had to climb.

When we returned to Chi Lang at lunchtime, we went through our usual refueling routine. As soon as we shut down, one of the Green Beret officers came down the hill to where all of us were parked and invited the officers to join them for lunch. As we got out of the ship, Sewell looked at me and said the Scout crews were always invited. I was shocked.

The SF guys had a small mess hall, capable of seating about twenty men. Steve and I let the six pilots take their seats, then we sat at the end of the table. Two Vietnamese ladies served us some form of French meal and the freshly baked French bread that I had learned to love. It did not matter to me that the bread always had a few gnats baked into the loaf. They added protein, and the bread was so delicious I never thought about the bugs.

All the pilots and the members of the SF A-team talked it up. The SF boys went on and on about the Scouts and all the chances we took. Steve and I said nothing, but it was nice to hear.

After about an hour, it was again our turn to hit the AO, so we took off to relieve the other team.

The ARVNs had been on the ground all day when we joined them. The group looked like it included forty to fifty men. We came in to clear an LZ so these soldiers could be extracted by our Lift platoon slicks.

The ARVNs had been busy. They had uncovered numerous arms caches spread over a large area. As the sun headed down, the leaders realized that the caches were too scattered to bring together into a single pickup spot. Someone decided to start a large fire to destroy the weapons and captured ammo.

The method was to have the two Scout ships fly from one end of the AO to the other, dropping Willie-Pete grenades as we went. We would fly along the windward side of the AO so the wind would carry the flames into the AO and into the caches. Sounded like fun.

When we reached the northern tree line on the windward side of the AO, Sewell and Coaley dove the Loaches to about fifteen feet above the ground.

When they gave us the word, Steve and I began pulling the pins on the Willie Petes and tossed the grenades out the door. As we low-leveled across the dry paddies at about eighty or ninety knots, our ship was positioned level with the lead ship and about forty feet behind, on the left, approximately the seven o'clock position from the lead ship's point of view. This was the standard position for this type of formation flying.

At this speed, it did not take us long to reach the opposite tree line, about three-quarters of a mile to the south. Both of us were out of grenades, so the lead ship started to climb to a safer altitude.

When we climbed to about two hundred feet, Sewell started to turn right, the rule when finishing a gun run or a grenade drop. As Sewell made his move, kicking the tail boom to the left as the nose went right, Oakley applied more power to remain in the seven o'clock position.

Sewell's ship was about ten feet above us and in our two o'clock high position as we continued to accelerate and climb.

Suddenly, I saw Steve's face come out of the door as he stared back at us. Sewell was now turning left, directly into our path.

Steve's eyes were as wide as saucers, and I could see his mouth open in a shouting motion. Coakley threw our Loach into a hard dive so suddenly that I could not get my heel down onto the floor-mounted mike button to warn him. I was weightless, pressing up into my shoulder straps. I was trying to say "Watch out!" when the Loach's sudden dive tossed me out of my seat.

As Steve and I stared at each other, the usually invisible main rotor blades of each ship slowed to extreme slow motion. I could see each rotor blade spinning so slowly that it might take a full minute to complete one rotation.

I could see Steve's mouth moving slowly but could hear nothing. I realized I was going to die. I clutched my CAR-15 to my chest, closed my eyes, and waited for the noise of the two ships coming together. I was calm and experiencing that serene feeling that so often came over me in stressful times.

Nothing.

Sewell's ship could not have missed us by more than one foot. About two seconds later, I hear Coakley over the intercom: "It won't pull up. It won't come up!" I opened my eyes and saw the rice paddy racing up toward us. I tried to find the horizon but saw nothing but brown dirt. Because of Coakley's instant reaction, we had avoided the midair collision with the other ship. Now we were going straight down in an uncontrolled dive. I looked up through the green-tinted Plexiglas of panel to find the horizon. All I saw was grass.

I simply stared through the bubble and thought, *Well, I'm dead. I hope someone tells my folks what happened to me.*

The fall probably lasted around five seconds, but just before we hit the ground, the Loach righted itself. As we pulled out of the dive, we dragged our skids through the paddy grass, lightly bounced twice, and bounded into the air doing about fifty knots!

What had happened? Coakley had the control stick pulled back as far as it would go, pinned against the rear stop. From my point of view, we were going straight down and appeared to be a little beyond vertical. Like an Olympic diver who overrotates, we seemed to be slightly upside down!

It had to be a puff of wind that struck the Loach at just the right speed and angle to alter its attitude. Suddenly we were flying straight and level about ten feet above the ground. I looked out the door to see if the skids were still attached to the ship. They were. However, they were draped in so many long strands of grass that the Loach looked like it was wearing a hula skirt.

The two ships made their way back to Chi Lang. As soon as we had refueled and parked, the two pilots jumped from their ships and headed toward each other. It looked like a fistfight was about to start. Steve and I ran to the pilots to keep them from doing something stupid.

As we approached, we could hear them yelling at each other. Coakley accused Sewell of swinging the ship into a right turn, then suddenly turning left and into our climbing ship. Sewell denied it, but he was wrong.

What he had done was to kick the tail boom to the left so he could watch the grenades exploding across the paddy. It provided him a good view of the show, but it made us think he was turning right, as the rules called for.

I knew Sewell was mistaken and said, "Sir, you turned right, and we pulled up to stay in position." He repeated his denial. I looked at Steve and said, "You know you went right. Tell him, Steve."

Steve told Sewell he *had* swung to the right before turning left. He went on to say that when he looked out the door to give Sewell the "clear left" call, there we were in the other ship, just feet away.

Tempers calmed, and there was no damage to our ship. Apache-Six had probably not even seen the near collision because he was watching the explosions too. When we returned to Vinh Long, no one mentioned it, and we went on with our normal routine.

However, the incident made a big and lasting impression on me. During my next two missions, I was a nervous wreck, fearing a midair collision. When we returned to Vinh Long with all thirteen ships in a trail formation, I could barely endure it. And I was flying the ship. Once we landed and all the formalities were taken care of, I approached Vernon Summerell and shared my experience with him. I suggested that I sit out the next couple of rotations until I could get my act together. He agreed. I was not doing anyone any good if I was concentrating on the other Loach instead of looking for Chuck.

Tranny Failure

Ask any helicopter pilot or crewmember what they fear most, and 90 percent of them will say a transmission failure. That's because in most army helicopters, going all the way back to the H-13 of MASH fame, a transmission failure usually results in the rotor head snapping the main mast and flying away. The helicopter then falls from the sky as rapidly as gravity can pull it. No one survives one of these incidents.

We were working out of Chi Lang again and I was flying for the first time with Warrant Officer 2 (WO2) White, a very nice guy. He had previously been an enlisted man, then went to flight school and eventually joined the Scouts. He had no ego.

White also enjoyed teaching us to fly, so he would hand control of the ship to the observer as soon as it was time to depart the AO.

We were returning to Chi Lang to refuel. We were casual about it, and the lead ship was probably three hundred yards ahead of us. For some reason, the lead pilot decide to take a shortcut, cutting between a mountain on our right and a small hill our left. The VC held the mountain, and it was against SOP to take this rout.

As we were cruising along, with me on the sticks, we noticed the lead ship suddenly dive to he left, then climb, then dive again. I looked at White as he said, "What was hat?" I told him I had no idea.

As soon as th words were out of my mouth, we started receiving fire from the mountain on our right. We could hear the pop, pop, pop, pop of a belt-fed machine gun as dove to the left and started zigzagging as fast as I could. The firing seemed to last forever. We waited for the sound of machine-gun rounds striking the ship but none did. We also noticed that we saw no tracers flying past the ship.

When the firing stopped, we understood what caused the lead ship to fly so erratically. However, we saw no tracers, and the lead crew did not call out that they were taking ire. We later found that they thought it would be a good joke for us to fly into he same thing and hope that Charlie's aim did not improve! We didn't think it was all that funny and told them not to pull that stunt gain.

Right after w refueled, we received a radio call that a Scout had been shot down, that one us had to return to the AO and initiate a three-ship rotation. White had not even turned the engine off yet, so he came up on the radio and told everyone that we would go back.

We took off, heading back to the border. I looked at White and said, "No shortcuts this time, right?" He said, "Roger fucking that," and we buzzed off.

We were less han ten minutes away from Chi Lang when I noticed a couple of drops of liqui running down the *inside* of the bubble, directly at eye level. I didn't know what it was, but I knew it wasn't supposed to be there. My eyes shifted to the lower instrument panel, where I saw a lot more drops sliding down the faces the instruments. The fluid was brown. It was oil. The only thing with any c near us was the transmission. The transmission was leaking oil! I looked over my shoulder at the transmission, just a foot or so away. As soon as I did, the seal on the transmission blew out, throwing warm oil into my face. Fortunately I had my visor down. Otherwise I would have been blinded.

Because my visor was covered with oil, I could not see a thing. I yelled into the intercom, "The transmission is blown. Set down right away!" White said something about the safety shaft and heading back to Chi Lang. I told him to forget it. I didn't want to see if the breakaway link really worked or not. I wanted down.

Because we were at 1,500 feet, it seemed to take forever to land. It was less than a minute but felt like an hour. As we headed down, White started giving a Mayday call and informed Apache-Six that we had lost our transmission and were landing about ten minutes south of Chi Lang.

When we landed and shut down, we could see that oil was all over the cargo compartment and the back of our seats. The seal had started blowing a small amount of oil forward, where we saw it, then failed completely. The transmission resembled a round hatbox about eighteen inches in diameter. The top of the tranny bolted to the top edge of the hatbox, and a large, circular seal kept the oil in its proper place. Usually. I had never heard of this happening before, so it wasn't something I suspected.

After an hour or so, Captain Sholtz, my old buddy from maintenance, and several other friends arrived in a LOH. Cpt. Sholtz commented on how rare it was for one of these seals to blow. He said that it was caused by an overfilled transmission and started accusing me of failing to check the oil level before the mission. Of course I would never fail to do that, and I corrected him. White came to my defense by telling Sholtz that we had *both* checked it, and the oil level was perfect before we took off. Sholtz relented.

Shortly thereafter, a slick came out and retrieved the LOH, White, and me. It had been an entertaining day, to say the least. I didn't know it at the time, but Sholtz and I would have another but less serious confrontation less than a week later.

Ricochets and Flying Mud

Another mission came up requiring us to operate close to Vinh Long. It was in the same general vicinity where we had found the large bunker after the Ninth Infantry Division was ambushed in the LZ.

I was flying with Cpt. Stark in the lead Loach when I spotted an armed VC hiding behind an elevated grave. This style of grave was popular in the Delta because the land flooded every year. The graves were concrete and similar to what you might find in New Orleans or on a Caribbean island.

As we approached, the VC slipped to the opposite side of the grave just as Stark began firing the minigun. As we flew past, I could see that he had pulled a grass mat over his body, trying to hide.

Stark made another run, and again the VC timed his jump and escaped behind the grave. Cort adjusted our path and ran the minigun over the grave, sending bullets bouncing everywhere. A tracer bounced off the grave right back at us. As I watched it come straight at me, it struck the left bubble just left of center and proceeded to exit the cabin through the left door. During its flight, I was mesmerized by the sight of it heading right for my forehead. Luckily, it missed me, but we had a large, jagged hole in the bubble. And we still had an armed Charlie waiting to get a shot at us.

I could not get a clear shot at him but suggested to Stark that we approach on an angle perpendicular to our previous gun run.

This did the trick.

When a minigun burst hits the ground, the dirt appears to boil. If the ground is moist or wet, the rounds can blow large chunks of earth and mud into the air, creating a small trench. This is especially true if the pilot keeps the Loach flying in a straight line. In this case, Cort flew the Loach dead straight, running the minigun rounds across the middle of the grass mat covering the VC. He was nearly hidden under the mat until the bullets struck.

As we flew past, I leaned out the door to provide covering fire. The VC appeared to have been cut in half just below his chest.

We swung around to make sure he was dead. He certainly was. The middle six inches of his torso was gone, turned into a red mass seeping into the ground. The AK-47 was smashed and the grass mat was off to the side, nearly severed in half. The scene looked like a gigantic chainsaw had descended from the sky and carved a trench across the spot where the VC lay.

We continued our patrol and found several sets of footprints in the mud of what had been a twenty-foot-wide canal. It was drying out, but the mud was still wet, making the footprints clearly visible. They led to one side of the canal and then disappeared.

Stark decided to "recon-by-fire" and see if we could get someone to fire back. He began a long gun run, during which he sprayed the side of the canal with minigun fire as we sped along at about eighty knots.

Because we were only six feet above the canal, the large chunks of mud blown into the air struck our ship at high speed, knocking softball- to basketball-sized holes into all four bubbles. The bubbles were almost gone, with as many holes as there was Plexiglas.

Where no hole existed, mud covered the glass, making it impossible to see.

As soon as our relief arrived, we headed back to Vinh Long. I told Stark he should land in the maintenance area and save us the effort of dragging the Loach over there for repair.

He radioed the tower, told them what we were doing, and asked them to radio our maintenance office and inform them.

When we pulled to a hover in the maintenance area, my second such trick in just a few days, Cpt. Sholtz was standing in front of the Loach tent with his arms crossed, staring at us. He did not look happy.

When we shut down and exited the ship, he approached and started chewing out Stark for blowing the bubbles out. Stark said something about us not having a choice because there were VC in the canal and we had to fire on them. Sholtz looked at me and gestured, indicating a "what the fuck" question. I just said, "Like Captain Stark said, VC in the canal," and began disarming and removing the minigun and ammo. Cpt. Sholtz continued his tirade as both Cort and I pretty much ignored him.

The Scout platoon truck showed up within a few minutes to pick us up. As we rode back to the line shack, Cort said, "Well, now we won't have to live with a crappy repair to that first bullet hole. They'll have to replace all the bubbles now."

I knew exactly what he meant. The typical repair for holes in the bubbles was to stitch in a piece of Plexiglas to cover the hole. It kept the wind out but created a distracting blind spot in the bubble. This was made worse by the safety wire used or the stitching, making a really ugly patch.

It occurred me that Cort probably had this all planned out when he decided to exect e the recon-by-fire gun run.

By this time, was accustomed to seeing mangled bodies and appreciated what a minigun ould do to a human being. I was quite thankful that Charlie did not have the or the ability to turn them on us.

Not long aft the ricochet-through-the-bubble incident, we were again working south o the Parrot's Beak. As Stark and I zigzagged over a paddy, one of the Cobra pi ts came up on the radio, telling us that an armed man was running to the st in a dry canal that we had just flown over.

That position d the man on Cort's side of the ship, so he began turning right. As he did , Six radioed, telling us to let the Cobras kill him, since they were the ones w spotted him.

Stark abortec is turn and headed for the edge of the paddy, maybe seventy meters from the nal.

While we fle over the tree line, parallel to the canal, the first Cobra rolled in and let loose ith its four wing-mounted miniguns.

Cobra-moun d miniguns were not restricted to the 2,000 rounds per minute limit, as r Loaches were. They could spit out 6,000 rounds per minute, an overwhelmin amount of firepower. The army reported that a Cobra could fly over a footb field at 150 feet of elevation and 150 knots of airspeed and place a bullet in every square foot of the field. I believed it.

From what w were seeing, this sounded like an understatement.

As the Cobr dove on the canal from about 1,000 feet and 180 knots, he opened fire. Th ntire canal bed appeared to be boiling. Small puffs of dust came up from t ground, carpeting the entire canal bed in a cloud of dust about eighteen i ches high. It was horrendous, and we thought the VC must have been killed

Not true, the an had crawled tight against the left canal bank. As soon as the Cobra stopp firing, we watched him jump up and start running toward the flooded can about a hundred meters away.

He was still r nning when the Cobra came around for a second run. Again,

Cpt. Cort Stark.

the canal and the man disappeared under a cloud of dust.

As soon as the Cobra ceased firing, the man jumped up and started running. Again, he had hidden against the bank of the canal and the miniguns missed him.

This time, Apache-Six told the Cobra pilot that he had missed his chance and ordered the second Cobra to make a run.

The second Cobra was armed with 2.75 rockets, and the pilot released them a little earlier than the previous miniguns had opened fire. Charlie did not hear any miniguns and kept running for the canal.

The first pair of rockets exploded about thirty meters behind the man but did not knock him down.

The second pair hit right next to him, with one rocket appearing to explode directly between his feet. He disappeared.

The third pair hit at the end of the dry canal, about twenty meters ahead of where the man had been, blowing huge chunks of mud and debris into the air.

Six told us to go down and confirm the kill. We dove to the canal and began to hover around the spot where we thought the body would be. Nothing. Charlie had disappeared in the proverbial flash.

We searched for another thirty seconds or so before I noticed a stump in the water of the flooded canal. I realized that there had been no trees around, so it could not be a stump.

I asked Cort to hover in that direction so I could inspect it more closely.

As soon as we got within twenty feet of the stump, I recognized that it certainly was not a stump; it was Charlie's remains.

It was burned black and was sitting in the shallow water at a forty-five-degree angle on what was left of his legs. They were both severed at the hips.

One arm was missing, as was his head. When we hovered over him, I could look down the tunnel that had been his neck. Inside his neck was the only place showing any blood. The exterior of his body had been completely charred by the blast. I could see why we both thought it was a stump.

Cort told Six and the Cobra pilots what we had found, then he asked me if I wanted to try to find the guy's head. I said, "Uh, no. I'm pretty sure he's dead," and we flew away. He was joking, of course.

Cort Stark, who was now our platoon leader, was the officer I came to admire most. Even though he was only three years older than I was, he became a father figure to me. As luck would have it, the majority of my most memorable and successful missions were carried out with Cpt. Stark in the right seat.

Japan

In early May, the time for my R&R arrived. I had chosen to go to Japan because I wanted to see a part of the Orient that had not been destroyed by (a recent) war.

Craig and I had planned to go together, so we coordinated our departure. We met in a place called camp Alpha, where we would prepare for our trip. We were allowed to travel in civilian clothes, so we bought khaki pants and short-sleeve sports shirts.

We left in the late evening. It was a direct, five-hour flight. What we did not know was the weather in Yokohama, Japan. We had not had to think about the weather for the past ten months, so it never occurred to us to plan for different conditions.

When we got off the plane, we were stunned to see that the weather was extremely cold – forty degrees, with a stiff wind blowing. No one had a jacket or sweater. I did not even have an undershirt on. My total protection was a short-sleeved cotton shirt designed for tropical wear.

We ran across the tarmac and into the travel center. Here you selected which city and hotel you wanted to visit while in Japan. The travel center provided a great deal of information on the various R&R destinations. The participating hotels in the destination cities offered an array of packages at varying price points. Travel center staff also offered many unofficial travel tips concerning which destinations catered to officers, which ones were safest, etc. We chose to stay in a moderately priced property in the city of Yokohama, thereby avoiding another flight to a distant city.

Once we made the selections, it was a matter of waiting for the designated bus.

The sun rose remarkably early: 4:45 a.m. This was a welcomed surprise because we wanted it to warm up as quickly as possible. As we rode a twenty-passenger minibus to the hotel, our guide had a young woman sing traditional Japanese folks songs to us. It was sweet, and we listened politely, but it wasn't exactly what we were looking for.

One of the GIs, an obnoxious, loudmouth redneck from somewhere in the South, was already drunk when he boarded the bus. After the serenade reached the fifteen-minute mark, this creep started yelling at the top of his lungs. He wanted to know "How much longer? Where's the hotel?" He was not yelling at anyone specific. He was yelling into space. The singing stopped.

The man appeared to be out of his mind. Fortunately, he was sitting in the front of the bus and we were in the rear. We did not have direct contact with him. I was embarrassed by his behavior.

After a few minutes of this tirade, he announced that he was sick and going to vomit. A mad scramble ensued, in which people tried to clear a path to the window so he could hurl outside.

We were on a freeway and probably doing seventy mph or more when he reached the window. He leaned out to his waist, so far that I thought he would fall out of the bus, then began Calling Ralph, as we called it in the Scouts.

Not only did he empty the contents of his stomach, he lost something valuable. "I lost my teeth. Stop the bus, goddammit! I puked out my f**ing teeth! Stop the bus!"

We did not stop. At the speed we were traveling, his false teeth probably shattered on impact or were crushed by one of the dozens of vehicles behind us.

After a few repetitions of his plea to stop the bus, he sat down with a thump and started crying. He kept this going for the remainder of the ride.

I looked at Craig and said, "Let's remember that guy. I don't want to be anywhere near him for the next week."

Japan turned out to be somewhat of a disappointment. It was far more modernized than I expected. It looked just like the US, except the people were shorter and the cars were smaller. It was also quite a bit more expensive than we had been led to believe.

I must have been envisioning Thailand when I thought about a trip to Japan.

The two-story hotel was actually a well-run and organized brothel. Everything could be arranged.

Craig and I toured the town and did a lot of walking. We went off the beaten path to see the less touristy parts of the city. While very interesting, communication was a problem. Very few people spoke English. Something as simple as ordering lunch became challenging.

In 1969, the restaurants in Japan had their dishes displayed in windows, similar to the way American stores display shoes in their windows. This allowed us to take the waitresses to the window and point out what we wanted.

It worked well until I tried to order dessert one evening. After finishing the entrée, I had the waitress accompany me to the window. I pointed to a piece of pastry covered in whipped cream.

The server looked at me with a puzzled expression and tilted her head as if to say, "Are you sure?"

I nodded my head in agreement and we returned to our table.

A few moments later, my dessert arrived. She stood to the side as I sliced off a sizeable portion with my fork and plopped it into my mouth.

My stomach and I panicked! Whatever it was, it was certainly not a pastry. It tasted like rotten fish. What I thought was whipped cream was some sort of bitter sauce. Now I had a mouthful of something I could not possibly swallow.

I gagged and simultaneously lost my breath. I could not inhale because my mouth was full, and the taste/smell had worked its way into my nose. I could not locate my napkin.

After watching eight to ten seconds of me flailing around and gurgling, the waitress came to my rescue by handing me a napkin that she had been dutifully holding as I attempted to poison myself. I quickly formed a small pocket in the napkin and transferred the poison mass from my mouth to the napkin. I struggled to catch my breath.

When I finally did, I caught a glimpse of Craig. He was sitting there with his mouth open, in awe of the scene before him. He was frozen in place.

I uttered, "Thanks. Thank you," and bowed my head to the waitress. She tried to stifle a laugh but had a hard time doing it.

I requested another beer and attempted to wash the taste out of my mouth. When she brought us the check, she politely pointed at the dessert, wagged her finger, and politely said, "No. No. No," as if trying to warn a four-year-old about a hot stove.

I did not order any more pastry in Japan.

On another evening, in the hotel bar, a GI sat down and we started to chat. He told me that he had just been released from rehab after recovering from a shrapnel wound. He went on to say that he was with the Ninth Infantry Division and had been wounded in the Delta.

I asked him when and where he had been hit. He said they had been searching for a VC hospital on such-and-such a date and that the VC had ambushed them in the LZ as they were awaiting extraction.

Apparently he had been wounded in the ambush that Sewell and I had helped break up when we found that huge bunker.

Here we were several weeks later and nearly 3,000 miles from the Delta, and we run into each other in a bar.

We exchanged memories, and I told him about finding the bunker. He had never seen it. I told him I was with A-Troop and we had Apache heads on our aircraft.

He said he remembered seeing the Apache head just before he passed out in the Huey that was evacuating him to the hospital.

One of my more surprising R&R experiences was my reaction to a shopping trip. We took a bus downtown to where many large department stores were located. I was mesmerized by the colors of the various goods on display. As we walked around the stores, I could not prevent myself from touching many of the clothes and other items, simply to see what they felt like. I came across a set of inflatable, nearly transparent vinyl furniture. I thought it was one of the most remarkable things I had ever seen.

I was surprised by my reaction. I kept stopping and touching items. This drew some strange stares. After seeing only green material and wooden, homemade furniture for ten months, I had forgotten what real furniture and normal clothes looked like.

When I returned to Vinh Long, Sgt. Smith informed me that I had guard duty that night. I was pissed because I would not have a chance to tell my buddies about R&R and the stuff I had seen there.

Smith went on to say there had been a considerable amount of VC activity in the area and we were trying something new tonight.

When I went to Guard Mount, the little gathering where the sergeant and officer of the guard make sure you are not drunk or missing any vital equipment, I noticed that another Apache Scout was there as well. This was odd, because only one individual from the Scout platoon pulled guard duty on any given night.

After the adults gave us their routine briefing and rules of engagement, he asked which of us were the Scouts. My companion, who shall remain nameless, and I raised our hands and yelled out.

He then told us that we would be assigned to a listening post outside the wire and to take a PRC-25 radio with us.

I wanted to yell, "What the fuck? Listening post? Outside the wire!" My companion told me that he had the same assignment about a week ago and didn't think much of it.

When the truck taking us out reached Bunker 9, we exited and went through a concealed gateway in the barbed wire. Approximately two hundred feet beyond the wire was a two-man fighting position that we were to occupy for the night. If we heard anything suspicious or saw any VC movement, we were to report back to the Ops Center, and they would decide what to do.

As we lay on the hard, dry ground and watched the sun go down, my companion pulled a joint from his pocket and lit up! He offered me a tug, which I refused, saying, "What in the fuck are you doing, man? We're outside the wire!"

I was amazed at his casual attitude and thought he was going to get me killed.

I took the first two-hour watch and woke him up at midnight for his two hours. You only half sleep when you're on your break, so you usually hear things around you and can be wide awake instantly if you need to be.

My sixth sense told me my two hours were up, but he had not awakened me. My first thought was he was giving me a break because I had just flown in from Japan. However, I soon saw that he was dead asleep and had slept through my wake-up call.

It was now 2:15, and I was as mad as a hornet. With him asleep, there was absolutely nothing preventing Charlie from coming up and slitting our throats. We were too far away from the guard tower and other bunkers for someone there to notice anything short of gunfire. We were pretty much on our own.

I asked if he wanted me to tuck him in, or was he OK to go nighty night? He got the point and woke up.

About two hours later, I got a small measure of revenge.

A couple of guys about three hundred yards east of us and inside the wire had spotted several armed VC slipping through the tree line. Under orders not to fire on them, they were told that a gunship was being dispatched. Listening on the PRC-25 radio, I thought this was a huge overkill, but what did I know? I've only been here ten months! I knew all hell was about to break loose but decided to let my companion sleep.

The Charlie-model gunship initiated his gun run about three hundred meters to our left and directed his fire over our heads at the VC located about three hundred yards to our right. This meant he would fly directly over our position when he was near the middle of his run. It was going to get loud.

Charlie models were not as fast or as loud as a Cobra. There was a little less sound to give you a warning before the rockets cut loose.

When he released his first pair of rockets, it sounded like he was inside the little bunker with us. The first rockets landed seconds later, sending out twin explosions that shook the ground. More rockets followed as the miniguns and door gunners opened up.

At this point, the ground was in a nearly continuous shake and roll as the explosions went off just seconds apart. My companion jumped up in sheer terror, unaware of what was happening and started yelling, "INCOMING! INCOMING!"

Of course it wasn't. I dragged him back down and into our fighting position. Otherwise, one of the door gunners might spot him and open fire. I have no idea if they knew we were down there or not, but I was not taking any chances.

As I was pulling him down, thousands of rounds of expended shell casings began raining down on us. These were the 7.62mm shell casings from the miniguns and door gunners' M-60s. The shells were falling at about a hundred miles per hour and were too hot to touch. They hurt when they struck us.

My companion jumped up and began yelling "Incoming" again, as if somebody could hear him. I told him what was happening and demanded that he lie still. He was still disoriented, but I did not want him to draw fire from the gunship, which might make a second run. I only had about sixty days to go.

Sure enough, the gunship came around for a second go. Flares were up this time, so we huddled in the little bunker and stayed as motionless as possible. By now, my companion knew where he was and what was happening.

As soon as the show was over, he wanted to know why I had not awakened him before the firing began.

I told him that I had thought about it but decided not to. I did not want to disturb his sleep again.

He had no trouble remaining awake for the rest of the night.

THE U MINH

"The Killer Awoke Before Dawn. He Put His Boots On"

The Doors, "The End"

The day, in mid-April 1969, had an unusual start. Rather than a sunrise takeoff, Apache Troop lifted off ninety minutes earlier. The eastern horizon wasn't showing even a hint of pink as our thirteen helicopters cruised south at 1,500 feet and eighty knots. The sky was pitch-black and the horizon invisible because the ground was equally black. No streetlights in the Delta. And that's what bothered me. Looking down, I could not distinguish solid ground from the rivers or wooded areas. There were no stars, and the moon was hidden by clouds. If our ship had a mechanical failure, picking out a safe landing spot would be impossible. If we were lucky enough to land in one piece, the other crews might never find us. You didn't want to be on the ground at night in the Delta. That had recently happened to a Cobra crew from B-Troop. They silently dropped out of formation and were never seen again. Charlie really did own the night.

I felt pretty confident about the prospects of a successful mission. The pilot was someone I had teamed with on several missions: Captain Cort Stark. A few weeks earlier, we had racked up our first confirmed kill together, working just south of the infamous Parrot's Beak. To make it even more memorable, we broke off from the rest of the Scout team and captured a VC flag I had spotted just before finding and killing a VC.

The pilot was a captain, and I was a Spec-5. Regardless of the gap in our ranks, Cpt. Stark often asked for my opinion when scouting an LZ, guessing the age of muddy footprints and VC fighting positions, or asking for directions to a specific spot in the AO. I was a good shot and had a reputation as a great grenade man. We made a good team – a duet – and would become a deadly duet.

We arrived on the Ca Mau Peninsula just as the sun broke above the horizon. The clouds had vanished. The sky was azure blue and the dry rice paddies a dull gold. The four slicks, four Cobras, and the other two Loaches departed for the staging area. The commanding officer of A-Troop, Apache-Six, took his command-and-control (C&C) ship to 2,000 feet so he could view the operation. The remaining two Cobras began orbiting the AO at 1,500 feet, out of small arms range, but low enough to dive on any significant targets the Scouts found.

I was flying the ship on the transit from the base and nosed over into a steep dive that would take us from 1,500 feet to the deck, about six feet above the grass. The enlisted men always flew to and from the AO to let the pilots sit back, smoke, and relax by listening to AFRN: Armed Forces Radio Network. Each Scout pilot would be under extreme stress for the next two hours. Giving them a break by having the crew chief or observer get some stick time was well worth it. Over time, the observers would be taught to land the ship in the event the pilot was shot, a fairly common event in the Scout platoon.

I handed the controls over to Cpt. Stark when we were about a hundred feet above the ground. We spotted a hooch and began a rhythmic slalom motion at ground level, swinging back and forth and moving at about five to ten knots. While I leaned far out the left door looking for tracks, Cpt. Stark looked out the right door, flying the Loach by pure feel.

The wing Loach began its nauseating high-low, elliptical orbit.

The sickening routine was needed to cover the lead Loach. If the lead ship received fire, the wing Loach would dive at the source of the fire as the lead ship pulled away. The wing Loach always circled to the right for two reasons.

First, the rotors' orque made right turns easier and faster. Second, by turning right, the pilot could look out his door and keep the lead ship constantly within his vision.

This continued for about an hour, during which our Loach hovered around the tree line that surrounded a field containing a house or hooch. Despite the hooch being relatively new and this area of the province designated a free-fire zone, we could find no signs of VC activity. The pilot flew over to the hooch so I could drop a Willie Pete grenade on it and burn it down. As we flew away from the hooch, the pilot turned over the controls and I flew the ship to the refueling point.

All thirteen ships sat on the ground while the officers discussed the next part of the mission. Our Loach sat near the front of the line, while all the officers and warrant officers huddled about thirty feet outside my door, looking at maps. I was still strapped into the left seat and taking advantage of the idle time to eat some canned pears, my favorite item on the C ration menu.

Just as I tossed the empty can aside, Cpt. Stark yelled over and gave me the crank sign, indicating that he wanted me to start the engine and get the ship ready to go. The other officers made a joke about letting the crew chief start the ship. Stark said something funny in return, but I couldn't hear it. I pulled on my flame-retardant flight gloves, reached down and switched the battery to the on position, checked all the instruments and circuit breakers, and hit the starter button.

The small turbine engine began its high-pitch whine, and within seconds the four aluminum blades were cutting through the air at 400 rpm, fast enough that they were nearly invisible.

As we took off and Stark guided the ship to cruising altitude, he keyed the intercom mic and said, "We're going into the U Minh. Make sure you know the way back. If I get hit, fly me straight back to the hospital. Don't land in here, no matter what Apache-Six tells you to do. This place is bad."

The U Minh was considered the southernmost rallying point from the Ho Chi Minh Trail. Located on the Ca Mau Peninsula, the name translates to "forest of darkness." The VC had bases there and the NVA frequented the area.

During the French Indochina War, a battalion of 500 French paratroopers jumped into the forest. They were never heard from again. They became the Lost Battalion in Vietnamese lore. As late as September 11, 1971, the *Lewiston Daily Sun* (Maine) reported a major battle between the ARVN and VC/NVA regulars in which 1,500 communists and 50 ARVNs were killed. The Dark Forest was never wrestled from communist control.

Stark then turned up the volume on the music, slouched back in his seat, and started taking potshots at the boats on the canal, 1,500 feet below. He was using his .38 revolver, a worthless weapon that all the pilots carried. At that altitude, hitting the canal was nearly impossible. By the time the bullets hit the ground, they were probably only falling under the force of gravity. The locals in the boats probably didn't even know they were being shot at! I could see no rounds splash into the canal.

The pilot invited me to take a turn. When I accepted, Stark took the stick and moved the Loach to the right side of the canal, giving me a better angle out the left door.

I pointed my .45 caliber model 1911 pistol out the left door and squeezed.

The entire Loach seemed to explode! I was deaf. Stark came out of his seat. His mouth was moving, but I could hear nothing.

The muzzle of the .45 was inside the door when the shot went off. It was still inside the cabin and not in the slipstream, like Stark's .38 was when he fired. The muzzle blast was confined to the cabin and the pressure was horrendous. I squeezed my nose and cleared my ears. Hearing returned, but slowly. Stark laughed as he handed over the controls and said, "Let's not try *that* again!"

After about ten minutes I could see coming up on the southwestern horizon a dark green mass that stretched from left to right as far as I could see: the U Minh Forest.

Just before gliding over the canal that surrounded the forest from the surrounding paddies, Cpt. Stark reminded me, "This is a free-fire zone. Hit anything you see moving." My optimism sank a little because free-fire zones were notorious for their lack of activity during daylight.

That thought was flushed from my mind as I saw a man with an AK-47 running away about fifty feet below us. I yelled, "Got a man! Break left!" We were not even fifty meters inside the forest.

Cort flung the ship into a hard left as I fired a short burst at the man. We were higher than normal because of the tall trees that made up this part of the U Minh. The man, dressed in an outfit I had never seen before, a blue-green top that looked like a hooded sweatshirt and khaki trousers, jumped into a narrow, deep ditch. His helmet went flying and landed beside the ditch. He held an AK-47 underneath him as he lay facedown in the bottom of the dry ditch.

As we circled at treetop level about fifty feet above the ground, I was having a tough time getting a clear shot at what I determined was an NVA soldier. The trees kept deflecting the bullets, sending the tracers spraying and bouncing among the trees. The ditch was deep and only as wide as the man's shoulders. I had to be at just the right angle to shoot down into the ditch effectively. I saw one of the rounds strike the man in the lower portion of his face. As it did, my CAR-15 jammed. I yelled, "I'm jammed," and Cort put the Loach into a hard right climbing turn.

I removed the magazine, cleared the jam, and was loading a fresh magazine when I heard Stark say, "Nine o'clock level. Quick! Quick." He was remarkably calm, giving no hint of the seriousness of the situation.

I looked to the left and saw we were hovering about six feet off the ground and about twenty feet from a tree line. Between us and the tree line was a muddy canal, about fifteen feet wide. Stepping out of the trees and onto the far bank of the canal were two NVA soldiers wearing those weird blue-green shirts and struggling with the shoulder straps of their AK-47s. They were obviously surprised by the proximity of the Loach as they fumbled with their weapons.

In one motion, I thumbed the release button and the spring-loaded bolt slammed a round into the chamber, slipped the safety into the full-auto position, and emptied the magazine in the direction of the two soldiers. While firing, I felt the ship lurch skyward as Stark executed a full-power, right pedal turn, spinning the Loach to the right and accelerating into a steep climb. After less than two seconds of fire, my CAR-15 was empty again.

I reloaded, and we were over the guy in the ditch. He was crawling rapidly but unable to extricate himself from the ditch; the shot to the face had taken a toll. The pilot lined up the Loach for a clear shot. I finished off the NVA with a short burst that struck the man in the middle of his back and the back of his head.

As Stark swung into a right turn, he said, "Let's go check the guys by the canal." Within seconds, I was into the scene that would come back to haunt me twenty years later.

We approached at about twenty feet high, doing fifty knots. The scene was so vivid that it would compare to today's HD TV: high contrast, crisp focus, saturated colors. The water in the canal was a light caramel and the mud on the bank was a dry, dusty brown. The undergrowth of the woods was dark green.

Stretching from one bank to the other was a huge, bright red stain that contrasted strongly with the caramel-colored water. Floating facedown in the middle of the stain were the two NVA soldiers, their blue-green shirts giving the scene a Christmas-like tone. One helmet floated motionless between the soldiers, who were dead. The water was like a mirror – not a ripple. The red stain, clearly blood, was shockingly huge, so huge I had a hard time believing it *was* blood. There was so much of it. Everything appeared to be in ultra-slow motion. I watched the canal disappear in the distance as Cpt. Stark said, "You ruined their day."

For years I wondered why we were hovering so low near the canal. I never got the answer because I forgot to ask Cort why. Had we been hovering at treetop level, Stark probably would not have seen the two NVA emerge from the forest. The NVA would have had a clear shot at the belly of the Loach. They would have hit either the engine, the fuel tanks, us, or all four. Stark had made a small, simple choice to hover just above the ground, and we were both alive because of it.

The patrol continued for about an hour. As we flew around, I saw the reason that Stark had ordered me not to land if he was hit. Every clearing that was large enough to accommodate a helicopter was surrounded by numerous so-called spider holes, foxholes that had small, camouflaged roofs. This made them hard to see unless you were right on top of them, as we were. We then headed back to a small camp to refuel. Another team of Scouts and Cobras took over but did not report any activity.

The minigun did not need to be reloaded, as it had not been used. But my CAR-15 magazines certainly did. I had emptied five of them and now had to go through the ordeal of loading each one by hand. Because the then-standard twenty-round clips could only be loaded with eighteen rounds, I was going to load a total of ninety rounds by hand. Not good for the fingertips.

After ninety minutes of rest, we lifted off and headed south again. I did not know what to expect. The earlier contact was a surprise because I wasn't that familiar with the U Minh. Would we be equally lucky or just cruise around, burning JP-4?

Upon entering the forest at a different point – you didn't fly over the same route twice – we began searching a large canal. From its width of about fifty feet, it was obviously one of the major thoroughfares in the forest.

Less than five minutes in, I spotted something I had not seen before; it looked like a huge plastic bag full of something important, probably rice. It was about six or seven feet in diameter, tied off at the top, and partially buried in a large hole. The dirt around the hole was fresh, indicating that whoever was trying to bury the bag had just left, with the job unfinished.

I then had one of those embarrassing experiences that added a little humor to the situation.

As we flew circles around the tree at about thirty feet off the ground, Stark agreed that it probably was rice and it was an NVA food store. Someone decided to let the Cobras destroy it with rockets, after I marked it with a smoke grenade.

The pilot pulled the Loach to a stop, then slipped it sideways to the left so I could drop the grenade on the bag. I leaned out the door, grenade in hand, ready to drop. Suddenly the Loach started going to the right! We were still over the canal. I tossed the grenade with a weak, left-handed flip motion. I knew it was not going to make it, but the pilot did not want to get closer to the bag, suspecting it might contain something more dangerous than rice.

The grenade plopped into the water, right beside the tree but twenty feet from the bag. From underwater, the spewing smoke turned into a red dye, creating a beautiful bull's-eye right beside the tree. Stark said, "Nice shot."

He radioed the Cobras and asked if they could see the red circle. They replied, "Yes. We're coming in hot. Move it."

Both our Loach and our wingman pulled away and orbited the scene at about five hundred feet, ready for the show.

Both Cobras rolled in, firing four or six rockets each. The tree and bag disappeared in fountains of dirt, fire, and smoke. Even from more than five hundred feet away, the concussions were strong.

We dove back to where the bag used to be and saw that the top had been blown away. The area around the tree, now a stump, was peppered with thousands of rice grains, making it look like someone had been throwing confetti.

We pulled away. All I could think about was my hope that everyone would soon forget that terrible grenade drop. I had a reputation to maintain.

As we went further west along the canal, we drew back into the deeper part of the forest and saw another sight new to us: bamboo and wooden sidewalks, running between a dozen or more hooches. It was a large NVA camp, obviously intended to be permanent. The communists operated VC training camps in the U Minh, and several American POWs had been held in the forest. Nick Rowe, a Green Beret captured in 1963, had been liberated from the U Minh in late '68 by a Loach and Cobra from B-Troop.

The camp was no longer occupied, and there were no signs of recent activity. We turned back toward the canal when the radio lit up. "You've got a male running away from you at seven o'clock," one of the Cobra pilots reported.

I looked left, saw a VC sprinting away, and said, "I got him!" The man was about 150 feet away and running hard, away from the Loach.

Stark put the Loach into a hard right-hand turn, which would cause the runner to disappear from sight behind our tail boom and tail rotor. Before that could happen, I stuck the CAR-15 out the door, pointed it at the guy with my right hand, and pulled the trigger. About four rounds came out and it jammed again.

WO2 Jones, the pilot of the wing Loach, yelled, "Damn! You hit him."

Now the big right turn was complete, and we were looking straight down at a dead NVA. One of the rounds had struck him in the left side of his head, killing him instantly.

The CAR-15 was small and light and capable of being fired with one hand, like a pistol. By leaning out the door and simply pointing it at the runner, I had pulled off what had to be one of the luckiest shots in the history of warfare.

After leaving another dead NVA behind, we returned to the canal and continued our search. The canal ran into a larger clearing, giving us a little more space to maneuver. While zigging and zagging to inspect the canal banks, we approached a small, elongated, wooded island in the middle of the canal. It was a couple of hundred feet long and twenty to twenty-five feet wide. The center of the island was sparsely covered with trees, creating a small, cleared area that ran along its banks, like a perimeter footpath.

Cpt. Stark gained enough altitude to skim over the forty-foot trees while maintaining about thirty knots of airspeed.

As we passed over the last tree on the west end of the island, I spotted about twenty NVA asleep in the cleared area. "I got twenty men! Break left! Break left! Break left!" I leaned out the door and sprayed them with the CAR-15. They were still asleep when I opened fire. They had not heard the Loach as it flew fifty feet overhead.

At that low speed, it was more of a pedal turn than a break. I reloaded and continued firing while Stark put the Loach in a short, shallow dive and opened up with the minigun. Again, a feeling of great calm came over me. I wasn't excited. It was like I was watching a movie of us in action.

The noise was horrendous. The minigun could spit out 2,000 rounds a minute, shooting a five-foot fireball out the muzzle as long as the pilot held the trigger. As we went over, I dropped the red smoke grenade on the group and fired my CAR-15 to cover our climb to the right. Jones in the wing Loach dove on the red smoke and let loose his minigun. The clearing looked like it was boiling and spitting fire as the bullets kicked up dust and the tracers bounced off the ground and the trees.

The NVA, trying to get organized, were either falling down or darting from one direction to another, probably trying to find their weapons, when the Cobras struck.

When the first Cobra dove in, the pilot fired a long volley of 2.75-inch rockets – maybe sixteen or twenty. The entire end of the island where the NVA were scrambling erupted into a ten-second series of explosions that shook the ground. Small ripples radiated away from the island and through the still, muddy water, creating a weird visual.

As soon as the explosions stopped, the second Cobra hit the island with his chin-mounted minigun and more rockets. That end of the island completely disappeared in the smoke and dust. Basketball-sized clumps of earth – and men – flew into the water.

When the smoke cleared, there was no movement or return gunfire. The NVA were all dead.

Apache-Six told us to go back down and assess the situation.

At first, we circled the island, flying at about eighty knots so as to be a hard-to-hit target. There were no signs of NVA who might have reached the partial safety of the thin woods. No one was attempting to swim away. Cpt. Stark made one quick pass over the end of the island, seeing more dead bodies than we could accurately count. Because of the mess caused by the rockets and miniguns, it was sometimes difficult to tell where one body ended and another began. Nothing moved or made a sound. All we could hear was the whirring sound from the Loach transmission, two feet behind our heads.

I turned to Cpt. Stark, flipped up my helmet visor, and said, "Wow." Stark said, "Take it" and leaned back into his seat for the ride back to the refueling point.

The Loaches landed at the fuel bladders. Both Tom Gery, the observer in the wing ship, and I hopped out and began pumping jet fuel into the ships' tanks. When done, we jumped back in, and the pilots moved the ships to a safe distance from the bladders. If a Chinook happened to come in for fuel, their rotor wash would blow the little Loaches over and roll them away like beach balls.

After shutting the engines down, I met Tom Gery at the ammo point. I took a look at Tom and said, "Man, you've been hit in the head! Lie down." I saw blood streaming from a dozen or more small wounds on the left side of Tom's face. The wounds were the size of BBs, and the entire left side of his face, including his nose, was pouring blood. Tom looked like rats had been feasting on his face.

When the bleeding eventually stopped, Tom explained the wounds.

"When we rolled in on the island I got so excited I accidently hit the minigun barrels when I fired my CAR-15. I shot a couple holes into the barrels of our minigun. Every time Jones fired the minigun, the bullets knocked little chunks of steel off of the barrels and they flew into my face."

Seeing me hovering over Tom and his bloody face, Jones and Cpt. Stark ran over to see what was going on. After a few choice cavalry expletives, we all started laughing and joked Tom about a self-inflicted wound. Stark leaned over and said, "I bet you were flying with your visor up, weren't you? Uh-huh. Uh-huh. They put that thing on your flight helmet for a reason, son. Use it next time." Tom was incredibly lucky that a chuck of steel had not struck his eyes.

When the other team of Loaches and Cobras returned to the refueling point, again having made no contact, it was time to crank up and head back to Vinh Long for the night. We had at least a one-hour flight, and it would be dark soon. We needed to get back before sunset.

When all thirteen ships had reached 1,500 feet, Apache-Six radioed the A-Troop tactical operations center, or TOC, with the report on the day's action. It was brief.

"A-Troop engaged several NVA regulars, mostly in small groups. Friendlies took no, repeat no casualties. Expended approximately twelve thousand rounds of 7.62, four dozen 2.75s, resulting in approximately thirty enemy killed. Also destroyed was one *very, very* large . . . bag of rice. Roger that. A bag of rice."

Upon our return to Fort Apache, we were greeted as heroes. Men from other platoons came over to offer their congratulations. Apache Troop's first sergeant (Top) came by with two six-packs of beer. Cpt. Lytle, my Christmas drinking buddy, came by to shake hands. It was an overwhelming moment for a twenty-year-old who believed in the war effort.

I had established a new kill record for a single sortie. It did not last long. Another U Minh raid was undertaken the next day, and Steve Holmes exceeded my KBA count by one.

One aspect of our U Minh raids that I found disturbing was that the US Army had declared this area as one that was "pacified and secured."

On Sunday mornings, the Armed Forces Vietnam Network (AFVN) broadcast a thirty-minute show called "Delta Nine." Produced by the Ninth Infantry Division Office of Public Affairs, the show reported on the activities of the division within the Mekong Delta region. Because we listened to the radio practically around the clock, we often heard this broadcast. I remembered distinctly that the show routinely carried glowing reports of how the division had cleared the U Minh Forest, and that the area was now safe for civilian settlement. This was my first personal exposure to the US Army's lies concerning the actual events of the war. When I heard another such report after I participated in the raid, I didn't know if I should laugh or cry.

My good friends Tom Gery (left) and Dave Raymond (right), returning from a mission. Both men wear armored vests (Chicken Plates) and carry the Colt CAR-15 automatic carbine.

SHORT

"I'm so short I can't see over my boot-tops!"

Anonymous GI

On June 24t we reached the thirty-days mark. Three of us knew we would be receivir our DEROS orders soon and would then know the exact date of our retur home.

We continu to perform our scheduled duties as required. When we reached the fifte -day mark, Vern, Dave, and I took ourselves out of the flight rotation. We ha done enough, and nothing good would come from taking more chances. F sh in our minds was the fate of Cpt. Cannon. He continued to fly up to the s ven-day mark and ended up being killed. Nobody wanted to end the tour lik hat.

Then, with n warning, I stopped receiving mail from Norma. Other mail was arriving, so knew the army had not cut off my mail. I feared the worst. I thought, *How uld she stick by me for eleven months, then ditch me when I'm two weeks f m home?* I knew that her mother had been trying to get her to dump m nd had spoken against me often. Had she finally won the argument?

As the days nt by, I got more and more angry when no letters showed up. After not re iving a reply to my many inquiries, I was on the verge of writing her a re rse Dear John letter when a letter from my folks arrived.

They explained that Norma had been stricken with rheumatic fever and was seriously ill. I was relieved at first but then concerned. I did not know what rheumatic fever was, but it sounded serious.

We received our DEROS orders with about ten or twelve days to go. Each of us got a three-day drop, meaning we would be departing Vietnam on July 21st, not the 24th. This was great news.

When we reached seven days, we would begin the clearing post process. This meant visiting the various administrative offices, turning in our weapons, and making sure that all of our payroll and personnel records were up-to-date.

But boredom raised its deadly head again.

The day before we were to begin the clearing process, Dave Raymond decided he wanted to fly one more mission. He attempted to talk Vern and me into flying with him, so we could all fly our last combat mission together.

Nice thought. Vernon and I both said, "NO!" and refused to even consider the idea.

Dave was all-in, and I helped him strap into the Loach the next morning. I was not required to do that. My replacement had arrived, and I was now retired from normal duties. However, I wanted to be there before the takeoff and wish Dave luck.

Dave knew that I thought he was foolishly tempting fate to get one more adrenaline fix.

A-Troop was again working from Vinh Long and did not have to go far to get to the AO. After an hour or so, we could hear radio traffic, indicating that they had located several VC and were in the process of engaging them. I felt like throwing up.

Within a few minutes, we heard that one of the Loaches had been hit and was on the way back to Vinh Long.

When the ship landed, I recognized it as Dave's. It did not look good. The top half of the left bubble had been shot away. The bulkhead behind Dave's seat appeared to have five or six bullet holes in it.

Dave was sitting upright in the seat and did not appear to be injured. When he stepped out of the ship, I could see that the rounds that had hit the bulkhead had passed through the armor plate and Dave's seat before blowing out the left bubble.

I could not understand why Dave was not hit. Then he told me what had happened.

While flying the lead Loach, he had seen an armed VC jump into a spider hole as they flew by. Dave could not get a shot, so the pilot, Sewell, swung the Loach around so Dave could line up a clear shot.

As they hovered over the spider hole and Dave opened fire, Charlie opened fire with his AK-47, striking the Loach and blowing Dave's seat away. Because Dave was leaning out the door to take his shot, he was no longer in the seat, and bullets passed through without touching him.

The VC was a poor shot. He was shooting at Dave's back but missed by two feet. Dave dropped red smoke, and the Cobras took care of the rest.

Dave said he had lost visual contact with the man as they executed their 180-degree turn to swing around. During that time, Charlie left his original hole and jumped into another one just six or eight feet away.

While the Loach hovered and Dave leaned out to fire on the first spider hole, he was presenting his back to the VC, only thirty feet away from him. Dave was firing into the wrong hole!

Charlie opened up with his AK-47, blowing up Dave's seat and the bubble. Fortunately, Dave was leaning out the door, so the AK rounds passed behind him and into the Loach. How Charlie missed was anyone's guess, but he did.

Dave laughed throughout telling this story. The incident had made a big impression on him, and he remained in a giggly mood for the rest of the evening.

Just after the barracks lights went down at bedtime, I yelled over to Dave and asked him if he was planning to fly again the next day. All I heard was, "No fucking way!"

Even a year later, when we were telling war stories at Ft. Knox, Dave could not tell the story without breaking into a sustained laugh. Reacting to trauma with humor was a pattern for each of us.

When we neared the seven-day mark, the army had another surprise for

Dave and me: guard duty one more time. This time we would be at the line shack, not in a fighting position or bunker on the perimeter.

The night was peaceful until 2 a.m., when we heard someone running across the PSP refueling pads behind our line shack. They were speaking Vietnamese and it was unmistakable. We went behind the shack and knelt to frame the runners against the barracks lights in the background. Sure enough, four VC were sprinting toward the west and stumbling over the PSP pads.

We reported it to the Ops Center, and they dispatched the officer of the day. We could not fire on them because we only had our pistols, and stray rounds could travel across the compound and strike the barracks buildings.

We were kneeling behind the shack when the OD pulled up behind us in a jeep. He had his headlights on, making Dave and me perfect targets. We yelled at him to kill the lights, which he did. He walked up behind us, and I saw that he was a second lieutenant. He had that little gold bar proudly stitched into his jungle fatigue collar.

By now, we had lost sight of the VC. They were headed west the last time we saw them, then they disappeared into the tall grass of a marsh that separated our area from the main runway.

I had never seen a second lieutenant before. They didn't exist in aviation units because all of the pilots made first lieutenant following flight school.

He then said, "What are you guys waiting for?"

Dave said, "Sir?"

The lieutenant motioned toward the tall grass and said, "Go in there and get them."

Dave started laughing.

I said, "Sir, how long have you been here?"

He said, "I got here last week."

I said, "Well, the specialist and I are clearing post today. We have seven days to go. There is no way we are chasing four VC through that grass with only our .45s and one clip of ammo."

He realized the stupidity of his order and said, "Oh. Yes. I see. That probably would not be a great idea. As you were."

We informed him that the grass where the men had disappeared ran into a culvert that went under the wire and outside the perimeter. We told him that the men had probably already exited and pointed out where the culvert intersected the wire. Before he drove away, we suggested that he and his driver not try to capture those guys.

He said, "OK. Thank you."

One of the experiences that had stuck with me ever since our first day on Vinh Long was how those guys in the faded fatigues and worn-out boots had treated us. It was evident from our new clothes that we were the newest guys on the block. They even had a universal term for it: FNGs, or Fucking New Guys.

I decided to get a little revenge, not on any FNGs, but on those individuals who *thought* they were short.

All I needed to do was replace my old jungle fatigues with new ones by going to the supply room and exchanging them – a process called DX-ing.

I went to the supply room and picked up a new ball cap, a pair of jungle boots, and spanking-new jungle fatigues.

When the three of us began walking between the various offices and tents we were required to visit, many GIs would look at me and say, "Hey, buddy, how many days you got left?" They always expected me to say, "Three hundred, plus."

Then Dave and Vern would jump in the guy's face, tell them that we were clearing post, and return the question. No matter what the number was, we would tease the GI and ask him if he really thought he would live that long. We would say, "No way, GI. You'll be dead *way* before that!"

While clearing post, we went into resort mode. While we were still on the A-Troop roster, we had no duties. We would spend a couple hours completing our office visits, then crawl to the roof of a bunker, strip to our skivvies, and soak up some sun. As soon as 5 p.m. rolled around and our refreshment stand opened for business, one of us would go down and fetch some cold beer. Life was good.

Late one afternoon, as we returned to the barracks, John Tillery, an observer from Texas, asked if we had heard the news. We said, "No, what news?"

Tillery then told us that he had heard about some trouble in the Congo, and the US was planning to send troops to put down the riots and violence. He went on to say the army would be supplying 10,000 troops to Africa, and they were planning to take experienced combat veterans straight from Nam to the Congo. This would likely include us, because all three of us had another full year of active duty.

We could not believe it. John had Doug Dietrich, one of our crew chiefs, verify that they had heard it on Doug's small black-and-white TV, the same TV on which we would later watch the replay of the moon landing.

John had us going for over an hour. The more we thought about it, the angrier we got.

He knew that the story would not hold up for long, so he eventually told us that it was BS. He just wanted to give us a hard time. We were now pissed at John. We held him down and covered him in shaving cream, knowing that the showers were out of water. He would have to sleep in the gooey mess.

Dave and Vernon "Clearing Post".

DEPARTURE

"True happiness is . . . to enjoy the present, without anxious dependence upon the future."

Lucius Annaeus Seneca

After we watched the moon landing replay, an event that did not impress us at the time, departure day arrived. We were all packed, said our goodbyes, and asked White to fly us to Bien Hoa in Vernon's Loach.

Before takeoff, we took three smoke grenades from the shack. Once in the air, White radioed the control tower and requested permission for a flyby.

We circled the pattern at four hundred feet before White dove for the center of the runway. As we screamed down the runway at a roaring eighty-five knots, the three of us held the smoking grenades out the door, trailing smoke in the finest Scout tradition. Of course, without flight gloves, the grenades became very hot and we ended up dropping them not far from the fuel bladders. Fortunately, nothing blew up.

We were heading home.

Bien Hoa

When we arrived at Bien Hoa to catch our flight back to the States, we found that the army was going to take one more opportunity to screw us over.

We checked in two days earlier than our ordered departure date and were assigned to a barracks building.

The staff sergeant who checked us in told us that we needed to get haircuts before *he* would send us home. We did not know that this was just the beginning of the harassment.

We had three formations per day in which all the people assigned to that company would wait to hear their name called. Again, people were being told to get another haircut.

When we went through customs, the sergeants confiscated many of our photographs, mainly on the grounds that they were contraband. I probably lost about 200 photographs that I had in the form of prints. Vern and Dave experienced the same thing.

It was quite evident that these a-holes were taking out their frustrations on the guys who had been closer to the action. None of these cadres wore any combat patches, and all of their uniforms were clean and pressed. All of their boots were still shiny black. It appeared that they had spent their entire tours at Bien Hoa and had never laid eyes on a VC. It made us seethe with anger.

Other individuals who had been part of our original 370th TC Detachment or our training classes at Ft. Eustis began to show up. One or two people came in who we thought had died, so those were pleasant surprises. We also learned of other friends who had been killed in action. Very sad.

After two days of this, we were really in a foul mood. Many of the grunts from units such as the 101st Airborne Division, the First, Ninth, or Twenty-Fifth Infantry Divisions, or the 173rd Airborne Brigade started to show their frustrations. There was a lot of loud grumbling and most of them had angry, black looks on their faces. It still amazes me that none of these guys beat the hell out of one or more of the cadres.

During one of the periods in which they allowed us to visit the PX, Dave and I had our Zippo lighters engraved with a morbid motto: *Death is my Business, And Business has been Good.*

On the third day of this, our scheduled departure date passed by as we sat. We considered trying to reach out to A-Troop and see if they could do anything for us. We knew that would be futile, so we killed the idea. We now belonged to the Eightieth Replacement Battalion.

Each formation came closer to a riot. Many people had no reason to be polite, so verbal threats started to come out of the group. This was frequent among the combat grunts who were not in the mood to put up with this treatment. Most of us had the attitude that these REMFs had no right to harass us after what we'd seen and done. It was getting ugly. It wasn't that the army could not get its act together and get us out on time. It was the pure delight that the cadre took in harassing us. I was surprised that no one got violent or that one of the cadres was not assaulted at night.

Finally, on July 23rd, we were scheduled for the departure flight. Craig Schmidt, Dave Raymond, Vern Summerell, Granville Oliver, Charley Sandt, Gary Buck, several guys from the 370th, and I boarded the plane for the ride home.

In the days leading up to the flight, we held healthy discussions of what the airline flight attendants would look like. After not seeing an American female for over a year, there was a great deal of attention and speculation on this.

As we walked across the tarmac, we spotted a Braniff Airlines 707 parked near us. Approaching the plane were about six or eight flight attendants, all stunningly beautiful.

Braniff was a relatively new airline in the late '60s. Their marketing campaign was filled with sexual overtones, and they flaunted the avant-garde (and revealing) uniforms worn by the female crewmembers.

As we neared the Braniff group, a bunch of good-natured whistles and catcalls came out of our group. The troops were amped up, but we walked straight past the Braniff plane and boarded an Eastern Airlines 707. The disappointment was palpable.

Awaiting our arrival was a group of flight attendants that were probably older than our mothers. These women were handpicked for their relative lack of sex appeal. They all resembled Aunt Bea from the *Andy Griffith Show*. It was an immediate downer.

For some reason, I was intensely anxious about the flight home. I could not help thinking about the irony of flying all those combat missions, then being killed in an airliner.

When we approached our first refueling stop, my anxiety appeared to be valid. The airstrip was surrounded by high mountains that were somewhat hidden behind scattered cumulous clouds. As we descended on our final approach, I could not stop fixating on the various mountain peaks surrounding our flight path. We were much lower than the mountaintops. We were actually flying between them, which heightened my anxiety.

We finally touched down with a thump. I am not sure I was ever so relieved, even when landing in a Loach.

Travis Air Force Base

We headed for Hawaii and our next fuel stop. On the way we watched what I thought was the funniest movie I had ever seen: *Support Your Local Sheriff*, starring James Garner. I loved it.

We arrived at Travis Air Force Base in San Francisco late in the afternoon and began our transition into the Stateside army or discharge for those soldiers who had less than six months of service left.

Our first stop was US Customs. The agent, a gentleman about my dad's age, could not have been nicer. He took a brief look inside my ten-dollar cloth suitcase and said, "OK. You're good to go." I asked him if he needed to check the paperwork on the weapon I was bringing in.

I thought he was going to flip out. In a tense voice, he said, "Weapon? What weapon? Do you have a weapon?"

I pulled the Chi-Com rifle from behind the suitcase and showed him the paperwork. Relieved, he said, "OK, son. You can go."

We received a new set of dress greens, with all the trimmings. They issued our various medals and awards, and even attached our First Aviation Brigade patches to the right shoulder of our dress coats. Believe it or not, my waist measurement was twenty-eight inches! I would never see that number again.

Like most of my friends, I came home with no orders for my next post. We were told the orders would be mailed to our address of record within two weeks. If they did not arrive after two weeks, we were to report to the nearest army installation personnel office, and the staff would retrieve them for us.

Unfortunately, several people on my flight received orders for Germany. They were to take their thirty-day leave and go overseas again!

Numerous individuals jumped on the phones to call their families and have them contact their congressional representatives. Fortunately, no one in my immediate group received such orders.

It was nearly midnight by the time we took a taxi to San Francisco International Airport. At that time, the terminal was semicircular. As soon as we reached the end of the terminal building, Vern told the driver to stop and let us out of the cab.

Surprised, the driver asked if we wanted him to take us to a specific airline, but we said we wanted out right away.

What a mistake.

We had no idea how large the airport was. We also had no way to know where the United or Eastern Airlines ticket desks were. We had a very long walk, carrying our suitcases and VC rifles.

We must have walked for close to a half hour before we reached the United desk. They were the only carrier with a flight that could get us to Norfolk at that time of night.

When I stepped up to the desk to buy the ticket, I was planning to pay the full fare ($180) to make sure I had a seat. Flying on standby would have cut the fare in half, but I was not taking any chances. The agent said, "Son, it's a red-eye 707, and there aren't twelve people holding tickets. Save your money." I followed his advice and saved $90.

The flight home was uneventful. We talked with the stewardesses for a while, then fell asleep. We slept through most of it. We changed planes at Washington National (now Reagan) and boarded a Piedmont Airlines flight to Norfolk.

HOME

"But listen to me first and swear an oath to use all your eloquence and strength to look after me and protect me."

Homer, The Iliad

My homecoming did not turn out as I had envisioned. I planned to surprise my folks, as I had seen in dozens of movies. Vernon killed this when he called his parents from Travis without me knowing about it. No surprises this time. When he told me he had called them and they were calling my parents, I gave up on the surprise and called my folks too.

When we deplaned, my parents, sister, and grandmother were there to greet me. John Wolford's family and Vern's were there too, along with his wife. Missing was Norma, my fiancée. To say I was disappointed does not begin to describe how I felt.

We retrieved our baggage and headed home. On the way, I had Dad stop at the neighborhood drive-in so I could buy a BBQ sandwich. I had not eaten one in over a year, and I was craving one. The taste was wonderful.

As soon as we reached home, I dropped my parents and drove the Road Runner over to Norma's house, less than a mile away.

She was much more ill than I had imagined, extremely pale and swollen, still taking regular penicillin shots, and restricted to bed until her SED count, a blood test, fell to a certain level, for which she was seeing the doctor weekly.

I spent my first night at home telling my parents about my war experiences and giving them updates on the people they knew from my days at Ft. Eustis. Like most of my friends, I had not told them that I was a Scout while I was in-country. I did not want them to worry needlessly.

A disturbing part of our conversation was my father's disbelief when I told him about the violence, especially on the part of the ARVNs. He even rejected several of the events involving GIs. He was expressing a naiveté that I knew he did not possess. He confirmed this years later when he told me about a couple of WWII events which proved he had seen plenty of American brutality. One such story involved the 101st Airborne Division. They were operating on my dad's unit's flank. Whenever either unit captured a German member of a certain Panzer division, the paratroopers would cut their throats. The Panzer division had murdered about seventy-five American troopers in the village of Malmedy just a few weeks before. The GIs were determined to avenge their deaths. I am sure this was on Dad's mind when he was later captured by that same Panzer division.

Why he reacted that way to me remained a mystery. I told him to imagine how he would have felt if, when he arrived in France in 1944, he found himself fighting on the side of the Nazis. He stayed away from the topic. His reaction, in light of that I was trying to live up to his model, crushed me.

Norma's illness severely restricted the time we could spend together. Any idea of getting married while I was on the thirty-day leave was out the window. She was so weak she could barely sit up.

I had to adjust my social plans drastically. I spent most of my days visiting with Norma until she got too tired. I hung out with John Wolford, who was on temporary assignment at the Portsmouth Naval Hospital. He had been shot down in November of '68 and was burned badly. He was sent home after only two months in-country. He had already been hospitalized for over nine months.

We spent our nights visiting all the Virginia Beach bars with old friends. I was quickly becoming bored. The next week, I took Norma to her doctor for an all-important blood test. I felt crushed when we learned that she was not even close to the number she had to reach. It was not her fault. It was strictly a matter of the time required for the antibiotics to kill the bacteria in her blood.

I tried to be noble and hide my disappointment, but I am sure she noticed how I felt.

The following week was more of the same, except for a road trip John and I took to the Pentagon.

He realized that his rehabilitation period was drawing to a close. He wanted to visit Army HQ in person and see if he could talk them into an assignment close to home.

He succeeded! Rather than being sent somewhere across the country, he was assigned to Ft. Belvoir, in Northern Virginia. Not only would he be three hours from home, he would also be responsible for the fort's weekly newspaper. *And*, he had a staff car at his disposal.

The following week's blood test showed that Norma's SED rate was being very stubborn. She was still restricted.

Because I would not be spending any money entertaining Norma, I decided to entertain myself by having a new exhaust system installed on my Road Runner. Norma wasn't real happy about it, but she got over it.

My parents threw a party in honor of Vern's, John's, and my return. Dad decided on a crab feast at the house. He brought in picnic tables, lots of beer, and crabs ready for steaming. We must have had twenty people stuffed around the tables and stuffing themselves with fresh crab meat. Many of our high school friends who were now in college attended. It was a great celebration.

Norma failed the next week's blood test also. The SED rate was declining, but not as fast as we wanted. This meant we were going to be down to one week of freedom, *if* she passed the next week's test. My leave was only thirty days, and we were now in the third week.

With this news, I decided mag wheels would really look good on my car, so I bought a set. The Road Runner would get even more attention as I cruised Shoney's, without Norma.

Now that I had been home for over two weeks and still had no orders, I visited the personnel office on Ft. Story. Remembering John's experience at the

Pentagon, I tried to talk the clerk into assigning me to Ft. Story. When he said they did not have any aviation units on the facility, I told him that was not a problem. I would take *any* assignment, as long as I could keep my E-5 rank. I tried for Ft. Eustis, too. Nope. They were overstaffed.

It was fruitless. He walked over to the teletype machine and ripped off a couple of sheets of paper. As he handed them to me, he said, "Fort Knox, Kentucky. Have fun."

Well, at least I would not be cold there, I thought.

Fort Knox

I left for Ft. Knox a week later. The Road Runner was a great road car, so at least I could look forward to an entertaining drive. The fort was about 700 miles from Chesapeake and Route 60 was not a superhighway. Interstate 64 terminated in Richmond, so I would be driving a two-lane highway through most of Virginia and all of West Virginia and Kentucky. This included the full breadth of the Blue Ridge Mountains.

I missed Norma terribly and I had only been on the road two hours when I reached Richmond. I was so depressed I felt like turning around but did not.

As I exited Richmond, the song "Jean" by Rod McKuen came on the radio. Jean. Norma Jean. The Oscar-nominated song made me cry.

When I arrived at the Ft. Knox airfield and parked in front of the hangar, Dave Raymond ran out to greet me. He had gotten married while on leave and had his wife, Cheryl, tucked away in a nearby apartment complex. He had also bought a '69 Road Runner while on leave and was quite proud that we both had the same model car.

When I went inside, I learned that I was again in an Air Cavalry unit – the Eighth of the First Air Cav this time – a Blackhawk again. I also learned that our entire fleet of aircraft was Korean War-era H-13s, the same as the ones later made famous by the movie and TV show *MASH*. They had six-cylinder, air-cooled piston engines, just like a Chevy Corvair, wooden main rotor blades, and leaked or burnt about a quart of oil every hour. This should be fun, I thought.

We provided helicopters and instructor pilots (IPs) to the officers attending the Armor School. It was like Hertz-for-Helicopters. This allowed the pilots to get their basic flight hour minimums and retain their flight pay.

Most pilots did not invite the crew chiefs to fly while they practiced, but a few did, and I got plenty of hours.

Later, we received the first of two UH-IH models, and it was assigned to me. This was a huge blessing. I could only assume it was because I had the oldest date of rank as an E-5, making me the senior crew chief in the platoon. I had no supervisory responsibilities associated with my rank, but I would certainly accept the assignment of the Huey! It meant daily flying and a lot less boredom.

In March, I applied for leave so I could go home and get married. Norma and I had settled on April 11th as D-Day.

Our first sergeant, an imbecilic E-7 who had spent twenty-two years as a grunt, denied my request. This was typical of his attitude toward non-career soldiers. If you weren't a lifer, nothing else counted. I had experienced this attitude among all of the lifers above me, and this was the main reason I decided to get out of the army. If you were not on your second enlistment, all of the more-senior NCOs treated you like crap. Absolutely zero respect. I did not want to join their group.

I asked "Top," the nickname given to all troop first sergeants, why not? He said, "Because it's up to me, and I haven't decided yet."

I knew he was screwing with me, but I did not feel like being passive about it. I told him that I had more than enough leave on the books to cover it and did not understand his attitude.

He replied, "It's my decision, *Specialist*, and I'll let you know if I change my mind."

"OK, Top," I said. "But you need to figure out how you're going to keep me here when April rolls around. Permission or no permission, I'm getting married."

He said nothing, but I was pissed. I decided to let the matter sit for a couple of days, then talk to the CO about it.

A few days later, the major approved my leave, and nothing else was said about it.

Jim Manley, the New Yorker who announced my perfect final exam score in Loach school was also assigned to this unit. He was still single and living in the barracks, as would be. Also assigned to the troop was Charley Sandt, who we thought was dead until he showed up for the flight home.

Jim Manley ended up as Scout crew chief with the Twenty-Third Infantry Division. He was now an E-6, so I thought he had reenlisted. Not so.

Jim had performed so many heroic stunts as a Scout that they promoted him to E-6. He had two Silver Stars, two Distinguished Flying Crosses, and so many other awards for valor that his dress uniform looked like it belonged to a general.

When he received his second Silver Star, his unit informed him that he had been nominated for the Medal of Honor. However, they would not approve the MoH unless he reenlisted! He refused, so they awarded another Silver Star and promoted him to E-6.

This promotion moved Jim up to the role of technical inspector, or TI, and as such he would not have a flying job.

This bored Jim terribly. He talked about it continuously, and his already strong drinking habit got worse, consuming all of his pay. At the end of the month, he would routinely pawn the spare tire of his Olds 4-4-2 to finance another trip to a bar.

We did not recognize the seriousness of his habit at the time, but things were getting worse.

WO4 Gautier, our platoon leader, restricted Jim to the base for thirty days and took his driver's license away after Jim got into a bar fight in Louisville.

WO4 Gautier was probably the toughest individual I met in the army. He was about six three and pure muscle. He was trim, and his waist looked to be about a size thirty. This, coupled with his broad shoulders and dark hair and eyes, made him look like a recruiting poster for the German SS. Gautier also liked to brag about his fitness and exploits at the post gym. He wanted everyone to know that violence was never far away. He would just as soon beat the hell out of you as write you up for disciplinary action.

After the third week of Jim's restriction, he begged us to take him to a bar for a cool one. No one wanted to do it, but he was desperate. Finally, Bob Hesse, another former Scout, Glen Borger, a former Chinook crew chief and now our troop clerk, and I agreed to drive him to a local bar for *one* quick beer.

We headed for the Last Chance bar, just across the county line. Meade County, where Ft. Knox is located, was a dry county at the time, meaning you had about a ten-mile drive to the nearest bar.

The bar was moderately crowded when we arrived, so we took a small, four-top table near the entrance. We quickly downed our first beer and ordered another round. The quick beer had turned into two.

As soon as the waitress sat the four glasses on the table, the entrance door swung open and in stepped a couple dressed in civilian clothes. I was facing the door. It took me about three seconds to recognize Gautier and his wife. It took him about five seconds to recognize me. We were doomed.

At first, his face turned scarlet and he stiffened like he was going to throw a punch. His eyes locked on mine as the other guys continued their chitchat.

As each one looked at me and saw me staring, they turned to see what I was so focused on. The table became silent.

Gautier's glare disappeared and a broad smile came over his face. He took his wife by the hand and said, "Step over here, dear. This is a group of my guys, and I'd like you to meet them." He slowly rounded the table, stopping at each chair so his wife could ask us where we were from. She shook hands with each of us.

This took about three or four minutes. I was so nervous, my head was about to wring itself off my shoulders. We were so tense, we could hardly speak well enough to exchange pleasantries with Mrs. Gautier.

Mr. Gautier was all smiles. We had never seen him like this. He asked if they could join us and, of course, we said, "Yes, please do."

They sat down, and it was like a family reunion. All merriment and old aviation stories. Having never seen Gautier drink, I did not know if a couple of beers would turn him into a mean drunk or what. I could not relax. Each of the four of us would occasionally sneak a glance at one another as if to ask, "What in the fuck is going on here?"

Gautier was in such a state of happiness he announced that all the drinks and food were on him. We proceed to drink and eat through the night.

We closed the bar at 2 a.m. and made our way into the parking lot. Everyone was stumbling, including the Gautiers.

When we arrived at my car, Bob Hesse, who was six six, flopped across the roof from the passenger's side and locked his fingers under the driver's side window. He couldn't move.

He was holding onto the window with all of his strength, and it took both Glen and Jim to pry him away from the door and get him situated in the back of the car.

It took forever to cover the ten miles back to Knox. I was barely awake and probably driving at twenty-five miles per hour, as drunks always do when they're being careful. It was about two thirty in the morning, and there were no other cars on the road. Gautier and his wife had disappeared as soon as they exited the bar.

Why a policeman did not stop us, I will never know. We made it back to the barracks and tried to catch some sleep before the 6 a.m. formation that our idiot top sergeant held every day, rain, shine, or snow.

As we gradually woke up, we began to dread what might await us at the hangar. Gautier usually beat us to the airstrip in the mornings, so we feared the welcome we were about to receive. I drove us to the airstrip and saw Gautier's car as soon as we rounded the corner. All four of us let out a moan or said, "Ah shit. He's here!"

We were severely hung over and it showed. We dragged ourselves into the office and there he sat at his desk, reading the paper. He looked like he had gotten eight hours of sound sleep and spent the last hour at the gym. Recruiting poster. He set his paper aside and asked if we were OK, that we looked a little under the weather. When we replied that we were fine, he said, "OK, get to work."

The bar scene was never mentioned again.

Jim eventually became so depressed, he decided to volunteer for another tour in Vietnam. However, he only had months to serve, and the army refused to deploy him.

Jim found a way. He got into his Olds 4-4-2 and headed toward Louisville.

Between Ft. Knox and Louisville was the small town of West Point. It occupied the southeastern bank of the Ohio River and was a notorious speed trap. Local residents claimed that the majority of the municipal budget was covered by speeding fines collected from the Ft. Knox troops.

Jim ran through the northbound radar trap in excess of 100 mph. After the policeman wrote him up for reckless driving, Jim turned around and ran through the southbound speed trap at 110. He was arrested immediately.

When it came time for his disciplinary process, he was busted back to E-4. He agreed to return to Vietnam rather than be sentenced to jail.

Right on schedule, I departed for Virginia and the big ceremony. Surprisingly, there was still snow on the ground at Ft. Knox. This was one of the conditions for which the lifers could cancel all leaves. I left town as soon as I could.

Craig Schmidt, my old pinochle partner, came in from Ft. Rucker and served as our best man. Glen Borger, who had left the army a couple of weeks before, came down from Pennsylvania to attend.

We had the ceremony at Epiphany Episcopal Church in Norfolk. Because Mrs. Potter, Norma's mother, was such a staunch Southern Baptist, she had been threatening not to attend, or if she did attend, to wear a black dress. She did all of this to punish Norma for changing from Baptist to Episcopalian. This was the final move in her two-year campaign to split us up. It was a great indicator of the way Sarah Potter would continue to abuse her children throughout their adult lives. Norma suffered greatly during this period, and I am forever grateful to Norma for persevering through it.

We arrived at Ft. Knox and moved into a brand-new, fully furnished apartment in Radcliff, Kentucky, a tiny town that bordered the fort.

We were married and on our own. It was a great feeling.

After our Ocean City honeymoon, we departed for Ft. Knox and our new apartment. It was more than brand-new; it was unfinished. The stairs going to the upper floors were still framed in, with no kickboards, walls, or handrails. The building was a four-story, with four apartments on each floor, and was ideal – only ten minutes away from the airfield.

A couple of days after our arrival, I took Norma to acquire her ID card. Because we only had one vehicle, she drove me to the airfield, planning to pick me up in a few hours so I could accompany her to the pass office.

While I was waiting in the tool room, a couple of guys said she had just driven up. I went to the office to let them know I was leaving, then went outside to join Norma.

When I arrived at the street, she was nowhere to be found. Several of my platoon mates were leaning out the tool room windows, yelling at me, telling me that she had driven off. Of course, this news was accompanied by several crude insults and jokes, most of which revolved around her leaving with some other man.

I waited about fifteen minutes, then called the apartment. As expected, she was there. I asked her why she drove off, leaving me. Her response: she had seen a Huey take off and figured that I was flying away in the ship. She was under the impression that my Huey was the only Huey at the fort, and therefore I had departed!

This was the first of several adventures Norma experienced at Ft. Knox, providing all the evidence she needed to conclude that staying in the army was not a good option for us.

On one occasion, she arrived at the airfield to pick me up at the end of the day. While she was sitting in the car waiting, one of my platoon members, SP/4 Gardner, left for the day. As he walked past Norma, he casually mentioned that I would be late because I had crashed during a training flight.

He provided no other details. In fact, we did have to make a forced landing about thirty miles from the field. One of the tanker drivers had accidently fueled my ship with Av-Gas instead of JP-4. This caused the engine to stop running at 5,500 feet as we were practicing a maneuver. Fortunately, our best instructor pilot was at the stick and he successfully executed a perfect autorotation, landing in a farmer's field.

An autorotation is an emergency procedure used by helicopter pilots when their aircraft loses power, as in an engine failure. It is difficult and risky. To autorotate, the pilot lowers the collective stick so that the blades are partially feathered. The ship descends at an angle of approximately seventy-five degrees. It is falling – not gliding. As the air flows past the rotor blades, the pilot controls their spin rate by adjusting the collective stick. He attempts to keep their spin rate at the approximate RPM that they would achieve if the engine was running: approximately 300 RPM.

The pilot dives toward the ground at approximately eighty knots of airspeed. At a point about ten to fifteen feet above the ground, he pulls the nose of the aircraft up into a "flare." This causes the loss of airspeed. Simultaneously with the elevation of the nose, he pulls up on the collective stick, adding pitch to the blades. The momentum that the blades have accumulated keeps them spinning, for a while. This causes the rotor to create temporary lift and slow down dramatically. The pilot lowers the collective and sets the aircraft on the ground.

The trick to this is twofold. First, it is all done by feel. It is a true seat-of-the-pants maneuver. Second, the timing of the flare and the application of the collective stick to introduce pitch to the blades has to be timed perfectly. If the pilot is a second or two late, the aircraft will continue its rapid descent and crash. If he pulls pitch too soon, the aircraft will come to hover too high above the ground, then crash. He has one shot to get it perfect. Do-overs are not allowed.

Pilots who successfully execute autorotations earn great praise. On this occasion, I felt like kissing the ground under his feet.

Of course, Norma had no way of knowing this. When we finally established telephone communication with the airfield, I requested that someone send Dave Raymond out to the parking lot and tell Norma I was OK. She was in a state of panic for nearly an hour.

During my one year at Ft. Knox, I suffered from intense anxiety over my future. I was married. I had zero college. I knew I was not going to make the army a career, so it made no sense to think about a possible reenlistment. I soon learned th in 1970, helicopter mechanics were a dime a dozen. Even experienced he opter pilots were having tough times locating decent employment. W en they did, the annual salaries were appallingly low.

My prospec looked bleak. I decided to enroll in the Armed Forces Correspondence School and take a class: Refrigeration and Air-Conditioning Basics. After jus few short classes and exams, I realized that I had no interest in pursuing this ne of study.

As the mont rolled by and my anxiety deepened, I heard that you could get an early disc arge if you enrolled in college. This had some appeal. I loved to read, and I w s a better-than-average writer. I felt that if I could complete college, I could prepare myself for a white-collar career and avoid the toil associated with mechanical work. After discussing it with Norma several times, we decid d that I would enroll in college and we'd live off her nursing salary and the ir ome provided by the GI Bill.

My anxiety l sened as I felt I now had a clearer path to our future.

While servin at Ft. Knox, several former Blackhawk pilots passed through our unit. Each l ought updates on the status of the people we left behind. I then realized th none of the Scouts who volunteered for an extra six months (extending their ours) made it home uninjured. I was even more glad that I had refused that ption.

I was able to aintain contact with Jim Lucido while he was still in Vietnam. We exchanged merous letters, but I lost track of him after he returned to the States. Desp e numerous attempts to locate him over the years, I never succeeded. This emains one of my deepest regrets.

SEPARATION

"A rebirth out of spiritual adversity causes us to become new creatures."

James E. Faust

My last twelve months in the army were filled with stress and worry. I had decided that my dreams of an army career were not to be fulfilled. I was not going to pursue the military career I had been counting on three years ago. Because my high school education included intense exposure to literature and the humanities, I anticipated becoming a warrior-poet. I would continue my education, seek a commission, and achieve a stable career. However, I simply could not tolerate an environment in which rank outweighed competence and where so many of the career soldiers did everything they could to express their lack of respect for their subordinates. It was a very well-defined caste system, and I wanted no part of it.

Interestingly, I got along much better with all of the officers. They demonstrated mutual respect and recognized that we were all human beings. I attribute much of the maltreatment by the NCOs to jealousy. Most of them had been in the army before the war. Promotions were hard to come by in the peacetime army. When the war got going and Army Aviation exploded, many of us had been promoted in as little as six months. The ranks we achieved, especially in aviation, were unthinkable to many of the old-timers. Several of us were promoted to E-5 after only six months – a rank that had taken many of the older soldier ten years to acquire. This seemed to be a permanent source of irritation for actically all of them. They seemed determined to make our lives miserable w ile they had power over us.

The army re ly suffered in the '70s. Some experts say it was virtually destroyed. Man competent soldiers chose to depart rather than stay. I was one of them.

I did have an therwise attractive option. One of the pilots, who had taught me to fly an H- 3, tried for months to convince me to enter the Bootstrap program. Under his program, the army would send me to college in return for me serving f six years after I graduated. It sounded good. I would receive my E-5 salary w le I was in school, along with any allowances that my marital status entitled m I would enroll in ROTC and graduate with a commission as a second lieuten: it. Financially, it was a very attractive package. It would allow me to pursue m original goal of becoming an officer. Since I had no plan B, I probably should ave considered it.

However, I w is so utterly disgusted with how the army ran things that I declined the off r. I served my remaining months, took my discharge, and decided to atten college in Norfolk. Norma could work at the hospital where she had attended nursing school and I would prepare to be a history teacher.

I applied for dmission to Old Dominion University, in my hometown. Much to my sur ise, they accepted me!

I then appli to the army for an early discharge under the guidelines of their existing olicy. It stated that if college classes started within the last ninety days of y ur enlistment, you could depart up to ninety days early to attend school.

The army ap roved my application and I paid my tuition. We arranged to have our belong gs packed and shipped home. Things were falling into line. But the army sti had one condom left, and I was the intended victim.

After approv g my application for early discharge, the army reversed the decision about t ee weeks before my revised ETS date.

To receive tl early discharge, army regulations stated that the school session had to gin within the enlistee's last ninety days of active duty. I was originally scheduled for a September 10th ETS. However, the first day of class was scheduled for September 11th: one day *after* my active duty ended. Some anonymous clerk had decided to veto my release. No one took into consideration that you have to appear and register for classes *before* they begin!

I was beyond livid. I had already paid my tuition and arranged housing. The packers were scheduled to begin the move in just a couple of weeks. I had given notice on my apartment and already began clearing post.

When I went to the personnel office, a second lieutenant informed me of the date problem. I tried to reason with him, explaining that you do not just show up at the college classroom. There is counseling and class registration required before classes start. He agreed, saying he was a college graduate, but that was the way the regulation was written.

I was ordered to begin reversing the clearing of post that I had begun less than a week earlier. As I revisited each office, every lifer in those offices had a snide remark for the college boy. The caste system was alive and well. I came close to physically assaulting several of them.

I called my parents and got in touch with the minister who had married Norma and me. He was a retired navy aviator and had a close personal relationship with our congressman, William Whitehurst. Mr. Whitehurst was not only a Navy WWII veteran, he was also the chair of the ODU History Department.

He had me copy, by hand, all of the relevant army regulations and send them to him. He then made a phone call to the Ft. Knox adjutant general, asking why they were screwing me. Both the adjutant general and the fort commanding general intervened to reverse the earlier veto.

The next day I started the clearing process again. I had many "kind words" for the lifers who had teased me the first time around.

It was at this point that I made a decision that would come back to haunt me forty years later.

While getting my last physical exam, we discovered that I had a significant hearing loss in my left ear. I was sure it was the result of the ear fungus that I had experienced during the wet season. It was certainly exacerbated by the minigun muzzle blast. I asked the medic to make a note of it in my medical record.

He replied th he was not authorized to do that. He could record normal test results, but only flight surgeon or audiologist could record a failure. He then went on to say i would take at least two weeks for me to get an appointment and I would ha to delay my discharge. Obviously, I could not do that, so I told him to fo et it. I was almost a free man. My only remaining military obligation was t ee years of inactive reserve. The critical term was "inactive." This meant no d lls, no summer camp, no lifers.

CIVILIAN

"Nothing in the affairs of men is worthy of great anxiety."

Plato

After an eighteen-hour drive across Kentucky, Ohio, Pennsylvania, and Maryland, Norma and I arrived at my parents' home in Chesapeake, Virginia. Because my GI Bill monthly allowance would not begin for a while, we were forced to stay with my parents for a couple of weeks. Norma began work at Norfolk General. As soon as she received her first paycheck, we moved into a two-bedroom apartment close to ODU. I could ride my bike to classes, and Norma only had a four-mile drive to the hospital.

We felt like we were beginning a race but were already three years behind.

Classes went well. I decided to major in history with the intent to eventually teach high school or maybe college. It had been over three years since I had pursued any type of academic effort, and I found myself having to study continuously. In biology, a subject Norma had promised would be easy, I was totally lost. Many of my classmates had three and four years of high school biology and could easily have taught the class. My previous, single biology class was six years ago and I did not retain much. I decided to write down every term the professor mentioned during the lectures, then look up each and every term in the index of my biology text.

It took hours, but it worked. I was able to score a B in biology and even made the dean's list in my first semester. I was stunned.

College also provided a deeper and more disturbing learning experience.

Many of our high school friends were now seniors in college. They returned home for the Christmas break. Several were with me at ODU. Naturally, we were invited to several holiday parties and were eager to catch up with our friends.

At the first party we attended, a couple of people we had known before approached and asked me where I had been; they had not seen me in a couple of years.

Without giving it a second thought, I said, "I've been in the army for three years. I was in Vietnam, then Kentucky. I just got out in August."

Their responses were not what I was expecting.

"Oh. Ohhh!" one said. They looked nervously at each other and said, "Let's go over and see what Terry is up to," then they hurried away without looking back.

Norma and I were both a bit baffled. When this pattern was repeated a couple of times during the rest of the evening, we got the clue: don't dare mention Vietnam. With the exception of another recently discharged veteran and a couple of our closest friends, we were left alone for the rest of the night.

I had never been treated like this before. I imagined it would have been a similar response if I told someone that I had just been released from prison. While I did not know it at the time, I would see this same response thousands of times throughout my business career. Nonveterans simply did not want to hear the war mentioned, even casually. This was especially true among my white-collar colleagues. Regardless of the setting, people simply did not care enough about the war or its veterans to hear about it. Utter indifference was the rule.

These were and continued to be very disturbing experiences for me. I could not reconcile this treatment with the respect and reverence given to the WWII veterans. Even after three years in the service, I was still naïve enough to believe that military service, especially combat service, would garner respect. Not so.

The My Lai massacre came to light right after I started college. This caused me unimaginable stress and led to some symptoms that would plague me for years.

I certainly did not agree with what Lt. Calley did. Nor could I devise any reasonable excuse for his behavior. However, I was utterly disgusted with how the army initially covered it up, then scapegoated Calley to the fullest extent possible. The actions of more senior officers and the entire command structure were ignored.

The media assisted with this persecution and failed to explore the violent atmosphere that drove everyone's actions in Vietnam. High body counts were all that mattered. Free-fire zones were prevalent. Harassment and interdiction "H&I" artillery fire missions, during which artillery units would randomly select road intersections or canals and fire a few dozen rounds of high explosives into these sites, were constant and deadly for the civilian population. Artillery or air strikes on villages containing civilians were also daily events. Thousands of civilians were killed by these practices, but this was considered a cost of war.

While this is not an excuse for Calley's actions, one can see where these practices established a psychological environment in which civilian casualties were somewhat acceptable.

After all, if it was permissible to bomb a village from which sniper fire originated, and if it happened to kill a couple of hundred people, so what? How much worse was it to kill a couple of hundred VC sympathizers who were sniping at and killing your comrades with booby traps? In the final analysis, they're all equally dead.

Because I was in college when the story erupted, I spent a great deal of time explaining that my unit had never participated in anything as gross as what happened at My Lai. However, we often killed people we found in free-fire zones, regardless of whether they fired at us or not. Unless we were operating with ARVN or American ground troops in the area, we did not take prisoners. Of course, these actions were never disclosed to my fellow students. I knew they would never understand the realities of combat and would look upon me as a murderer.

I felt extremely confused about all this. I was having trouble sleeping. One day while I was sitting with a couple of friends waiting to go to a class, I imagined that I saw bugs crawling across our table. When I pointed out the bugs to my friends, they asked if I was OK and told me that I did not look well.

Suddenly I experienced a numbness creeping into my face and hands. I left campus and headed to our apartment. I lay down on the bed, believing I was having a stroke. When Norma arrived an hour later, I could not understand anything she was saying. I did not recognize any of the words. When I tried to speak, completely irrelevant words came out. My vision was blurred and my hearing was impaired. Something bad was happening, and I had no idea what it was. Norma also feared that I might be having a stroke.

Norma took me to the emergency room, where they were unable to diagnose me. The doctors decided to give me an injection of Demerol and keep me overnight for observation.

The Demerol knocked me out. When I awoke, I was back to normal. I was told to go home and stay in bed and rest for a couple of days. No further explanation was given.

After returning home and resting for a couple of days, I found that I could not get the My Lai incident out of my mind. I remained very upset and could not reconcile the events with the situation in Vietnam that I knew.

After several similar, debilitating episodes over the next few months, my family doctor referred me to a neurologist. He ran a series of tests, including a CT scan of my brain. He determined that I was suffering from atypical migraine headaches, brought on by stress.

Because no effective medication for migraines existed at the time, my wife and I came up with a routine that would at least give me some relief from the symptoms. If the situation would allow it, I would go to a darkened room, take four aspirin, drink a caffeinated drink, and lie down until the symptoms subsided.

Little did I know, these events would plague me for the rest of my life.

Tina Drops In

During the summer of 1971, at which time I had achieved sophomore status and was considering switching my major to German, Norma came home with a big surprise: she was pregnant.

While I was happy about the prospect of becoming a father, this meant a big change had to occur – I needed employment and needed it NOW!

I had worked some miscellaneous jobs during my first year and a half of school. Now I needed a job with significantly more income than these odd, part-time jobs had provided. I started an intensive job search, starting at the Virginia Employment Commission.

They had nothing to offer. The only jobs even remotely related to mechanical work were openings as gas station attendants at minimum wage – $1.60. This was significantly less than I had earned in the army, and it was not enough to raise a family.

Of course, as soon as I started the search, I also cut my shoulder-length hair to a more conservative, just-over-the-ears look. I certainly was not in a position to argue over hairstyles. I needed a job.

A couple of weeks of searching turned up nothing. I was getting desperate and decided to get another, shorter haircut. Norma was convinced that I was becoming paranoid and insisted that my hair was already short enough.

Another week of futility followed. I considered becoming a taxi driver, but we decided this might be a little too dangerous. I considered life insurance sales. However, watching my dad struggle in this business for over ten years convinced me to avoid it.

Another haircut followed shortly thereafter.

In late August, after nearly ten weeks of frustration, a family friend arranged for me to take a temporary clerical job at a computer service bureau. This was truly a godsend because I had no clerical experience, could not identify a computer if I was sitting on one, and I could not type. However, the army had shown me that I was a fast learner and adaptable. I entered my new profession hopeful that I could make it a success.

The temporary nature of the job followed from the company being exclusively dedicated to providing data processing services to the Norfolk International Terminals and several port-related companies around the Hampton Roads area. The Longshoremen's Union was scheduled to begin a strike when their contract expired on September 30th. Everyone predicted the strike was certain to occur.

My employment was starting on September 13th, giving me just three weeks of employment. They were willing to hire me to accomplish as much data processing as possible before the strike began. Once the strike began, it was probable that my employment would end.

I was assigned to make financial projections of port activity, assuming certain levels of continued business. Luckily, I found that I had a knack for this type of work. When September 30th came and the strike began, I was retained and remained employed throughout the strike. When the union returned to work, I had a permanent job at $2.25 per hour – not much, but far better than nothing.

I remained with that small company for nine years. I found a niche and decided to return to college and pursue a degree in accounting. I couldn't foresee it at the time, but this first step led to a successful forty-five-year career in information technology.

I remember the evening we drove to my parents' to give them the news that we were expecting a child. My mother was ecstatic. My father, ever the supportive, encouraging dad, said, "You'll never finish college now!"

Tina was born that January. These were the days of anesthetized mothers and dads banished from the delivery room. My parents, Norma's parents, my sister Terry, Norma's siblings Geraldine and Raymond, and I stood by in the waiting room. After a short period, the doctor arrived and announced that we were now the parents of a beautiful baby girl! I was tremendously happy and thankful that Norma had come through OK. After her earlier bout with rheumatic fever, I was worried the delivery would be fraught with complications.

As soon as permitted, I went to the nursery for my first look at Tina. I was surprised by her dark skin and later told Norma that she looked like raw liver. Bad move! Norma did not find that funny in the slightest and reminded me of my stupid remark for decades after. Strangely, Tina inherited my fair skin and had by far the fairest complexion of our two children.

She would grow up to be a tremendous source of pride and wonderment for her mother and me.

Research, Research, Research

My confusion about my Vietnam experiences persisted. Two simple questions remained foremost in my mind: How did the US get involved in Vietnam, and why did the South Vietnamese people seem so ambivalent about the fight? They had been invaded, right? They were trying to preserve their freedom against a communist onslaught, much like the South Koreans, right? We were only trying to help, right?

I had gone to Vietnam expecting to be treated like a liberator. Images of Paris and Rome in 1944 dominated my thoughts. It certainly had not turned out that way, and I wanted to know why.

As soon as I returned home and while I was on leave before my next stateside, post-Vietnam assignment, I visited the Norfolk Public Library. I reviewed every issue of *Life* and *Time* magazines, looking for clues about the Vietnam War. While there were plenty of photo essays documenting all types of in-country events, I could find nothing that helped me understand what had led us into this disaster.

My experiences had shown me that the South Vietnamese population was either indifferent to the war, or worse, opposed to the Saigon government. I had been led to believe that North Vietnam had invaded South Vietnam, and the Saigon government had asked the US for help. If that was the case, why did the rural population show such disdain, and often hostility, toward us? Why would the ARVNs consistently fail to fight? I was baffled.

For nearly ten years, I despised the South Vietnamese because of what I perceived as their cowardice. This intensified during the fall of Saigon in 1975, when the ARVN collapsed, leaving their population at the mercy of the NVA and Viet Cong. I simply could not understand it.

Our country remained divided over the war for several decades. The right wing wanted to blame the press and what they saw as a cowardly Congress. They blamed Congress for pulling the rug out from under the Saigon government. The left put forward the opinion that the war was doomed from the beginning and the US should never have made commitments we were unable to keep. Unfortunately, the right was far more vocal and passionate about their view, causing their opinion to gain a great deal of traction with the US populace. That view offered a simple solution, identified a readily available scapegoat, and preserved the myth that the US could do no wrong. The right repeatedly identified the Vietnam War as a "noble cause" led astray by a liberal press.

We watched the collapse of South Vietnam at my parents' home in 1975. While I felt a certain degree of resignation about the collapse, I was still disgusted to watch it unfold. As we watched helicopters being pushed overboard from US Navy ships and the ARVN fleeing in panic, I thought of all the wasted lives and effort that had gone into creating this debacle. It was deeply disturbing.

When the broadcast paused for a commercial break, my mother leaped off the couch, approached the television, and screamed, "I'll never buy Chinese food again!" That broke the tension, and we all had a good laugh. Why she thought the Chinese were involved remained a mystery to me.

Shortly after the fall of Saigon, I discovered David Halberstam's landmark work, *The Best and the Brightest*. Published in 1970 before the outcome of the war was known, the book presented an unbiased look at the members of the Kennedy and Johnson administrations and how their belief system led to our intervention in Vietnam. It was an unflinching revelation about how the US betrayed Ho Chi Minh in 1945.

The western powers split Vietnam in two after Ho Chi Minh defeated the French in 1954. We were not fighting invaders. We were fighting the Vietnamese patriots who were trying to reunify their country. As Animal declared in *Full Metal Jacket*, we were killing the wrong gooks! We were dying and killing to defeat self-determination, not foster it. What made this finding even more disturbing was that LBJ was told by the Joint Chiefs of Staff that the war was unwinnable. Documentation proved that this occurred in 1965, *before* he ordered the troop buildup.

There was no invasion by the North Vietnamese. They were merely attempting to put their country back together under a popular, nationalist leader who had defeated the French. The conclusion was painfully clear. *We* were the invading force.

Later, the publication of the *Pentagon Papers* erased all doubt. Still, the die-hard right-wingers clung to their fable, despite overwhelming evidence about the loss of the war. Numerous publications and scholarly texts emerged over the next four decades. All made the same case: the US was wrong to intervene in the manner we chose. The Vietnamese were committed to their independence far more than we were committed to the puppet government we established. Regardless of the amount of violence we leveled against the Vietnamese people, they were never going to give up.

The more I learned, the more sympathetic I became toward the South Vietnamese soldiers. I no longer despised them but looked upon them as victims. The anger I had directed toward the ARVN became focused on the Johnson administration, especially Secretary of Defense McNamara and General William Westmoreland.

This called my entire participation in the war into question. Our role was not that of the WWII GI liberating Paris. We were the foreign invaders attempting to force our way of life on an independent-minded people. I became ashamed.

This knowledge led me to question my morality and the value of my service.

Kevin Arrives

In mid-1979, we learned Norma was pregnant again. I was working as a manager in a division of ITT. Financial security was not the issue it was in 1971, when we learned of Tina's pending arrival.

Like Tina, this birth was projected for January.

A new birthing method was just coming into vogue: Lamaze. I had barely heard of it, but Norma was fully versed. When I learned more about it and saw Norma's enthusiasm for the method, I agreed we should try it.

As the months passed, I learned more. Classes were required. No anesthesia was used. I would participate as a coach and be present in the delivery room.

A great deal of practice was required. The more I heard, the more skeptical I became.

It soon became time to attend the Lamaze classes. These did little to soothe my nerves.

The class was comprised of about ten couples. Not only were we the oldest at thirty and thirty-one, but we were also the only rookies in the class. The other students looked at us as if we were wearing animal skins and had just emerged from a prehistoric cave.

As the class got underway, the instructor asked each couple to introduce themselves and tell everyone why they chose Lamaze. I hated these exercises because they felt like what I imagined AA meetings to be.

As the rotation made its way toward us, one of the fathers, sporting shoulder-length hair, bell-bottoms, flip-flops, and a flowered tank top, began evangelizing why he chose Lamaze. He told us this was their second childbirth and the previous one (just ten months earlier!) had been "inspirational." It was so inspirational that he and his wife had decided to become Lamaze instructors. They were, from this moment forward, dedicating the rest of their lives to Lamaze.

I did not know whether I should throw up or run from the room.

I am not known for having a poker face, and I cannot imagine what my facial expression might have been. Judging from the force of Norma's elbow digging into my ribs, I can only assume that my face must have contorted into something hideous.

We got through the class, and January finally rolled around. About two weeks before the anticipated due date, Norma visited her ob-gyn for a routine visit. I remained at work, and she drove herself to the office.

Shortly thereafter, I received a call from the ob-gyn office informing me that Norma's blood pressure was very high and they were transporting her to the hospital. I should get there ASAP.

A big part of the Lamaze training was the need to prepare a "Baby Day" kit. This was to provide the lucky couple with a few odds and ends that would come in handy over the first couple days in the hospital. In addition to the spare clothes, comfortable shoes, and toiletries, cash and loose change for the pay phones were paramount. Cell phones did not exist in 1980.

Because Norma had believed she was going in for a routine checkup and I was going directly to the hospital from work on an ASAP basis, neither of us had time to pick up the Baby Day kit.

I hated to be unprepared for anything, and today was going to be a big trial.

I arrived at the hospital shortly before five p.m. I found Norma hooked up to several monitors and tubes. Her blood pressure was about 300 over something, and the doctor was very concerned. Norma did not look good.

She stayed in this condition until nearly midnight, when the doctor decided to induce labor with a drug. I had nothing to eat or drink since noon. I was wearing cheap shoes and my feet were on fire. I was still dressed in a business suit. One of the nurses noticed my plight and offered me a glass of orange juice. I accepted. Norma was unable to eat or drink anything. When she noticed my orange juice, she got angry.

The initiation of labor seemed to take forever. Again, the doctor was concerned. When labor finally started around three a.m., it was slow and painful. I attempted to act as the well-trained Lamaze coach and help Norma with her breathing. She would not hear it. Instead, she kept telling me that I had been allowed to drink orange juice and she was not. Little did I know that this topic would be brought up in every discussion of Kevin's birth for the next four decades!

Kevin finally arrived around seven a.m., more than twelve hours after Norma first reached the hospital. I was present in the delivery room and was able to cut the umbilical cord. After that, I stood around and felt totally useless, but also full of joy. Norma and I now had two perfect children. Kevin went on to join Tina as another source of immeasurable pride and delight.

The VVA

Not long after Kevin's birth, I happened to see a fellow named Robert Muller on a TV talk show. He was a former marine and Vietnam combat veteran. He was wounded in Vietnam and was a paraplegic, now confined to a wheelchair

He was describing a new organization he was forming for Vietnam veterans: the Vietnam Veterans of America, or VVA.

He was creating the VVA to give our generation of veterans a voice in national policy toward the Vietnam veteran community. He described an extensive pattern of mistreatment of Nam vets by the VA, the need for changes in the legislation that governed the VA, and the addition of Agent Orange-induced ailment to the list of service-connected injuries that the VA would recognize and treat.

Muller had his act together. I began following his speeches and TV appearances. I resolved to join the VVA as soon as possible. I did so in 1984, becoming member number 679.

The VVA became a great experience for me. I became the VP for Legislative Affairs in Chapter 48, located in Norfolk, Virginia. I was able to interact with the Virginia congressional delegation regularly. This confirmed the belief I had developed in 1980, when President Reagan tried to cut the funding of the new Veterans' Outreach centers, commonly referred to as Vet Centers. Republicans talked a good game. They loved memorials and parades. But when it came time to provide the resources required to truly help veterans, they failed repeatedly.

I moved into the presidency of VVA Chapter 48 in 1986 with a clear goal: change the public's perception of Vietnam veterans. Media portrayals of Vietnam veterans were consistently derogatory. Regardless of the source – TV, movies, or literature – we were always shown to be whacked-out, unstable individuals, living in the woods and ready to kill anyone who looked at us the wrong way.

This was far from the truth and negatively affected anything we wanted to do regarding legislation and veteran benefits. Large numbers of the population either held a negative opinion of veterans or at best were indifferent toward us. This needed to change.

We began a series of initiatives directed toward improving our communications and providing various services to needy and hospitalized veterans. As these programs gained momentum, people became aware of

Chapter 48 and our positive activities. We gained support from the business community and local media.

Indifference toward Vietnam veterans continued for many years and only partially reversed itself in 1986 when the movie *Platoon* was released. It suddenly became cool to be a veteran. This timing proved beneficial to me because of my involvement in the veterans' movement. The sudden burst of support for Nam vets enabled us to grow the chapter from seventy to over three hundred members. We initiated several veterans' service programs and established a scholarship fund for the children of Vietnam veterans. Norma's support was critical to our success in building one of the best VVA chapters in the country. This was one of the most memorable experiences of my life and provided opportunities to meet Admiral Elmo Zumwalt, Senator John Warner, and numerous other elected officials.

Fortunately, I never experienced the types of abuse some veterans suffered upon their return from Vietnam: no spitting in the face, no name-calling. Most of my negative experiences involved the subtle indifference peers expressed about the war and about those who participated in it. People were not interested and simply did not want to hear about it.

The Wall

I visited the Vietnam Veterans Memorial in 1982, an extremely emotional event. As we topped the crest of a small hill and observed the size and scope of the memorial, I was nearly overcome by a panic attack. My heart raced. I began sweating and breathing rapidly. I did not know if I would be able to continue. Thanks to help from Norma and my close friend and fellow Nam vet John Wolford, I was able to proceed to the wall. My reaction on seeing the number of names engraved upon the wall was, "What a waste of human life!"

I found both Captain Cannon's and Mark Hansen's names, only a few lines apart and on the same panel.

Since that initial visit, I have returned to the wall numerous times. It is still an emotional undertaking. However, I can now get through it without the risk of a panic attack.

In 2009, I found Mark Hansen's name on the Vietnam Veterans Memorial website. The facts were clearly and coolly stated:

MARK JOHN HANSEN
SP4 Army
1st Aviation Brigade, 7th Squadron, First Cavalry
Length of service: 0 years
Tour Began: Oct 14, 1968
Casualty Date: Apr 26, 1969
KIEN GIANG PROVINCE
HOSTILE, HELICOPTER CREW
AIR LOSS
BODY RECOVERED
Panel 26W - Line 54

I posted a short remembrance of Mark, noting his courage, sense of duty, and gentle nature. When I saved the message, I felt better but did not expect to hear any more about Mark.

That changed a year later. In August of 2010, an email arrived from California. Mark's older sister and only sibling, Pam, had seen the posting.

I called her and we began a series of communications that sounded like a tragic screenplay.

Mark's family never understood how he came to be killed in a helicopter. They thought he was in the supply room, probably flying resupply missions to outlying camps. Like many of us, Mark never told his parents about his real job. He did not want to upset them. Despite the troop commander's death letter and the posthumous Silver Star citation, they never connected the dots.

Because Pam was studying on the East Coast and unable to return to California when Mark came home for his predeployment visit, she never said goodbye.

Support for parents who lost children to the Vietnam War was rare. Losing

Pam (Hansen) Cipriotti and the author.

their youngest child was too much for the Hansens to bear. His mom, for whom Mark had been the light of her life, committed suicide a year after Mark's death. His dad, who taught Mark patriotism and marksmanship, could not live with the responsibility he felt over Mark's death. After multiple failed marriages, he grieved himself to death.

Despite the sad memories, our communication presented an opportunity. We visited California in September 2011 and met Mark's family. Pam's children and grandchildren were extremely curious about "Uncle Mark" – the handsome boy-soldier in the black-framed picture. Her husband hoped a visit could bring Pam some degree of peace.

It did. The family asked many questions. I answered frankly but gently. After a six-hour visit, Pam learned what she had wanted to know for forty years. One could see the relief spread across her face.

And for me? It created the chance to do something for Mark that was long, long overdue.

Blackhawk Reunions

In 1989, one of the former Blackhawks, Paul Hansen, took the initiative to organize a reunion in Washington, D.C. I immediately registered to attend.

The reunion took place in a hotel bar. Approximately fifteen Blackhawks attended. Most, if not all, had decided not to bring their wives. This was probably a wise choice because no one knew what to expect.

I made the four-hour drive to DC, checked into the hotel, and headed down to the bar. As I approached it, my heart started pounding and I began to sweat. I was in a near panic attack as I crossed the threshold into the open space in the middle of the room.

I had taken no more than three steps into the room when I heard, "Hey! I know you! You were an Apache Scout. I came in about a week before you left. You wouldn't speak to me because I had not killed any VC!"

I had no idea who this guy was. He was practically yelling at me as he walked rapidly toward me. Silence fell across the room as everyone turned to see what would happen next.

I expected him to take a swing at me. I had never refused to talk to someone because of their lack of kills. I was not built that way. He had obviously confused me with someone else.

We sat down and talked, and I learned his name was Joe Vernengo. I did remember him coming into the Scout platoon, but it was so close to my departure that we never established a relationship. Also, he was not a crew chief. He transferred from D-Troop as an observer and would not be in my squad.

Joe went to his room and retrieved a small box, maybe one cubic foot in size, which contained dozens of small black-and-white Polaroid photographs. We sat on the floor and spent an hour going through the pictures. It was amazing to see some of the places where we had operated twenty years ago.

Joe and I were the only former Scouts in attendance. Near the end of the evening, after we had talked to just about everyone, Joe mentioned something that remained with me for years. He told me how glad he was that I had shown up. He explained the reason. "Al, I was beginning to believe that I had only dreamed these experiences. As years went by I found it hard to accept that we had done all these things and lived to tell about it."

This reunion began a pattern of semiannual then annual gatherings of the former Blackhawks. Attendance regularly exceeded one hundred and fifty people because family members often attended. We gathered in such cities as St. Louis, Ft. Knox, San Diego, Sacramento, Reno, Norfolk, San Antonio, Traverse City, MI, Charleston, WV, Phoenix, and Boise.

Finding Dave

I located and contacted Dave Raymond in 1975. Dave and his wife Cheryl relocated from LA to Oregon, where Dave became a detective on the Cave Junction police force. We exchanged Christmas cards and spoke a couple of times. He and Cheryl divorced in the late '80s. He moved to Las Vegas for a year, at which time I lost track of him.

Around 2005 I located him on Facebook, and we started exchanging emails. He had returned to Oregon and rejoined the police force. Despite many attempts to get him to attend the Blackhawk reunions, he consistently refused. I soon learned the reason.

Dave said that when Mark Hansen was killed in 1969, Mark was substituting for Dave. Dave had an ear infection and was grounded, so Mark was tapped for the mission. Dave suffered a lifelong sense of guilt because he was supposed to be in the ship with Lt. Tanner, not Mark. He further said that he did not want to deal with that at the reunions. I assured him that no one would bring that up and that most people had probably forgotten about it, as I had. He would not hear it.

In 2013, Dave was diagnosed with ALS. I was stunned. The VA informed Dave that his case was caused by a bad reaction to the smallpox vaccination we received in Nam. The army had added an accelerant to shorten the incubation period. Some individuals were intolerant to the accelerant and developed ALS as a result.

In 2015, I succeeded in convincing Dave and his wife Jamie to attend the Blackhawk reunion in Sacramento, California. When I saw him, I was shocked again. He was thin and weak. He could not stand or walk without a cane. A wheelchair was required for longer distances.

What made this particularly sad for me was Dave's previous condition and level of activity.

Dave was always much more muscular than I was. He was a great athlete, shown by his performance in innumerable touch football games at Ft. Knox. He also took great care of himself and surfed regularly, well past the age of sixty. He rode a Harley.

His arms and legs had shrunk to a size much smaller than mine. He appeared to be skin and bones. He was incredibly depressed and would break into tears at the lightest provocation. I could not blame him. Knowing that one has a terminal, incurable disease would crush anyone. I told my wife that Dave had been killed in Vietnam, but no one knew it at the time.

The reunion gave us plenty of time to exchange memories and catch up. Unfortunately, Dave was so easily fatigued that he could only chat for about an hour before needing a two- or three-hour nap.

One of my most rewarding memories of Dave was the happiness he showed when we had a chance to fly in a restored Huey H model at the reunion. Our wives joined us, and Dave and Jamie sat in the crew chief's seats on the port side of the aircraft, immediately behind Norma and me.

Something that made the flight especially meaningful for us was the pilot. A former B-Troop Scout pilot was at the controls. Rather than a leisurely cruise at 500 feet, Fred dropped the Huey to the deck as soon as we cleared the airport perimeter. We zoomed around the terrain at about ten feet high! At one point, Fred took the ship below ground level by diving into a nearly dry riverbed. We stayed at this height for about five minutes before Fred pulled up to ground level and we headed back to the airport, about five minutes away. As we did so, Fred selected various trees along the way. Steering toward each tree at ten feet of altitude, Fred would hop the Huey over each tree. All the passengers would be momentarily weightless as he dove back to the ground. Norma loved it – not.

When we landed, I looked back at Dave and saw him crying. He was so happy he could not contain himself. He was sobbing like a baby. I will always remember that sight.

Jamie (center, holding M60!) and Dave Raymond (far right).
The author in sunglasses (far left) watching Norma (left) secure her seat belt.

Dave died in early 2017. I had lost a great friend and the man with whom I had spent thirty-three of the thirty-five months of my army service. An important link to my past was gone.

In 2001, Lt. Tucker died from alcohol and drug abuse. Norma and I attended his Arlington funeral about a week after the 9/11 attack on the Pentagon. We ate lunch with his wife and son and received more information than we should have.

My memories of Lt. Tucker were positive and he was one of my three or four favorite officers. His defense of me against Sgt. Saunders and our discussion on the South Vietnam prospects for success stuck with me for a long time. Unfortunately, he made some disastrous post-war decisions. According to his wife, he became involved in drug running, flying drugs across the US-Mexico border. Another Vietnam casualty?

REVELATION

"You talkin' to me?"

Travis Bickel, Taxi Driver

I had been experiencing symptoms since my return from Nam in 1969. During that time, PTSD was an unknown concept. It would only emerge as a recognized mental health issue in 1980, when it was adopted into the Diagnostic and Statistical Manual of Mental Disorders (DSM), the definitive guide to diagnosis within the psychological professions. Prior to that time, afflicted soldiers were said to be suffering from Soldier's Heart (Civil War), War Neurosis (Russian-Japanese War of 1904), Shell Shock (WWI), and Combat Fatigue (WWII and Korean War). Ancient literature as early as Homer's *Iliad* mentions combat trauma. During these earlier periods, many lay people considered these veterans as lacking in character or possessing defective personalities. We now know that PTSD is a normal response to an unnaturally traumatic experience.

My symptoms included the classics: nightmares and other sleep disturbances, anxiety, depression, and flashbacks. In one remarkable episode in the mid-1980s, I woke up in a cold sweat, breathing hard, sitting straight up in bed, remembering a scene from the raid into the U Minh Forest. This was the killing of the two NVA who stepped out of the woods, surprising both Cort and me.

In my dream the intensity of the colors overwhelmed me. The bright red bloodstain contrasting with the muddy canal water was striking.

What made the dream extraordinary was that I had completely forgotten about this experience, despite its intensity. I believe I remembered everything else that happened that day, but not this. I had experienced numerous nightmares about my other experiences, but these incidents were always present in my memory. For some unknown reason, I must have repressed this memory for years.

In the mid-1990s, after a recent promotion to a managerial position in a national consulting firm, I began experiencing several symptoms that I could not understand and could barely describe. I had weird visualizations, the inability to "turn off" my mind and go to sleep, and strange distortions of time and space. Because of the inability to sleep, I felt exhausted for weeks at a time.

I collected a short list of notes so I could present them to my family doctor in an orderly fashion. He diagnosed me with anxiety/depression and prescribed a mild antianxiety drug. Fortunately, this provided instant relief and the symptoms declined.

After a couple of years on the drug, I began to think there must be a better solution. I was not a big fan of medications and thought there had to be a better method to defeat these symptoms. I sought treatment from a psychologist and from a psychiatrist.

I underwent about six weeks of counseling and a medication review. I never brought up that I was a combat veteran. We never discussed Vietnam because I purposefully drove the conversations away from it. I was irrationally afraid that the mention of Vietnam would make its way back to my employer and I would fall subject to all the prejudices associated with being a veteran. This was a mistake as it prevented me from participating in the kind of treatment that would have helped me. The medications continued.

Agent Orange - Worst Friendly-Fire Incident Ever

In 2009, I received a diagnosis of ischemic heart disease and underwent quadruple bypass surgery. Unfortunately, I also experienced post-operative delirium and was placed into an induced coma for a week. This caused immense stress for my wife and family.

While in the coma, a nurse asked Norma if I was an alcoholic and explained that post-op delirium was common among alcoholics. When Norma replied that I was not, the nurse asked if I was a combat veteran. Norma answered that I was. The nurse said, "That's it then! We operate on a lot of combat veterans here, and many, if not most of them, suffer from post-op delirium when we try to bring them out of the anesthesia." This was only partially reassuring. There was talk of brain swelling and other horrific outcomes over the course of the week.

When I finally awoke, I believed that it was the Friday afternoon of my surgery. It was more than a week later. They avoided telling me this for about three days and would not answer my questions about the wall calendar. The staff had scrawled June 4 on the whiteboard. I thought it was still May 29th.

Norma and the kids told me about my behavior before they induced the coma. I had acted like an animal, growling and snorting at people. I pulled my chest tube out. I was so disturbed they had to tie me to the bed.

I had no memory of this. Nor did I have any memory of being in the coma. I heard nothing and felt nothing. It was a complete, black void. Later I imagined it to be like death. I was simply no longer present. No awareness whatsoever.

When Norma told me about her conversation with the nurse, I wanted an answer. I had never heard of post-op delirium in veterans and wanted to know more. I asked my family physician. He knew nothing about it.

I looked at every website I could find. I did not see any mention of combat-related post-op delirium. I was baffled.

Thirty days after my discharge from Sentara Heart Hospital, I had a follow-up visit with my cardiac surgeon. He reviewed the results of the surgery but did not bring up the delirium or the coma. Because it was his nurse who had informed Norma about the combat link, I asked him what he could tell me about it. I did not share any facts about my own experience, either while suffering delirium or while in a coma.

He went into a lengthy explanation about the preponderance of combat veterans in the Norfolk area and the many times his patients experienced the delirium. He described it as "an everyday experience," saying he thought it happened more often than not. He further explained that the delirium appeared to be linked to PTSD and was a good indicator that the patient might be suffering from that disorder.

I confirmed that I was a combat veteran but had not been diagnosed with PTSD. He said that I might have a mild case because, "The really crazy guys can't remember anything about their delirium or the coma."

I thought I might fall out of the chair. I had not told him that I had no memory of the event.

The surgeon suggested that I contact the VA and get checked out.

We later learned from a VVA friend that my heart disease was a result of Agent Orange exposure, making me eligible for assistance from the Veteran's Administration.

I decided to look into what type of assistance was available from the VA. Because I was still employed as the president of an IT consulting firm, I limited my research to the disability compensation benefits. I was not interested in seeking any kind of therapy. I did not feel it was necessary. Nor did I want it to affect my career.

I filed two compensation claims with the VA: one for ischemic heart disease, and one for PTSD. My cardiologist's report was sufficient to earn a disability rating of 30 percent. After a one-hour psychological exam by a government contractor, the VA awarded me another 30 percent for PTSD.

HELP

"I am aware that I, without realizing it, have lost my feelings – I don't belong here anymore. I live in an alien world. I prefer to be left alone, not disturbed by anybody. They talk too much – I can't relate to them – they are only busy with superficial things."

Erich Maria Remarque, All Quiet on the Western Front

Prior to this episode, I did not realize that I might have a diagnosable case of PTSD. While I had suffered from nightmares, flashbacks, anxiety, and a strong feeling of alienation from my nonveteran peers, I had never sought therapy for PTSD.

"Trauma" was, to me, some kind of terrifying experience, based on extreme fear and disturbing one's mental health to a significant degree and for a long time. My combat experiences, during which I came face-to-face with Viet Cong and North Vietnamese Army soldiers on numerous occasions, were never characterized by terror. My training and mindset never allowed me to become terrorized. I simply reacted to the situation. The fear often occurred at night, after the actual event had long passed. My most terrifying experience during my combat role was a near midair collision with another helicopter. While extremely intense, the sensation only lasted about ten seconds. I was convinced I was about to crash and die but did not have time to experience fear. I was simply resigned to the fact that I was dead.

I did not feel all that traumatized. Despite decades of nightmares, flashbacks, anxiety, depression, migraines, and a strong sense of alienation, I had successfully risen above all that and never considered the possibility that my experiences had affected me. I certainly did not feel that I needed any kind of special treatment or medication.

In terms of being terrified, my worst experiences were the frequent, two a.m. mortar attacks that often occurred at Vinh Long, our airbase in the middle of the Mekong River Delta. Being awakened by the sound of explosions, some quite close, was frightening. The disorientation and fear during such an event are something one does not forget. However, it was not life-altering.

My post-war experiences also included a decade of intense involvement with the veterans' movement, primarily directed at obtaining adequate services for the tens of thousands of Vietnam veterans who needed significant help. I was frequently close to needy veterans as well as care providers. The psychology of post-traumatic stress disorder (PTSD) was just coming to the fore. I participated in numerous discussions of the science as it went from being considered a "character flaw" to being recognized as a valid response to abnormal stressors. Despite this knowledge, it never occurred to me that I might also need some help.

I had plenty of evidence to the contrary. I had left the army after three years and attained a bachelors' degree in business administration. I had a successful business career in the information technology industry, reflecting numerous promotions and above-average performance. Most importantly, my wife and I had a very happy marriage and two wonderful adult children. Both attained college degrees and were experiencing successful careers of their own. We had never suffered from any form of spousal abuse or violence of any type. No one was addicted to drugs. The only notable carryovers from my combat experience were the aforementioned nightmares, anxiety, depression, etc.

Cort Stark's sudden death changed all that.

In 2015, we lost Cort Stark to a motorcycle accident in Arizona. He was attempting to make it to a friend's house after a long ride. He decided to do something that he once told me he never did: ride through a downpour. A cloudburst caused him to lose visibility, and he failed to see a truck stop in his path. He struck the rear of the truck, and according to witnesses, was killed instantly.

He had enjoyed a successful career after Vietnam. He retired as a lieutenant colonel after being awarded three Distinguished Flying Crosses. Prior to his retirement, he was assigned to serve as the chief administrator of the Panama Canal Zone while the US prepared to return the canal to the Panamanian government.

Fortunately, Cort and I reconnected at a Blackhawk reunion in 1995. This was wonderful for me because we had shared so many intense experiences as Scouts.

We remained in touch until his death. Cort hosted a Blackhawk reunion in San Diego, and he continued to attend reunions regularly.

On one occasion, I met him in DC for a Memorial Day celebration. We rode our motorcycles back to Virginia Beach, where he spent the weekend at our house.

Cort Stark and the author - 2014.

Upon his death, I was invited to attend his memorial service in San Diego. His daughter, Carolyn Cox, lived near us in Chesapeake, Virginia. She needed help in sorting through his military memorabilia and asked if I would mind doing it. I happily said yes.

When I arrived in San Diego, I was very happily surprised by several events. First and foremost, I learned that Cort had been engaged in a lifelong search for the meaning of our lives on earth and the impact of spirituality. He had dozens of books and tapes on the subject.

Cort's search was far more than simple reading. He routinely visited the elderly and terminally ill in various San Diego hospitals and hospice facilities. One of his local friends told me that he could not even attempt to estimate how many people passed away while holding hands with Cort Stark. He said it was probably several hundred. He traveled the world, spending months in underdeveloped countries providing carpentry services to poor villages in need of sturdy buildings.

Cort was also socially active. He belonged to the local chapter of the Harley Owners' Association ("HOG"). He also was an active participant in the San Diego chapter of the "Old, Bold Pilots' Association." This was a worldwide group and a play on the platitude often stated by experienced aviators. *There are Old pilots. There are Bold pilots. However, there are no Old, Bold pilots.*

About a dozen of the members attended the memorial service and luncheon. Most were WWII aviators and the majority of them were combat aces. A couple were retired air force general officers. I had the honor of meeting all of them.

This was a real treat. It was obvious that Cort had told our flag story many times. Everyone I met would greet me with something like, "Oh! You're the Moore guy we've heard so much about."

After lunch, I was asked to retell the flag story from the podium. I did so but omitted the grislier aspects. When finished, I received a standing ovation from the entire audience, led by the Old-Bold crew.

I think it would be impossible for me to receive a higher compliment from a more qualified group of people.

Cort's daughter presented the flag to me at the close of the ceremony. Right after Cort's death, I was surprised by the arrival of a small package from the Department of the Army. I had not requested or ordered anything, so I had no idea what it might be.

I opened the box to find a letter of about ten pages in length and a smaller case containing an Air Medal. It was adorned with the number "6" and a bright "V." The letter explained that the Department of the Army had completed a review of my service records as part of my 2009 claim for PTSD compensation. Upon review, they discovered that Cort Stark had initiated a citation for valor after our capture of the VC flag in March of 1969. The Air Medal had been "awarded" in June of '69 but was never presented to me. This oversight occurred despite my remaining in the army for another nineteen months after the "award." I guessed the army could not find me.

The numeral 6 was authorized because I had completed enough combat flight hours to earn five Air Medals. Those five, plus the one for valor, qualified me to display the 6 on the medal and accompanying ribbon.

The army succeeded in getting the medal to me, but it was about forty-six years late! It was also too late for me to thank Cort for recommending the award.

Cort's death was a major blow to me. I had lost the man with whom I shared my most memorable war experiences. He, like Dave Raymond, was a strong link to my past and someone I could count on to remember and validate our crazy deeds. We had recently strengthened our relationship, and I garnered a great level of reassurance from that. Now he was gone.

His loss sent me into a psychological tailspin.

The symptoms that had caused me to seek medical help in the mid-1990s returned. However, they were far more intense and frequent this time. I could not concentrate at work because I could not keep thoughts about Vietnam out of my mind. These flashbacks were occurring a dozen or more times per day. My short-term memory deserted me. My feelings of alienation got worse.

When sitting in meetings or across a table from another individual, I had the visual sensation that they were sitting fifteen or twenty feet away. It appeared as though I was looking at them through the wrong end of a pair of binoculars!

One of the recurring feelings that deeply disturbed me was a strong sense of alienation. These feelings were often present, especially during a family gathering or a large business networking event. During these gatherings, I often thought that those present had no idea who I was or what I had done in my earlier life. While there was nothing in particular about these settings that caused these feelings, the mere presence of so many nonveterans sparked the feeling that I would surely be an outcast if they had the slightest inkling of what I'd done. These feelings often morphed into contempt for those around me. My mind was telling me that these nerds had never faced the situations I had, that none of them knew what it was like to beat someone to the draw and kill them before they could kill you.

This feeling was especially intense when I was around the chicken-hawks who promoted wars and kicking ass in any country we chose. Of course, none of them had served in the military, despite numerous opportunities to do so. I often felt like screaming, "You pussies! I used to be a dangerous man! I used to hang around with guys who were ten times the man any of you even hope to be. Show us some goddam respect!" I felt head and shoulders above them when contemplating our relative places in the world. Of course, we were living in separate worlds. Fortunately, I never allowed such an outburst to happen.

I was becoming less effective at work. Without telling my partners what was happening, I decided to pass the president's job to the other senior partner and entered a part-time, as-needed employment status. I blamed it on burnout and the desire to travel. I committed to a two-year part-time role, with full retirement planned for 2017.

With a great deal of trepidation, I contacted the local Vet Center and made an appointment for an intake interview. The Vet Centers are a form of outreach centers allowing veterans to participate in various types of outpatient psychological counseling without having to travel to a regional VA hospital. While initiated for use by Vietnam veterans, they now serve veterans from all of the subsequent wars.

After four initial individual counselling sessions, I agreed to participate in group therapy. Ten veterans were already taking part, and they had a slot open. I took it.

Several of the other therapies offered by the VA tended to focus on discrete traumatic events. Two that stood out were Prolonged Exposure Therapy and Eye Movement Desensitization and Reprocessing (EMDR).

During Prolonged Exposure Therapy, a therapist guides the veteran through a detailed reliving of the traumatic event. According to the American Psychological Association (APA), the therapist asks a series of probing, detailed questions about the trauma, with the veteran describing the event in detail in the present tense with guidance from the therapist. Together, the veteran and therapist discuss and process the emotion raised by the imagined exposure in session. The veteran is recorded while describing the event so that she or he can listen to the recording between sessions, further process the emotions, and practice the breathing techniques.

EMDR, again according to the APA, relies on a retelling of the trauma while the veteran executes a series of standardized rapid eye movements. The therapist guides a discussion of the veteran's memories, rather than focusing on the associated feelings and emotions. This therapy leads to an alteration of the way the memory is stored in the brain, thereby reducing PTSD symptoms.

When presented with these options, I faced a significant dilemma. These therapies focused on overcoming a single traumatic event. My trauma was spread over hundreds of events that most people would consider traumatic: killing individuals in face-to-face settings, seeing dozens of mangled and dead bodies, and even watching the heart being cut out of a living man. None of these events lasted more than a few minutes. However, they were disturbing enough to cause decades of nightmares and flashbacks.

Entering the group therapy session was intimidating, to say the least. The only thing I knew about the group was that they were all Vietnam veterans and most had seen combat. The group had been meeting for over a year, so I was the FNG. I wondered how they would treat me. Would they be standoffish, waiting for me to earn admission? Or would they be welcoming and glad to have a new member?

Fortunately, they were open and welcoming and I was immediately at ease with them.

We worked on various exercises that fell within the Cognitive Behavioral Therapy (CBT) classification of treatment. This was based on talk therapy during which we learned to identify our triggers – those daily life events that might cause the onset of a panic attack, a flashback, or even an episode of depression. Emphasis was placed on the mindfulness technique, which we could use to reground ourselves when we felt anxious or under stress.

We also performed periodic self-assessment surveys to track our response to therapy over time.

This weekly therapy was supported by monthly individual counselling sessions. I also participated in classes that taught the basics of PTSD, the effects of trauma on the brain, and an orientation to the various therapies offered by the VA.

RECOVERY & REWARD

---

*"The only person you are destined to become
is the person you decide to be."*

Ralph Waldo Emerson

One of the most revealing lessons of these therapy sessions was learning that combat trauma can cause the brain to alter its circuitry – the so-called Lizard Brain effect. The change takes place in the most primitive section of the brain. It results from extended periods of stress or hyper-alertness. The brain learns to maintain a constant high level of alertness as a defense mechanism. Once learned, it cannot be unlearned. This leads to many types of psychological damage, including anxiety and depression. The key for the veteran is to recognize when this is happening and learn to manage the experience.

This state of mind also accounts for what is often mistaken for memory loss. Because the veteran is often hyper-alert, he or she is unable to live in the moment. This subconscious behavior prevents the brain from recording a clear memory of the event at hand, causing it to fade over time. I suffered from this effect for years, often listening to my wife berate me for failing to remember some aspect of a significant family event.

I participated in the PTSD therapy program for about two years and found it remarkably helpful. In addition to the advice and group exercises provided by the counsellors, I received a huge benefit from learning that many of the other veterans were experiencing the same disturbing symptoms and feelings that I had experienced. Because of these efforts, I was better able to understand the nature of my condition, as related to PTSD. I no longer felt alone in my misery. While the symptoms did not completely disappear, I understood what was behind the episodes and was better able to manage them. We learned that our feelings were the natural result of combat trauma, not the result of a character defect.

After two years on this program, and numerous conversations with my counsellor about my feelings of guilt, she recommended that I look into a relatively new line of VA treatment: Moral Injury (MI) therapy.

From the late 70s, when I learned the true history of the US involvement in Vietnam, I suffered from intense feelings of guilt. I recognized the immorality of our involvement and had a difficult time dealing with my participation in it. I felt I should have known better. Such thoughts haunted me for years.

Another counsellor in another Vet Center had formed a small Moral Injury group. We arranged a series of in-person interviews where we discussed my feelings of guilt and how I might benefit from the group. I decided to join and began attending the weekly meetings. I essentially replaced the PTSD group with this new MI group.

The results far exceeded my expectations. I was somewhat skeptical going in. I could not conceive how someone was going to talk me out of my guilt. I was pleasantly surprised. After a year of participation, I had to agree that the therapy had worked.

One of my biggest benefits was gaining the ability to forgive myself for my enthusiastic participation in so much violence. There were many times when I questioned my morality and wondered if I was any better than the German SS troops of WWII who murdered so many innocent people. Fortunately, the Moral Injury therapy enabled me to get beyond these feelings.

When discussing my guilt feelings with my wife, she often said I did not have a choice. She often said that I was in a "kill or be killed" situation and had no other option. I knew that to be untrue. I had volunteered for the army, chosen aviation, and forced my way into the Scout Platoon. I could have stayed in maintenance and avoided all the violence.

The MI therapy helped me understand that I had no other choice. My upbringing, the post-WWII propaganda environment, and Kennedy's "Do not ask what your country can do for you . . ." speech all created a force that I could not overcome, even if I wanted to.

Despite my Vietnam disappointments, I went on to have a wonderful life. I attribute all of our successes to the person I chose to be my wife: Norma Potter, my high school sweetheart.

Norma's presence gave me the motivation I needed to focus on the future and put the unpleasantness and confusion of my war experiences behind me. Thanks to her twenty-seven years of hard work as a nurse, I was able to complete my college education and prepare myself for a rewarding business career.

It was not easy. She often worked nights, and we split the responsibilities of raising our two children: Tina and Kevin. Fortunately, they were nine years apart and presented different demands on our time. I say fortunately because none of this was planned! Both of them are quite wonderful in their own right. Both completed college, and Tina earned a master's degree. We now have two highly successful teenage grandsons and cherish our opportunities to spend time with them.

While in college, I was able to contribute to our income by working as a part-time photographer. This allowed me to meet several celebrities. This included Willie Mays, Arthur Ashe, Jimmy Connors, and Ilie Nastase.

While I was largely unaware of it at the time, my war experiences harmed my immediate family. In recent discussions with my wife, she told me how my various mood swings, periods of depression, social withdrawal, and fatigue were noticed by Tina and Kevin. These issues often led to frustrations and hurt feelings on their part. I was clueless about this.

Another aspect of my behavior that affected Norma was my near-obsession with researching the war and my participation. Unbeknownst to me, Norma often felt that my research was robbing her and the kids of my attention.

This was shocki g to me because I often felt that I overindulged the kids. I always made su that they both had my unflinching support and whatever resources they r eded to pursue their desires. Because my childhood was one of limited oppor inities, leading to great frustrations, I did everything I could to make sure ou kids did not experience that. While both my parents tended toward discoura ement and faultfinding, I always tried to be supportive and encouraging. Ui ortunately, this behavior did not fully offset the effects of my concentration o the war.

My family lift definitely improved as a result of my therapy. I can make a conscious effort > be more attentive. I am able to stay in the moment and get more satisfactio from daily events. While I still suffer from bouts of anxiety, I am less depress than I was prior to therapy. The nightmares continue.

My business ireer was one of uninterrupted responsibility and personal growth. Having arted work as a temporary hire in a small, local IT service bureau, and ev itually working as a director in a global, publicly held enterprise, I ha many opportunities to observe and learn from numerous leaders. I learne something from every one of them. This included what to do and what *not* > do in almost every business situation. I drew heavily on my army days and t great officers I had served under.

I also drew i my Vietnam experiences as a source of motivation and strength. Makin life-and-death decisions at twenty years of age went a long way toward red cing the stress associated with routine business challenges. I often consider the complaints of my colleagues to be trivial distractions. After my experi nces overseas, pulling an all-nighter in the computer room just did not seer that tough. I often thought, *If I could survive Nam, what I'm facing now is a c kewalk.*

Despite the r ghtmares and other PTSD issues, I know that I would have never been satis ed with my life had I not pursued my military aspirations. After all is said d done, I know I volunteered for virtually every assignment and can blame > one else for the consequences. I do not consider myself a victim in any wa shape, or form. As I look back at those thirty-five months in the army, it is h d to reconcile the thoughts and aspirations of that eighteen-year-old with the values and aspirations I held later in life. As my fellow Scout Tom Gery told me recently, we were heavily invested in the business of "killing and counting." I have to live with the knowledge that we were pawns in our country's and Vietnam's history, and on the wrong side morally and politically.

I now accept the factors that led to the US invasion of Vietnam and my enthusiastic participation in it. I am no longer as angry about Vietnam as I used to be. I consider it a horrendous mistake and hope that we will stop repeating it, someday.

Now, with the US troops having departed Afghanistan, we see the third US failure at nation-building in my lifetime. First, the Vietnam War. Then the invasion of Iraq and the attempt to establish a pro-western democracy. Lastly, Afghanistan, the longest war in US history, is another monumental failure. We have consistently repeated similar mistakes, resulting in the deaths of hundreds of thousands of the people we were allegedly trying to help. Why?

To me, the reasons are clear:

1. **We are a more militaristic nation than we care to admit.** We too often see military action as the first and best course of action.
2. **We are delusional in our belief that everyone wants to live like we do.** When we find otherwise, we attempt to persuade them at the point of a gun.
3. **We are willing to jump into these adventures before we fully understand the culture of the people we are trying to convert**. This creates conditions that doom us to failure.

All three mistakes are the results of our widespread belief in the concept of "American Exceptionalism." We see ourselves as God's Chosen People, infallible and immune from failure.

After seeing our country at its worst, I can say with confidence: we have not been chosen by anyone.

We now have three groups of veterans who gave their all in futile efforts. I hope these men and women come to understand their roles in these efforts

EPILOGUE

"Even a fool may be wise after the event."

Homer, The Iliad

Craig Schmidt, **Vernon Summerell**, and **Dave Raymond** left the army after their initial three-year enlistment.

Craig pursued a career in sales. I served as his best man when he was married in September 1971. Norma, who was four months pregnant with our first child, and I flew to St. Louis for the ceremony. My grandmother loaned us the money for the airfare. We did this in return for **Craig's** participation as my best man when Norma and I were married, in April of 1970. We reconnected at a reunion in the mid-1990s. We correspond and see each other regularly.

Vernon returned to college to complete his education. Instead of returning to Old Dominion, he chose to attend East Carolina University, where his younger brother was the starting quarterback. He became a CPA and moved back to Virginia. We reconnected in the mid-1980s. **Vernon** was not interested in joining the veteran's movement and I eventually lost track of him.

Dave Raymond went into law enforcement, divorced his wife Cheryl, remarried, and moved to Oregon. He passed away in 2017 as a result of ALS.

Tom Gery, my   Minh wingman, pursued a career as a social worker and retired to the Ea   rn Shore of Virginia. He attended the 2017 reunion and was instrumental in   lping me recall the names of pilots I had long forgotten. We correspond and   eet regularly.

After I left Nan   **Jim Lucido** and I exchanged several letters. I successfully contacted **Jim** i   the mid-1970s while he was living in Montana and Utah. He was not inte   sted in discussing our time in the Blackhawks. I eventually lost track of hir   . Several attempts between 2017 and 2021 were fruitless. I continue to sear   .

Steve Holmes,   Scout observer and our source for pot, disappeared. I attempted to fin   him in Cocoa Beach, Florida, but failed.

Glenn O'Leary   a D-Troop medic I met at the reunions, contacted **Jimmy Heller**. Jim wan   d no part of the Blackhawks and went as far as denying some of the conversat   ns he had with **Glenn** while in the Scouts.

   Glenn and I   came close friends, visiting each other's homes on occasion. His wife Carole   as an independent travel agent and assisted Norma and me with several maj   r trips.

John Tillery, t   Congo joker, was seriously wounded right after I went home. One of J   Lucido's letters told me that John was hit in the foot by two AK-47 rou   ls. Both bullets also passed through his tibia and his femur. One of the two   destroyed his knee. I tried to locate John years later but could not.

Frenchy Lemoy   was also seriously injured after I left. He was flying with Lt. Tucker when th   were shot down. Frenchy suffered a serious back injury in the crash and w   forced to use a cane for the rest of his life. He attended one of our reunions   the late-1990s.

SFC Saunders survived the war and attended one or two reunions in the late nineties. Interestingly, Saunders perpetrated a "stolen valor" fraud, actually claiming to be flying with Cpt. Stark when Stark and Tom Gery were shot down in June 1969. Saunders included this falsehood on his resume, informing folks that he was flying when Tom was the real crewman that day. After the behavior I observed while we were in the Scout platoon, this scam did not surprise me.

Cpt. Sholtz, one of my favorite officers, retired to Florida. I retrieved his address from the Blackhawk Association and wrote to him. However, he did not respond. I later learned that he passed away about three years after my attempt to contact him.

Lt. Tucker, another of my favorites, took a big turn toward the dark side after his departure from the army. He became involved in drug running, flying drug-laden helicopters into the US from Mexico. He got busted and divorced. His lifelong best friend from high school told us that he was injured during a drunk driving episode and spent his last twenty years confined to a wheelchair. Sadly, he told people that his injury was from a helicopter crash in Vietnam. He had virtually abandoned his son, who had dropped out of high school and was in the process of arranging his marriage to his pregnant girlfriend. It was obvious that the young man was lost.

His widow described several incidents of extremely strange and violent behavior. I was deeply saddened to hear it.

Granville Oliver and I had one conversation around the year 2000.

I was unable to connect with **Mike Wells**, **Rich Ward**, or **Jim Manley**, despite several search attempts.

APPENDIX "A"
GLOSSARY

2.75-inch Rocket

An aerial-launch weapon fired from tubes mounted on Huey C-Model gunships and Cobras. Very effective as aerial artillery in close ground support actions.

106mm Recoilless Rifle

A light artillery weapon designed to eliminate recoil. This allowed the weapon to be mounted on portable platforms such as jeeps and trucks. Primarily designed as an anti-tank weapon, it was often used to attack enemy bunker fortifications.

122mm Rocket

Primarily a Communist block weapon, based on the Katyusha rockets of WWII.

40mm Grenade

A low-velocity projectile fired from a single-shot, shoulder-fired grenade launcher. The grenade is quite short, measuring only 46 millimeters in height. The grenades used in the Vietnam War had two configurations: high explosive, and scattershot. Gunships and Cobras often carried auto-loading grenade launchers, utilizing a belt-fed loading device.

40mm Grenade Launcher

A single-shot, shoulder-fired infantry weapon resembling a small shotgun. It utilized a breech loading, folding barrel, similar to a single-shot shotgun.

AH-1 Cobra

A two-man attack helicopter armed with a variety of weapons, including miniguns, 2.75 rocket launchers, and 40mm auto-loading grenade launchers. Cobras were designed to replace the UH-1C model gunships in order to achieve higher top speeds and more lift capability. The two-man crew was comprised of fully trained and certified pilots. The pilot flew the ship while the weapons officer operated the weapon systems. The weapons officer occupied the front seat while the pilot sat directly behind him in a slightly elevated rear seat. Both seats were equipped with flight controls, allowing either pilot to fly the ship.

AK-47

A Russian/Chinese automatic assault rifle in 7.62 x 39 mm caliber. Most were equipped with thirty-round magazines. While not as accurate as an M-16, they were more reliable and able to stand more physical abuse.

AO

The geographic Area of Operation; the AO would vary in size according to the mission and the size of the unit assigned to undertake the mission.

Battalion

This encompasses four to six companies and between 300 and 1,000 soldiers. A battalion normally is commanded by a lieutenant colonel, and a command sergeant major serves as principal NCO assistant. A battalion can conduct independent operations, if they're of limited scope and duration, and operates its own administration. An armored or air cavalry unit of equivalent size is known as a squadron.

Blackhawks

The nickname given to the First Regiment of Dragoons in 1833. It was based upon the regiment's participation in the Blackhawk War. The regiment eventually became the US First Cavalry Regiment.

Brigade

A brigade includes 1,500 to 3,200 soldiers, and a brigade headquarters commands the tactical operation of two to five combat battalions. Brigades normally are employed on independent or semi-independent operations, and normally are commanded by a colonel or general with a command sergeant major as senior NCO.

Bunker

A protective structure used to provide cover from small arms, rocket, and mortar fire. Construction materials included sandbags, wooden frames, or steel plating. Bunkers could range in size from a small four-man structure to one large enough to house fifty men. VC and NVA bunkers were often comprised of dried mud.

C-123

The Provider. Twin-engine cargo plane designed for short runway takeoffs and landings.

C-130

The Hercules. A larger, four-engine cargo plane, also designed for runways.

C&C Ship

The UH-1H used by the Troop commander to oversee operations in the AO.

CAR-15 Auto-Carbine

A shortened version of the M-16 rifle. Equipped with a telescoping stock and a twelve-inch barrel. Semi-auto and full-auto selectability.

Chicken Plate

An element of body armor designed for use by aircrew. It was designed to protect against .30 caliber small arms fire at a range of 100 yards. It consisted of a ceramic plate to protect the front of the torso and was worn by slipping it over the wearer's head. It weighed approximately twenty pounds.

Company

A company contains three to five platoons and a total of 60 to 200 soldiers. It is commanded by a captain (a major in an aviation or air cavalry unit) with a first sergeant as the commander's principal NCO assistant. If the element is an artillery unit, it is called a "battery" rather than a company. If it is armored or air cavalry, it is called a "troop." A company is a tactical sized unit and can perform a battlefield function on its own.

Crew Chief

A trained aircraft mechanic who has primary responsibility for the first level of maintenance on a single aircraft. Most crew chief billets are flying assignments. However, Cobra crew chiefs did not fly with their ships.

Division

With 10,000 to 15,000 soldiers, a division usually consists of three brigade-sized elements and is commanded by a major general, who is assisted by two brigadier generals. It can conduct major tactical operations and sustained battlefield operations and engagements. Divisions are numbered and are assigned missions based on their structures. Divisions perform major tactical operations for the corps and can conduct sustained battles and engagements.

Gun Platoon

The casual name for a platoon of Cobra or gunship personnel.

Hooch

Army slang for any residential structure, from simple lean-tos, to two-story, tropical barracks.

Hooch Boy

A male, South Vietnamese national hired to perform housekeeping duties in army barracks.

Hooch Maid

A female, South Vietnamese national hired to perform housekeeping duties in army barracks.

Lift Platoon

In an air cavalry or air assault unit, the platoon that flew UH-1H models to transport ground troops to and from the AO.

LZ

Landing Zone. An area designated for the aerial insertion (or retrieval) of ground troops.

Loach

Army slang for the OH-6A. Based on the full description, Light Observation Helicopter.

M-16 Auto-Rifle

The standard issue infantry weapon of the US military during the Vietnam War. It utilized a twenty-round box magazine and a twenty-two-inch barrel. Caliber was NATO 5.56mm. A selector switch allowed semi- or full-auto operation.

M-79 Grenade Launcher

A single-shot, shoulder-fired infantry weapon resembling a small shotgun. It utilized a breech-loading, folding barrel, similar to a single-shot shotgun.

Mike-Mike

Army phonetic representation of millimeter.

Military Aged Male

A male Vietnamese national of approximately military age (sixteen to forty years). They were often suspected of being VC or NVA infiltrators.

Minigun

An electrically driven, multi-barreled, 7.62mm machine gun, similar to a Gatling gun. Mounted on a pylon on the port side of the Loach, the gun had a maximum rate of fire of 6,000 rounds per minute. This was electrically reduced to 2,000 RPM on Loaches.

MOS

Military Occupational Specialty. An area of expertise in which the individual soldier is trained. '67V20" was the MOS of an OH-6A crew chief or mechanic.

OH-6A Cayuse

The Light Observation Helicopter used for Scout operations and other support tasks.

Orderly Room

The company or troop office.

Platoon

A platoon is comprised of twenty to forty soldiers and is commanded by a lieutenant. In a cavalry or aviation unit, the platoon is usually commanded by a captain.

POL Point

Petroleum, Oil, and Lubrication point, where a ship could refuel and sometimes reload ammo if the POL point was so equipped.

PSP

Portable Steel Plating used to construct runways.

Puff the Magic Dragon

A C-47 cargo plane converted to function as a gunship. Miniguns mounted inside the fuselage fired laterally through portholes in the side of the ship. Later models carried 20mm cannon and even 105mm artillery pieces.

Spec-4

A rank designation equal to an E-4 on the army pay scale. The "specialist" term refers to a technical specialty, as opposed to a "corporal" holding an infantry or artillery MOS.

Spec-5

A rank designation equal to an E-5 on the army pay scale.

Unit-"six"

Leaders of army units down to platoon level were referred to as the unit's "six". Therefore, Apache-Six was the designated call sign of Apache Troop's commanding officer. Blackhawk-Six referred to the squadron commander.

Slick

Usually a troop-carrying UH-1D or H model. The only weapon systems carried were two M-60 machine guns mounted on pylons. When compared to a UH-1 gunship, the silhouette had a relatively "slick" appearance. The H model could carry approximately eight armed infantrymen.

Spider Hole

A concealed, shallow foxhole, typically equipped with a camouflaged roof.

Squad

Smallest organizational unit in the army. Usually comprised of eight to twelve soldiers and commanded by a sergeant; squads were sometimes divided into fire teams for tactical purposes.

Squadron

The cavalry equivalent of an infantry battalion.

Thermite Grenade

A non-explosive incendiary grenade based on a thermite filler, capable of burning through steel. The grenade resembles a welding torch when burning. It can function underwater and was particularly effective when starting fires in damp or wet conditions.

Troop

The cavalry equivalent of an infantry company.

UH-1 Iroquois A & B Models

The first two models of the famous Huey. Initially used for air ambulance and troop-carrying operations, they were somewhat underpowered. Their troop-carrying capability was limited. This led to the development of the more powerful C Model.

UH-1 Iroquois C Model

Referred to as the Charlie model, and sometimes as the Hog, the Charlie model was designed for the gunship role. It was equipped with an 1,100 HP engine and a newly designed rotor system.

UH-1 Iroquois D Model

This was the stretched model, intended to carry eight to ten infantrymen. The passenger compartment was forty-one inches longer than a Charlie model, and two side-facing seats were added beside the transmission well. These were occupied by the crew chief and the gunner.

UH-1 Iroquois - H Model

An upgraded D model with a 1,400 HP engine.

Willie Pete

A white phosphorous incendiary grenade used as an anti-personnel weapon and marking device. When ignited, white phosphorous would burn through skin and bone. Extinguishing the burn required total immersion in water.

APPENDIX "B"
QUOTED AUTHORS

"War is delightful to those who have had no experience of it."
Desiderius Erasmus (1469 – 1536) - Dutch humanist who was the greatest scholar of the northern Renaissance, the first editor of the New Testament, and an important figure in patristics and classical literature.

"It is forbidden to kill. Therefore, all murderers are punished, unless they kill in large numbers and to the sound of trumpets."
Voltaire (1694 – 1778) - Author of the satirical novella *Candide*, Voltaire is widely considered one of France's greatest Enlightenment writers.

"It has become appallingly obvious that our technology has exceeded our humanity."
Unknown

"The key is to keep company only with people who uplift you, whose presence calls forth your best."
Epictetus (AD 55 – AD 135) - Greek philosopher associated with the Stoics.

"War makes strange giant creatures out of us little routine men who inhabit the earth."
Ernie Pyle (190 – 1945) - American WWII journalist. Killed during the battle for Okinawa.

"Courage is knowing what not to fear."
Plato (~429 – 317 BC) - Athenian philosopher during the Classical period in Ancient Greece.

"The Beatles saved the world from boredom."
George Harrison (1943 – 2001) Be serious! (You'd be surprised how many people under forty don't know him.)

"Only the dead have seen the end of the war."
George Santayana (1863 – 1952) - Spanish novelist and philosopher.

"There is no hunting like the hunting of man, and those who have hunted armed men long enough and liked it, never care for anything else thereafter."
Ernest Hemingway (1899 – 1961)

"The killer awoke before dawn. He put his boots on."
The Doors - American rock band from the late '60s and early '70s.

"I'm so short I can't see over my boot-tops!"
Anonymous GI

"True happiness is . . . to enjoy the present, without anxious dependence upon the future"
Lucius Annaeus Seneca (Circa AD 65) - A Roman Stoic philosopher, statesman, and dramatist.

"But listen to me first and swear an oath to use all your eloquence and strength to look after me and protect me."

Homer, The Iliad **Circa 750 BC** - Homer is believed to be the author of the *Iliad* and the *Odyssey*, two epic poems of ancient Greek literature.

"A rebirth out of spiritual adversity causes us to become new creatures."

James E. Faust (1920 – 2007) - An American religious leader, lawyer, and politician.

"Nothing in the affairs of men is worthy of great anxiety."

Plato (~429 – 347 BC) - Athenian philosopher during the Classical period in Ancient Greece.

"You talkin' to me?"

Travis Bickel, Taxi Driver - A fictional character and protagonist of the 1976 film *Taxi Driver*, directed by Martin Scorsese.

"I am aware that I, without realizing it, have lost my feelings – I don't belong here anymore. I live in an alien world. I prefer to be left alone, not disturbed by anybody. They talk too much – I can't relate to them – they are only busy with superficial things."

Erich Maria Remarque (1898 - 1970) *All Quiet on the Western Front,* German WWI veteran and novelist.

"The only person you are destined to become is the person you decide to be."

Ralph Waldo Emerson (1803 – 1882) - American author, philosopher, poet, and essayist.

ABOUT THE AUTHOR

AJ Moore was an avid historian who, at the age of twenty, found himself deeply involved in a grave national mistake: the Vietnam War. When he enlisted in the US Army in 1967, he was a patriotic "true believer" in the war effort. His combat experience changed that. The disillusionment and confusion over his role in the war motivated him to undertake years of research and soul searching in order to reconcile his beliefs with reality. This enabled him to understand his experience and ease the feelings of personal guilt that had plagued him for decades.

AJ spent years as a leader in the IT industry, working for national and international consulting organizations. In 2006, he and three partners formed a new consultancy in Virginia Beach, Virginia. Under his leadership as president, the firm grew rapidly and in 2010 was named to the prestigious *Inc. 500* list, an annual compilation of the most entrepreneurial and fastest growing, privately held U.S. companies.

During the mid-'80s, AJ served as president of Chapter 48 of the Vietnam Veterans of America (VVA) in Norfolk, Virginia. Al focused the chapter's activities on elevating the public perception of Vietnam veterans, recognizing that most veterans are productive, stable members of the community: not the Rambo-like personas often portrayed in the media. This led to the growth of the chapter and enabled it to offer a wide range of assistance to veterans, including college scholarships for veterans' children.

AJ holds a BS degree in Business Administration from Old Dominion University. He resides in Virginia Beach with his wife, Norma, a former nurse. Their two adult children also reside in Virginia Beach with their families.

If you would like to learn more about AJ and his activities, more information can be found at:

www.apachepressbooks.com

You can also connect with him via the following social media:

ww.facebook.com/ajmoorevietnamauthor
www.instagram.com/apachepress

Manufactured by Amazon.ca
Bolton, ON

32010978R00168